Trustworthy AI:
From Theory to Practice

Ferhat Ozgur Catak and Murat Kuzlu

Preface

Artificial intelligence (AI) has been integrated into a variety of fields from healthcare, to energy, finance, autonomous vehicle, manufacturing, etc., and opened up potential opportunities. However, it also causes challenges related to the trustworthiness of AI systems in terms of fairness, transparency, privacy, and security. This book aims to address these challenges and bridge the gap between the theoretical concepts of trustworthy AI and their practical applications using Python and open-source libraries.

"Trustworthy AI: From Theory to Practice" is more than just a book. It is a comprehensive guide for creating AI systems that are not only efficient and powerful, but also ethical, fair, equitable, and responsible. It is expected that this book will serve as a valuable resource for all interested in shaping AI's future, emphasizing security, privacy, robustness, and ethical principles.

The book provides practical insights and code examples, in addition to theoretical discussions. It covers various relevant topics, including uncertainty quantification, adversarial machine learning, and privacy-preserving techniques, such as federated learning and homomorphic encryption. With this book, the readers gain a theoretical understanding of Trustworthy AI and practical skills to apply these principles in real-world applications. The final chapter discusses the future directions and challenges of Trustworthy AI.

In this book, each chapter provides fundamental knowledge of the primary principles of trustworthy AI, including reliability, transparency, fairness, accountability, inclusiveness, privacy, and security. Readers will gain a solid understanding of these principles as they are explored in detail, giving them a comprehensive understanding of the challenges and strategies involved in putting them into practice.

This book is written for readers with and without a background in mathematics. Appendix A provides a summary of the primary symbols utilized throughout the book to aid those who may be unfamiliar with mathematical notation. It is designed to align with the course "DAT945: Secure and Robust AI Model Development" offered at the University of Stavanger, Norway.

For additional resources, updates, and code examples, readers are encouraged to visit the book's GitHub repository: https://github.com/ocatak/trustworthyai.

Contents

Contents

Contents

1 Trustworthy AI

1.1 Introduction to Trustworthy AI

In recent years, Artificial Intelligence (AI) methods have been significantly utilized in various applications, including healthcare, manufacturing, next generation communication, energy, finance, law, education, and self-driving cars [1]. However, AI methods are often obscure, vulnerable to prejudice, and may provide incorrect answers [2]. Furthermore, the industry does not trust the results of AI-based approaches due to a lack of clarity on the inner workings of the model and a lack of transparency and explainability. This raises several concerns about the trustworthiness of the model, i.e., "Trustworthy AI". Trustworthy AI refers to reliable, transparent, explainable, accountable, secure, and fair AI systems [3]. Researchers, developers, and decision-makers have typically focused on the performance of AI-based applications, especially precision, while missing the trustworthiness of AI.

The main focus of current academic research on AI trustworthiness lies in examining the algorithmic characteristics of models. However, progress in algorithmic research alone proves inadequate to create reliable AI products. The life cycle of an AI product encompasses various phases, from data preparation, model development, deployment, operation, evaluation, and monitoring to governance. Enhancing trustworthiness in any dimension, e.g., robustness, requires interventions across multiple life cycle stages, including data refinement, resilient algorithms, anomaly surveillance, and risk assessment. On the contrary, a breach of trust in any single component or facet can erode the trustworthiness of the entire system. Therefore, establishing and systematically evaluating AI trustworthiness should cover the entire life cycle of an AI system.

Trustworthy AI has been investigated in many studies in the literature. The survey [4] offers a detailed examination of existing approaches to confirm and verify current standardization efforts for reliable AI. It also provides a comprehensive perspective on recent progress in trustworthy AI to help researchers interested in the subject quickly understand the essential elements and suggest potential future research directions. With advanced computing and communication technologies, AI-based applications have also become more dominant, reshaping industries and redefining human-machine interactions, e.g., the autonomous precision of self-driving cars, personalized medical diagnoses, surgical robots, and financial advice. All these advancements are necessary to develop and employ AI systems that are not only powerful and efficient, but also reliable, transparent, and fair. Trustworthy AI can address these requirements, along with the promise of bridging the gap between the mysterious workings of AI algorithms and the principles of human values and ethics [5]. The paper by Li et al. [6] offers a detailed overview of how to create trustworthy AI systems, including key components of AI trustworthiness, such as robustness, generalization, explainability, transparency, reproducibility, fairness, privacy protection, and accountability. Additionally, it provides practical steps for practitioners and social stakeholders (e.g., researchers, engineers, and regulators) to enhance the trustworthiness of AI.

There is no single or best approach to meet the requirements of AI trustworthiness for all applications and fields. The best approach can be selected to improve the trustworthiness of AI models based on the application and field. However, the approach must meet several or all trustworthy AI principles, including reliability, transparency, fairness, accountability, inclusion, privacy, and security. Among these principles, reliability is the most important principle of the trustworthy AI paradigm, which should perform consistently and predictably within established limits. A reliable AI system ensures that machine-made decisions are grounded in robust data collection and processing, model training and evaluation, as well as interpretability and explainability [7]. Researchers and AI engineers can gain confidence in the requirements with rigorous testing, evaluation, and an iterative feedback loop. Transparency emerges as an important factor in building trust in AI [8]. It requires that AI's internal working principles be accessible and understandable, similar to deciphering the logic behind a human decision-maker's choices. Techniques such as explainable AI, interpretable machine learning models, and intuitive visualizations make easy-to-understand machine learning models, and clear visuals help us understand how AI works [9]. Transparency lets users examine, ask questions about, and trust the results that AI systems produce. Trustworthy AI goes beyond reliability and transparency. An AI model is also expected to deal with biases, distort outcomes, and perpetuate inequalities, i.e., ensure fairness. Fairness in trustworthy AI means that AI models make unbiased decisions. They don't favor or discriminate against any group based on factors like race, gender, or age [6]. This ensures that the AI system behaves ethically and builds trust in its use.

Gaining an understanding of the overall concept of AI trustworthiness is essential. This requires cooperation among experts from different fields, each handling various aspects and stages of the system's development to ensure its trustworthiness [3]. Recently, significant advances in multidisciplinary research on trustworthiness AI have been made. From a technological standpoint, trustworthy AI has spurred the growth of adversarial learning, privacy-preserving learning, and the fairness and explainability of machine learning (ML). Numerous studies are focusing on these advances from a research or engineering perspective [10, 11, 12, 13].

AI has grown significantly with advanced computing technologies. At the same time, trustworthy AI is also becoming quite vast due to increasing requirements from the industry and governments. In the following sections, we will briefly describe each principle of Trustworthy AI along with the organization of the book. By embracing the principles of Trustworthy AI, it is expected to provide a path toward a future where AI stands as a reliable, transparent, and fair partner in advancing human-centered AI applications.

1.2 Principles of Trustworthy AI

AI-based methods have been widely used in academia and industry for a long time. However, many AI-based applications are vulnerable to several attacks, i.e., adversarial, biased against underrepresented groups, and lacking user privacy protection. This results in a decrease in trust in AI systems. The six principles of Trustworthy AI are given in Figure 1.1, i.e., reliability, transparency, fairness, accountability, inclusiveness, privacy, and security. Each principle will be briefly explained in this section.

Figure 1.1: The principles of Trustworthy AI

1.2.1 Reliability

Reliability is one of the fundamental principles of trustworthy AI. In practice, AI-based methods are expected to make the right decisions and predictions to build trust and belief in the system. To be reliable in terms of trustworthiness, those systems must consistently deliver accurate and predictable results within defined parameters, especially in critical applications such as healthcare, e.g., identifying abnormalities in brain scans and prescribing appropriate treatment. The reliability of trustworthy AI requires rigorous testing, validation, and ongoing monitoring. Monitoring AI systems is the key to guaranteeing their dependability. This way, problems can be reported immediately, and steps can be taken to reduce risks. The research paper [14] outlines the requirements and provides an overview of various methods that can reduce AI risks and increase the trust and acceptance of systems. It also examines existing strategies for validating and verifying these systems and current standards for trustworthy AI. In order to achieve reliable AI, companies must ensure that their AI algorithms generate the correct results for each new data set. They must also create procedures to address issues and inconsistencies when they arise.

1.2.2 Transparency

Transparency in trustworthy AI is the ability to open and understand the models, decision-making, or prediction processes used by AI systems. It involves making the inner workings of AI systems understandable and accessible to stakeholders, including developers, researchers, and end-users, i.e., all stakeholders can clearly understand the inner workings of an AI system, including how it makes decisions and processes data [15]. It is one of the key features in building trust between humans and AI-based systems. Transparency in Trustworthy AI can be achieved through various methods, such as explainable AI (XAI), interpretable machine learning models, and intuitive visualizations by providing insights into data sources and model training procedures. They help us to understand algorithms by showing how they turn inputs into results. Through transparency, users are able to examine and understand AI-generated outcomes, eliminating the mystery that has surrounded AI. Transparent AI ensures that the logic and reasoning behind AI-generated outcomes can be analyzed and verified, contributing to accountability, fairness, and trustworthiness in the use of AI methods. The study [16] raises concerns about the reliability of AI applications, particularly in crucial fields such as healthcare. For example, even a small 0.5% error in the detection of cancer by an AI model could pose life-threatening risks. It also indicates that increasing trustworthiness in AI-based systems, i.e., transparency and explainability, is a more effective way to establish trust in AI.

1.2.3 Fairness

Fairness is one of the main principles of trustworthy AI to prevent potential biases, which can be classified into two forms, i.e., explicit and implicit. Explicit bias refers to discriminatory data, while implicit bias refers to choices made during model design. Achieving fairness involves designing and deploying AI systems by considering and mitigating potential biases, i.e., arising from race, gender, ethnicity, religion, income, family status, and others. The outcomes of AI are expected to not lead to discriminatory or unfair treatment of individuals or groups to be able to provide equal opportunities and treatment for all individuals, regardless of their background or identity. To achieve this goal, it is essential to conduct bias audits, examine data sources, and perform fairness-aware techniques in the development of trustworthy AI. In the literature, the study [17] explores the concept of fairness in trustworthy AI with respect to the social impact of AI to understand how concepts such as prejudice, discrimination, equity, inclusion, and similar factors can be integrated into the development of trustworthy algorithmic decision-making systems. It also indicates the importance of fairness in creating a trustworthy AI.

1.2.4 Accountability

Accountability is one of the key principles of trustworthy AI, which refers to holding individuals, organizations, or entities responsible for the design, development, deployment, and outcomes of AI-based systems. Accountability in trustworthy AI identifies the responsibilities of each party for AI-based decisions and actions, i.e., both developers and users, and ensures that any potential harm or ethical issues may originate from AI systems. Each party is expected to be held accountable at each stage of the process, not just after the AI is already operating, and to ensure that AI technologies are deployed ethically and responsibly, building trust in their capabilities. External entities are also suggested to review whether an AI system is used for sensitive purposes, such as public services. Other principles of trustworthy AI, including transparency, ethical behavior, and trust, are promoted in the development and use of AI systems with accountability. The authors in [18] emphasize the significance of accountability in reliable AI due to the complex nature of AI systems. To tackle this, they provide a more precise definition of accountability based on answerability. They describe three crucial conditions for establishing accountability, i.e., recognition of authority, the ability to question, and limitations on power. Additionally, they propose a framework consisting of seven essential elements (context, scope, agent, forum, standards, process, and implications). The authors also examine four accountability goals (compliance, report, oversight, and enforcement), emphasizing that policymakers can prioritize different goals depending on the proactive or reactive use of accountability and the particular objectives of AI governance.

1.2.5 Inclusiveness

Inclusiveness is one of the fundamental principles of trustworthy AI. There is an expectation formed in recent years, i.e., AI-based systems should benefit all members of society, including minority, marginalized, and underrepresented groups. It involves a wide range of stakeholders, including groups who may be affected by the AI system, in the decision-making process. This includes individuals from different cultural, social, economic, and demographic backgrounds. The main goal of inclusiveness is to prevent biases, discrimination along with promoting fairness, equity, and accessibility in the trustworthy AI concept. The integration of inclusiveness into AI-based solutions can help developers understand and address potential barriers by providing unbiased outcomes, and accessible to everyone. There is an important research conducted by Microsoft [19] for trustworthy AI, which introduces a guideline to categorize AI biases and tools to identify issues and potential challenges in AI-based systems. This research also expands inclusive approaches to address various conditions of exclusion, including cognitive challenges, different learning preferences, and social biases.

1.2.6 Privacy and Security

Privacy and security are the main principles of trustworthy AI. Privacy refers to protecting personal information, while security refers to protecting information from unauthorized access. A secure data process using encryption is essential to meet the privacy and security requirements of trustworthy AI. In addition, there are several requirements along with privacy and security, such as addressing system security weaknesses, protecting against malicious activities, and a secure data collection. Organizations can guarantee that their AI-based systems can meet the trustworthy AI criteria by considering concerns related to privacy and security. The study [20] emphasizes the vulnerability of numerous AI models to sophisticated hacking techniques, which requires concentrated research on adversarial AI. It also provides a comprehensive cybersecurity assessment by showcasing adversarial attacks on AI applications, including adversarial knowledge, capabilities, and current defense methods.

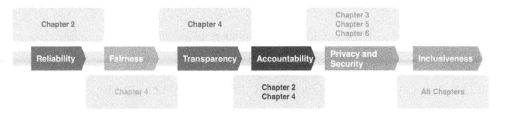

Figure 1.2: The relationship between the principle of trustworthy AI and each chapter

1.3 Organization of the Book

The main objective of this book is to explore the main principles of trustworthy AI and how they can be applied to the development of AI systems. It also investigates the opportunities, challenges, and future directions of trustworthy AI.

Figure 1.2 shows the relationship between the main six principles of trustworthy AI and each chapter. The six principles are linked to each chapter in the following way.

- Reliability: Chapter 2
- Fairness: Chapter 4
- Transparency: Chapter 4
- Accountability: Chapters 2 and 4
- Privacy and security: Chapters 3, 5 and 6
- Inclusiveness: All Chapters

This book covers the following chapters.

Chapter 1: Trustworthy AI
This chapter provides a fundamental overview of trustworthy AI along with its main principles from reliability, transparency, fairness, accountability, inclusiveness, to privacy and security. This chapter will give readers an understanding of those main principles of trustworthy AI and their importance.

Chapter 2: Reliability: Uncertainty Quantification in Artificial Intelligence
This chapter provides the fundamentals of uncertainty and then classifies it into epistemic (knowledge-based) and aleatoric (randomness-based) uncertainty. Monte Carlo Dropout and Ensemble Models are discussed, which can manage uncertainty. In addition, the chapter illustrates the relationship between uncertainty and adversarial machine learning, providing readers with a guide and practical examples for building trustworthy AI systems.

Chapter 3: Security of Artificial Intelligence: Adversarial Attacks
This chapter provides a comprehensive overview of adversarial attacks in AI along with the various types of attacks, i.e., targeted and untargeted attacks. It also introduces widely-used adversarial machine learning attacks (Fast Gradient Sign Method, Basic Iterative Method, Projected Gradient Descent, and others), and the mitigation methods (Adversarial Training, Defensive Distillation, and others). This chapter provides readers with practical examples of how to launch adversarial attacks against AI systems, as well as how to protect AI systems from such attacks.

Chapter 4: Transparency and Explainability
This chapter provides the overview of Explainable AI (XAI), and discusses several popular XAI methods, such as LIME (Local Interpretable Model-agnostic Explanations), SHAP (SHapley Additive exPlanations), and Contrastive Explanations Method (CEM). This chapter offers readers practical examples of selected XAI methods to make the AI method more understandable and to improve the trustworthiness of AI systems.

Chapter 5: Privacy-Preserving Artificial Intelligence: Federated Learning
This chapter provides a comprehensive understanding of Federated Learning

(FL) and covers the different types of FL, strategies, and horizontal and vertical FL in terms of Privacy-Preserving. At the end of this chapter, the readers will gain the skill to apply Federated Learning (FL) using FL strategies to AI-based applications.

Chapter 6: Privacy-Preserving Artificial Intelligence: Homomorphic Encryption

This chapter provides an overview of cryptography along with encryption and decryption. Additionally, the foundations of Homomorphic Encryption (HE) are introduced, accompanied by practical examples. Readers gain the ability to implement Homomorphic Encryption (HE) in AI applications through this chapter.

Chapter 7: Opportunities, Challenges, and Future Directions

The final chapter provides a brief overview of the opportunities, challenges, and future directions of trustworthy AI. Readers gain a broad understanding of opportunities, challenges, and future directions in trustworthy AI through this chapter.

1.4 Target Readership

This book is written for readers, i.e., developers, researchers, and end-users, who need to understand the concept of trustworthy AI and how to achieve trustworthy AI in real-world scenarios. Readers will gain the skills and create effective strategies for trustworthy AI. This book provides both theoretical and practical examples.

Finally, this book is a guide for developers to create AI systems that are powerful, efficient, ethical, reliable, and equitable. After reading this book, readers will have a theoretical understanding of trustworthy AI and will be able to put it into practice, leading to positive changes in the field of AI. This book is a tool to transform AI from a powerful tool into a force for good, ensuring it is in line with human values, fairness, and transparency.

Bibliography

[1] Darrell M West and John R Allen. How artificial intelligence is transforming the world. *Report. April*, 24:2018, 2018.

[2] Reva Schwartz, Apostol Vassilev, Kristen Greene, Lori Perine, Andrew Burt, Patrick Hall, et al. Towards a standard for identifying and managing bias in artificial intelligence. *NIST special publication*, 1270(10.6028), 2022.

[3] Ehsan Toreini, Mhairi Aitken, Kovila Coopamootoo, Karen Elliott, Carlos Gonzalez Zelaya, and Aad Van Moorsel. The relationship between trust in ai and trustworthy machine learning technologies. In *Proceedings of the 2020 conference on fairness, accountability, and transparency*, pages 272–283, 2020.

[4] Caesar Wu, Yuan-Fang Lib, and Pascal Bouvry. The survey, taxonomy, and future directions of trustworthy ai: A meta decision of strategic decisions. *arXiv preprint arXiv:2306.00380*, 2023.

[5] Ben Shneiderman. Bridging the gap between ethics and practice: guidelines for reliable, safe, and trustworthy human-centered ai systems. *ACM Transactions on Interactive Intelligent Systems (TiiS)*, 10(4):1–31, 2020.

[6] Bo Li, Peng Qi, Bo Liu, Shuai Di, Jingen Liu, Jiquan Pei, Jinfeng Yi, and Bowen Zhou. Trustworthy ai: From principles to practices. *ACM Computing Surveys*, 55(9):1–46, 2023.

[7] Diogo V Carvalho, Eduardo M Pereira, and Jaime S Cardoso. Machine learning interpretability: A survey on methods and metrics. *Electronics*, 8 (8):832, 2019.

[8] Heike Felzmann, Eduard Fosch Villaronga, Christoph Lutz, and Aurelia Tamò-Larrieux. Transparency you can trust: Transparency requirements

for artificial intelligence between legal norms and contextual concerns. *Big Data & Society*, 6(1):2053951719860542, 2019.

[9] Umit Cali, Murat Kuzlu, Manisa Pipattanasomporn, James Kempf, and Linquan Bai. Foundations of big data, machine learning, and artificial intelligence and explainable artificial intelligence. *Digitalization of Power Markets and Systems Using Energy Informatics*, pages 115–137, 2021.

[10] Davinder Kaur, Suleyman Uslu, and Arjan Durresi. Requirements for trustworthy artificial intelligence–a review. In *Advances in Networked-Based Information Systems: The 23rd International Conference on Network-Based Information Systems (NBiS-2020) 23*, pages 105–115. Springer, 2021.

[11] Haochen Liu, Yiqi Wang, Wenqi Fan, Xiaorui Liu, Yaxin Li, Shaili Jain, Yunhao Liu, Anil Jain, and Jiliang Tang. Trustworthy ai: A computational perspective. *ACM Transactions on Intelligent Systems and Technology*, 14 (1):1–59, 2022.

[12] Abhishek Kumar, Tristan Braud, Sasu Tarkoma, and Pan Hui. Trustworthy ai in the age of pervasive computing and big data. In *2020 IEEE International Conference on Pervasive Computing and Communications Workshops (PerCom Workshops)*, pages 1–6. IEEE, 2020.

[13] Rosario Cammarota, Matthias Schunter, Anand Rajan, Fabian Boemer, Ágnes Kiss, Amos Treiber, Christian Weinert, Thomas Schneider, Emmanuel Stapf, Ahmad-Reza Sadeghi, et al. Trustworthy ai inference systems: An industry research view. *arXiv preprint arXiv:2008.04449*, 2020.

[14] Davinder Kaur, Suleyman Uslu, Kaley J Rittichier, and Arjan Durresi. Trustworthy artificial intelligence: a review. *ACM Computing Surveys (CSUR)*, 55(2):1–38, 2022.

[15] Philipp Schmidt, Felix Biessmann, and Timm Teubner. Transparency and trust in artificial intelligence systems. *Journal of Decision Systems*, 29(4): 260–278, 2020.

[16] Warren J von Eschenbach. Transparency and the black box problem: Why we do not trust ai. *Philosophy & Technology*, 34(4):1607–1622, 2021.

[17] Daniel Varona and Juan Luis Suárez. Discrimination, bias, fairness, and trustworthy ai. *Applied Sciences*, 12(12):5826, 2022.

[18] Claudio Novelli, Mariarosaria Taddeo, and Luciano Floridi. Accountability in artificial intelligence: what it is and how it works. *AI & SOCIETY*, pages 1–12, 2023.

[19] Joyce Chou, Roger Ibars, and Oscar Murillo. In pursuit of inclusive ai. *Microsoft Res. Microsoft*, 2018.

[20] Ayodeji Oseni, Nour Moustafa, Helge Janicke, Peng Liu, Zahir Tari, and Athanasios Vasilakos. Security and privacy for artificial intelligence: Opportunities and challenges. *arXiv preprint arXiv:2102.04661*, 2021.

2 Reliability: Uncertainty Quantification in Artificial Intelligence

Let's imagine you are teaching a computer to recognize traffic signs, like stop signs or speed limit signs like in Figure 2.1. This computer is like a smart student, but it's not perfect, it's still learning.

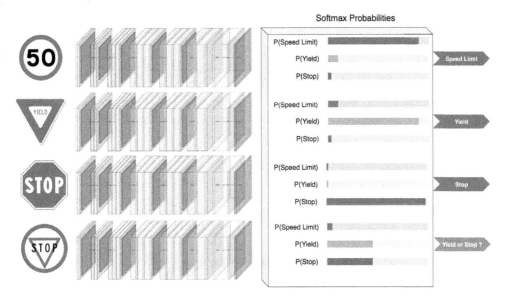

Figure 2.1: Uncertainty in AI model decisions

Uncertainty in AI is like the computer admitting it doesn't know everything for sure. For example, when it sees a traffic sign, it might be unsure about what it is or what it means. This uncertainty comes from a few places.

First, think about the pictures the computer has learned from. They might be taken in different lights and weather conditions, or even with some objects blocking the view. So, the computer has to deal with this uncertainty because the real world sometimes differs from the pictures it learned from.

Then, there needs to be more certainty in how the computer was trained. It is like teaching the computer some rules, which might only cover some situations. So, it needs clarification when it sees a new sign or something different.

Lastly, the computer might have to make decisions based on partial information. Imagine that it sees a sign, but a tree branch covers part of it, or there is a bit of fog. In such cases, it can only be partially specific about the sign.

Uncertainty in AI is like the computer saying, "I'm doing my best, but I can't be 100% sure about everything." This honesty about not being perfect is important, mainly when the computer is used in things like self-driving cars. It helps us understand when the computer might need extra help or when we should be more cautious.

2.1 Introduction

Uncertainty Quantification (UQ) is one of the challenging topics in the context of trustworthy AI. It involves the study of the effects of uncertainty on the output of AI-based models [1]. In recent years, UQ has become more crucial, particularly high-risk applications significantly depended on AI/ML-based models, including healthcare [2, 3], robotics [4], self-driving cars [5], finance [6], smart grids [7], space weather predictions [8], and next-generation communication (5G and beyond) [9].

In the literature, to deal with model uncertainty using ML techniques, a variety of methods have been developed to quantify, estimate and propagate uncertainty in AI/ML-based models. Uncertainty can arise from different sources, such as model architecture, training data, and inference algorithms [10, 11, 12, 13]. For the model architecture, the selection of layers, their connections, and hyperparameters that control their behavior in the model architecture can lead to uncertainty. It should be carefully adjusted to navigate the uncertain terrain. For training data, it is also a source of uncertainty due to its complexity and diversity. The model learns from the data provided, trying to identify relationships between data points and features with a degree of uncertainty. Additionally, the uncertainty is higher, especially for deep learning (DL) models [14, 15] due to the nature of neural networks. For DL models, each neuron's activation and weight can cause a slight change in the model training. The study [16] provides a comprehensive overview of uncertainty estimation, covering recent advances, challenges, and potential research directions. It also introduces key sources of uncertainty, categorizing them into model and data uncertainty. Various modeling approaches, including deterministic and Bayesian neural networks, are discussed, along with measures of uncertainty and methods for calibration. It also emphasizes limitations in high-risk applications and suggests future steps toward a wider adoption of uncertainty quantification methods. The methods allow researchers to estimate the probability distributions of the model parameters and generate samples of input variables, and understanding these methods is essential to develop accurate and reliable AI models. The state-of-the-art UQ approaches are provided in [17]. However, it is clear that two widely used types of uncertainty quantification (UQ) methods, i.e., Bayesian approximation and Ensemble methods, are more promising than other methods. Bayesian approximation methods refer to using computational methods [18], such as Monte Carlo, to estimate complex probability distributions in Bayesian statistics, while ensemble methods model uncertainty using multiple models [19]. The authors in [20] proposed a novel approach method for model uncertainty estimation using ML techniques, applied specifically in rainfall-runoff modeling. The proposed method consists of two main steps, i.e., (1) estimating the probability distribution of model errors for various hydrological cases and (2) aggregating the parameters of these distributions to create target values for training ML models. The model is trained to encapsulate past information concerning model errors in different hydrological conditions, and then the trained model is used to estimate the probability distribution of model errors for new hydrological model. According to the results, the proposed method can provide consistent, interpretable, and improved model uncertainty estimates.

This chapter provides an overview of uncertainty quantification or UQ along with practical examples in Python for readers who have a background in data science and ML but limited experience with probability and uncertainty theories. If you have knowledge of probability and uncertainty in AI, you can bypass the initial sections and go directly to the practical examples.

2.2 Types of Uncertainty

These are various forms of uncertainty based on the behavior and reliability of AI/ML-based models. In this section, two main types of uncertainty in AI/ML concept, i.e., epistemic and aleatoric uncertainty, will be explained.

2.2.1 Epistemic Uncertainty

Epistemic uncertainty refers to the uncertainty that originates from the lack of knowledge in the model [21], which captures the uncertainty associated with lack of information or ambiguity in the model parameters.

Consider a supervised learning problem where we have a dataset consisting of input-output pairs, denoted as $(\mathbf{X}, \mathbf{y})$, where $\mathbf{X} = \{x_1, x_2, \ldots, x_n\}$ represents the input features and $\mathbf{y} = \{y_1, y_2, \ldots, y_n\}$ represents the corresponding output labels or targets. It is assumed that a parametric model $f(\mathbf{x}; \theta)$ that maps the input features to the output labels, where θ represents the model parameters. The goal is to estimate the optimal set of parameters that best fits the observed data.

In the context of epistemic uncertainty, it is acknowledged that the true model may not be captured perfectly by the chosen model $f(\mathbf{x}; \theta)$. Therefore, we introduce an additional level of uncertainty by treating the model parameters θ as random variables instead of fixed values, e.g., Bayes' theorem is given below.

$$P(\theta|D) = \frac{P(D|\theta)P(\theta)}{P(D)} \qquad (2.1)$$

where $P(\theta|D)$ is the posterior probability of the model parameters, i.e., θ, given the observed data D, $P(D|\theta)$ is the likelihood of the observed data that given the model parameters, $P(\theta)$ is the prior probability of the model parameters, and $P(D)$ is the marginal likelihood of the observed data.

To incorporate this uncertainty, we assign a prior distribution $P(\theta)$ over the model parameters θ, representing the initial beliefs or knowledge about the parameter values before observing the data. The prior distribution captures our prior uncertainty about the parameter values.

After observing the data, we update the beliefs about the parameter values using Bayes' theorem. The posterior distribution $P(\theta|\mathbf{X}, \mathbf{y})$ represents the updated distribution over the parameters given the observed data. It combines the prior distribution with the likelihood function $P(\mathbf{y}|\mathbf{X}, \theta)$, which measures the probability of the observed data given the model parameters.

The posterior distribution encapsulates the epistemic uncertainty by reflecting the updated knowledge about the parameter values after observing the data. It provides a distribution of plausible parameter values, quantifying our uncertainty about the true values of the parameters.

In practice, obtaining the exact posterior distribution is often analytically intractable due to the complexity of the likelihood function and the prior. Therefore, various approximation methods, such as Markov Chain Monte Carlo or variational inference, are commonly used to approximate the posterior distribution.

By characterizing the posterior distribution, we can estimate epistemic uncertainty in various ways. For example, we can compute the predictive distribution $P(\mathbf{y}_{\text{new}}|\mathbf{x}_{\text{new}}, \mathbf{X}, \mathbf{y})$ for a new input $\mathbf{x}_{\text{new}}$ by marginalizing the parameter uncertainty. This predictive distribution provides a measure of uncertainty associated with the model's predictions for new, unseen data points.

Epistemic uncertainty helps us understand the limitations of our model and provides a way to make more informed decisions by accounting for the uncertainty due to the lack of model knowledge about the true underlying data-generating process.

2.2.2 Aleatoric Uncertainty

Aleatoric uncertainty refers to the inherent variability or noise present in the data. It is characterized by the uncertainty that remains even when the model is given complete information about the inputs. In statistical terms, aleatoric uncertainty captures the irreducible randomness in observations [22]. Coin flipping is a classic example of aleatoric uncertainty. The data-generating process in this experiment has a random element that cannot be reduced by any extra information (except Laplace's demon). Therefore, even the most accurate model of this process will only be able to give probabilities for the two possible results, heads and tails, but not a definitive answer [21].

Let's consider a regression task where we have input-output pairs $(\mathbf{X}, \mathbf{y})$ as follows:

- Input data: $\mathbf{X} = \{\mathbf{x}_1, \mathbf{x}_2, \cdots, \mathbf{x}_n\}$
- Output data: $\mathbf{y} = \{y_1, y_2, \cdots, y_n\}$

The goal is to learn a function $f(\mathbf{x}; \theta)$ that maps the inputs to the outputs, where θ represents the parameters of the model. In the context of aleatoric uncertainty, we introduce a noise term ϵ, which captures the inherent variability or randomness in the observations. It is typically assumed that the noise term follows a certain distribution, such as the Gaussian distribution with mean zero and variance σ^2.

Thus, the observed outputs can be modeled as:

$$y_i = f(\mathbf{x}_i; \theta) + \epsilon_i, \quad for\ i = 1, 2, \cdots, n \tag{2.2}$$

Here, ϵ_i represents the noise term associated with the i_{th} observation.

To quantify the aleatoric uncertainty, it is needed to estimate the parameters of the noise distribution. This can be done by maximizing the likelihood of the observed data given the model parameters and the noise distribution. In mathematical terms, the distribution can be estimated as follows:

$$P(\epsilon|\mathbf{X}, \mathbf{y}; \theta) \tag{2.3}$$

By modeling the noise term ϵ, it can be obtained a probabilistic representation of the results can be obtained, taking into account the inherent variability of the data.

2.3 Quantifying Uncertainty

Quantifying uncertainty is a crucial task in the concept of trustworthy AI, especially for applications requiring high reliability, i.e., healthcare, self-driving cars, or finance. As mentioned earlier, uncertainty can arise from various sources, including noise in the input data, model architecture, and parameter initialization. As mentioned earlier, two common types of uncertainty in the concept of trustworthy AI have already been explained, i.e., epistemic and aleatoric uncertainty. Quantifying both epistemic and aleatoric uncertainty is crucial for building reliable AI models. By understanding and modeling uncertainty, robust models can be built that not only make accurate predictions, but also provide insights into the reliability and limitations of those predictions.

There are several approaches and strategies to accomplish this [23, 24]. In this subsection, the most two popular methods, i.e., Monte Carlo Dropout and Ensemble, will briefly be explained.

2.3.1 Monte Carlo Dropout

Monte Carlo Dropout approach is used to estimate the epistemic uncertainty by approximating the distribution of the model output by sampling multiple predictions with different dropout masks, thereby introducing randomness in the model prediction. It can be obtained by setting the dropout rate to 0 during the testing and generating multiple predictions with dropout applied during training.

During training, dropout is applied to the output of each layer with probability p. This can be given as follows:

$$y = f(\mathbf{x}, \theta) \cdot m, \quad m \sim Bernoulli(p) \tag{2.4}$$

where θ denotes the set of model parameters, $\mathbf{x}$ the input, and y the output, $f(\mathbf{x}, \theta)$ is the model prediction, f is the neural network function and m is a binary mask sampled from a Bernoulli distribution with probability p.

During testing, the dropout rate is set to 0, and the model prediction is obtained by averaging the output of T stochastic forward passes through the network:

$$y = \frac{1}{T} \sum_{t=1}^{T} f(\mathbf{x}, \theta_t) \tag{2.5}$$

where θ_t is a set of randomly sampled weights for the $t_t h$ forward pass.

The predictive distribution can be approximated by calculating the output mean and variance over several samples, θ, with dropout applied during inference time. It can be given as follows:

$$E_{p(y|\mathbf{x})}[\hat{y}] \approx \frac{1}{T} \sum_{t=1}^{T} f(\mathbf{x}, \theta_t)$$
$$V_{p(y|\mathbf{x})}[\hat{y}] \approx \frac{1}{T} \sum_{t=1}^{T} (f(\mathbf{x}, \theta_t) - E_{p(y|\mathbf{x})}[\hat{y}])^2 \tag{2.6}$$

where $\hat{y}$ is the model prediction with activated dropout, $\mathbb{E}_{p(y|\mathbf{x})}[\hat{y}]$ and $V_{p(y|\mathbf{x})}[\hat{y}]$ are the mean and variance of the predictive distribution, respectively.

2.3.2 Ensemble Models

Ensemble models include multiple trained models on the same dataset and then combine their predictions to obtain a final prediction. This typically involves training multiple models with the same architecture but different initial weights on the different portions of the dataset. Each model produces a softmax output for a given input instance and combines all models' outputs to obtain a final prediction.

Quantifying the uncertainty in the ensemble models uses the variance of the softmax outputs produced by the individual models. Specifically, given an input $\mathbf{x}$, it can be obtained T different softmax outputs from T different models: $\{y_1, y_2, ..., y_T\}$. Then it can be calculated the mean softmax output as follows:

$$\bar{y} = \frac{1}{T} \sum_{t=1}^{T} y_t \tag{2.7}$$

The variance of the softmax output(s) can be calculated as follows:

$$\sigma_y^2 = \frac{1}{T-1} \sum_{t=1}^{T} (y_t - \bar{y})^2 \tag{2.8}$$

This variance represents the uncertainty in the ensemble prediction. Suppose the slight variance indicates that the individual models produce similar outputs, which gives greater confidence in the ensemble prediction. On the other hand, if the variance is significant, it indicates that the individual models produce diverse outputs, suggesting that the prediction is more uncertain.

Ensemble models based on uncertainty quantification can provide more accurate uncertainty estimates than other methods, such as Monte Carlo dropout. Ensemble models can capture a broader range of possible models, whereas Monte Carlo dropout only captures the uncertainty associated with the weights in a single model. However, they require training and maintaining multiple models, which can be computationally expensive and time-consuming. Additionally, it can take time to determine the optimal number of models to include in the ensemble. Finally, the ensemble can be less effective if the individual models are too similar.

The Figure 2.2 shows different model variants created as an ensemble, each trained with a subset of the input data. A total of six models are displayed,

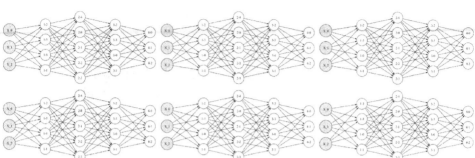

Figure 2.2: Ensemble-Based Model Variants

with three models per row. The visual representation of each model is provided, emphasizing the diversity within the ensemble.

2.3.3 Quantifiers

Quantifiers in uncertainties are used to calculate the degree of uncertainty associated with a particular statement, prediction, or measurement. The most common quantifiers, i.e., the variation ratio, predictive entropy, mean softmax, and standard deviation, are explained as follows:

2.3.3.1 Variation Ratio

The Variation Ratio (VR) is a measure of the concentration of probability masses in the predictive distribution. It is defined as the difference between the maximum predicted probability and the average predicted probability [25]. It is given as follows:

$$\text{VR} = 1 - \max_{y} p(y|\mathbf{x}, \theta) \tag{2.9}$$

It is supposed that there is a classification task with three possible classes: $y = 0, 1, 2$. The model is trained the Monte Carlo Dropout neural network with $T = 5$ dropout samples per input, and the softmax outputs are given in Table 2.1 for an input $\mathbf{x}$.

Table 2.1: VR: Softmax outputs of the trained Monte Carlo Dropout neural network with $T = 5$ dropout samples

Sample t	Class 0	Class 1	Class 2	Most Probable Class
1	0.1	0.4	0.5	2
2	0.2	0.3	0.5	2
3	0.15	0.35	0.5	2
4	0.45	0.3	0.25	0
5	0.05	0.6	0.35	1

To calculate the variation ratio, the most probable class for each dropout sample and then the frequency of the most probable class across all T samples are calculated, sequentially. In this case, the most probable class is 2 for three out of the five samples, so the Variation Ratio (VR) is 0.4, i.e., $\text{VR} = 1 - 3/5 = 0.4$. This means that there is a 40% chance that the most probable class is incorrect. A lower VR indicates greater confidence in terms of model prediction.

2.3.3.2 Predictive Entropy

The Predictive Entropy (PE) is a measure of uncertainty in the predictive distribution, which is defined as the negative sum of predicted probabilities weighted by their algorithms [26]. It can simply be given as follows:

$$PE = -\sum_y p(y|\mathbf{x}, \theta) \log_2 p(y|\mathbf{x}, \theta) \qquad (2.10)$$

Suppose we have a classification task with three possible classes: $y = 0, 1, 2$, and train a Monte Carlo Dropout neural network with $T = 5$ dropout samples per input, and the softmax outputs are given in Table 2.2 for an input $\mathbf{x}$.

Sample t	Class 0	Class 1	Class 2
1	0.2	0.3	0.5
2	0.3	0.3	0.4
3	0.25	0.25	0.5
4	0.1	0.2	0.7
5	0.4	0.1	0.5
Avg	0.25	0.24	0.52

Table 2.2: PE: Softmax outputs of the trained Monte Carlo Dropout neural network with $T = 5$ dropout samples

To calculate the predictive entropy using the given table and show the uncertainty value for each class and the overall uncertainty, we can calculate the entropy for each class separately and then take the average.

$$
\begin{aligned}
H(y = 0) &= -(0.2 \cdot \log_2(0.2) + 0.3 \cdot \log_2(0.3) + 0.25 \cdot \log_2(0.25) \\
&\quad + 0.1 \cdot \log_2(0.1) + 0.4 \cdot \log_2(0.4)) = 1.881 \\
H(y = 1) &= -(0.3 \cdot \log_2(0.3) + 0.3 \cdot \log_2(0.3) + 0.25 \cdot \log_2(0.25) \\
&\quad + 0.2 \cdot \log_2(0.2) + 0.1 \cdot \log_2(0.1)) = 1.901 \\
H(y = 2) &= -(0.5 \cdot \log_2(0.5) + 0.4 \cdot \log_2(0.4) + 0.5 \cdot \log_2(0.5) \\
&\quad + 0.7 \cdot \log_2(0.7) + 0.5 \cdot \log_2(0.5)) = 1.912
\end{aligned}
\qquad (2.11)
$$

To calculate the overall uncertainty, we can take the average of the individual entropies:

$$H(y) = \frac{1}{3}\cdot(H(y=0)+H(y=1)+H(y=2)) = \frac{1}{3}\cdot(1.881+1.901+1.912) = 1.898$$

$$(2.12)$$

2.3.3.3 Mean Softmax

The Mean Softmax-based uncertainty for a given deep learning model measures the average uncertainty or unpredictability of the model's predictions based on the softmax probabilities [27]. It provides an indication of how confident or uncertain the model is regarding its predictions. To calculate the Mean Softmax-based uncertainty, these steps are followed:

1. Calculate the mean probability for each class:

$$c : \bar{p}_c = \frac{1}{N}\sum i = 1^N p_c^{(i)}$$

$$(2.13)$$

   where $p_c^{(i)}$ is the softmax probability of Class c for the i_{th} input instance, c ranges from 1 to C, C is the total number of classes, and N is the total number of input instances.

2. Calculate the uncertainty for each class using the mean probabilities:

$$c : U_c = 1 - \bar{p}_c$$

$$(2.14)$$

3. Calculate the mean uncertainty:

$$\bar{U} = \frac{1}{C}\sum_{c=1}^{C} U_c$$

$$(2.15)$$

The amount of uncertainty in a model prediction can be determined by subtracting the mean probability from 1. A higher uncertainty implies a less certain prediction, while a lower uncertainty implies a more confident prediction.

In order to determine the mean softmax-based uncertainty value for the prediction output using Monte Carlo dropouts, it is needed to calculate the mean softmax probability for each class and then use these probabilities to calculate the uncertainty. It is given in the following example how you can calculate as follows:

1. Calculate the mean probability for each class:
   - Class 0 = (0.2 + 0.3 + 0.25 + 0.1 + 0.4) / 5 = 0.25
   - Class 1 = (0.3 + 0.3 + 0.25 + 0.2 + 0.1) / 5 = 0.24
   - Class 2 = (0.5 + 0.4 + 0.5 + 0.7 + 0.5) / 5 = 0.52.
2. Calculate the uncertainty for each class using the mean probabilities:
   - Uncertainty for Class 0 = 1 - 0.25 = 0.75
   - Uncertainty for Class 1 = 1 - 0.24 = 0.76
   - Uncertainty for Class 2 = 1 - 0.52 = 0.48.
3. Calculate the mean uncertainty:
   Mean uncertainty = (Uncertainty for Class 0 + Uncertainty for Class 1 + Uncertainty for Class 2) / 3 = (0.75 + 0.76 + 0.48) / 3 = 0.66333333333

Therefore, the mean softmax based uncertainty value for the Monte Carlo dropout results given is approximately 0.6633.

2.3.3.4 Standard Deviation

The Standard Deviation-based uncertainty measures the variation or spread of the model predictions based on softmax probabilities. It quantifies how much the predictions deviate from the average or mean prediction [28]. To calculate the Standard Deviation-based uncertainty, these steps are followed:

1. Calculate the mean probability for each class:

$$c : \bar{p}_c = \frac{1}{N} \sum i = 1^N p_c^{(i)} \tag{2.16}$$

where $p_c^{(i)}$ is the softmax probability of Class c for the i_{th} input instance, c ranges from 1 to C, C is the total number of classes, and N is the total number of input instances.

2. Calculate the squared deviation from the mean for each class:

$$c : (p_c^{(i)} - \bar{p}_c)^2 \tag{2.17}$$

3. Calculate the variance for each class:

$$c : V_c = \frac{1}{N} \sum_{i=1}^{N} (p_c^{(i)} - \bar{p}_c)^2 \tag{2.18}$$

4. Calculate the standard deviation for each class:

$$c : SD_c = \sqrt{V_c} \tag{2.19}$$

5. Calculate the mean standard deviation:

$$\bar{SD} = \frac{1}{C} \sum_{c=1}^{C} SD_c \tag{2.20}$$

In summary, the standard deviation-based uncertainty is obtained by calculating the standard deviation for each class based on the softmax probabilities from the model's predictions and then calculating the mean standard deviation. The standard deviation measures the dispersion of the probabilities around the mean, and the mean standard deviation represents the average dispersion across all classes. Note that a higher standard deviation indicates a higher degree of variation or uncertainty in the predictions, while a lower standard deviation suggests a more consistent or certain set of predictions.

To calculate the standard deviation-based uncertainty value for the prediction output using Monte Carlo dropouts, it is needed to compute the standard deviation of the softmax probabilities for each class. It is given in the following example how you can calculate as follows:

1. Calculate the mean probability for each class:
   - Mean probability for Class 0: $\bar{p}_0 = \frac{0.2+0.3+0.25+0.1+0.4}{5} = 0.25$
   - Mean probability for Class 1: $\bar{p}_1 = \frac{0.3+0.3+0.25+0.2+0.1}{5} = 0.24$
   - Mean probability for Class 2: $\bar{p}_2 = \frac{0.5+0.4+0.5+0.7+0.5}{5} = 0.52$
2. Calculate the squared deviation from the mean for each class:
   - Squared deviation for Class 0: $(0.2 - 0.25)^2 = 0.0025$
   - Squared deviation for Class 1: $(0.3 - 0.24)^2 = 0.0036$
   - Squared deviation for Class 2: $(0.5 - 0.52)^2 = 0.0004$
3. Calculate the variance for each class:
   - Variance for Class 0: $V_0 = \frac{0.0025+0.0036+0.0025+0.0121+0.01}{5} = 0.00614$
   - Variance for Class 1: $V_1 = \frac{0.0036+0.0036+0.0025+0.0016+0.0144}{5} = 0.00594$
   - Variance for Class 2: $V_2 = \frac{0.01+0.0025+0.01+0.0001+0.01}{5} = 0.00672$
4. Calculate the standard deviation for each class:
   - Standard deviation for Class 0: $SD_0 = \sqrt{0.00614} \approx 0.0783$
   - Standard deviation for Class 1: $SD_1 = \sqrt{0.00594} \approx 0.0771$
   - Standard deviation for Class 2: $SD_2 = \sqrt{0.00672} \approx 0.082$
5. Calculate the mean standard deviation:
   - Mean standard deviation: $\bar{SD} = \frac{0.0783+0.0771+0.082}{3} \approx 0.0798$

Therefore, the standard deviation-based uncertainty value for the given Monte Carlo dropout results is approximately 0.0798.

2.3.4 Practical Example for Monte Carlo Dropout

The following code focusing on *Monte Carlo Dropout* method combines traditional deep learning techniques with uncertainty quantification to obtain probabilistic predictions and measure different aspects of uncertainty in the model output. The code demonstrates the usage of the *uncertainty_wizard* library to train and evaluate a stochastic neural network model on the MNIST digits dataset. The code performs the following steps. Every step will be thoroughly explained since this is Part 1 of the first example.

1. **Importing Libraries:** Import the necessary libraries, including *tensorflow, uncertainty_ wizard, and tqdm*. These libraries are typically used in ML projects, with *tensorflow* serving as the core deep learning framework, *uncertainty_ wizard* potentially providing tools for handling uncertainty, and *tqdm* enhancing the training process with progress bars for better user feedback.

```
1  # ================================================
2  ### Part 1
3  #Import common libraries
4  import tensorflow as tf
5  import uncertainty_wizard as uwiz
6  from tqdm.keras import TqdmCallback
```

2. **Loading Dataset and Data Preparation:** Load the *MNIST* digits dataset, and prepare the *MNIST* dataset for training a ML model, ensuring the input images are properly formatted and the labels are in the appropriate representation for training.

```
1  # Load the MNIST digits dataset
2  (x_train, y_train), (x_test, y_test) =
       tf.keras.datasets.mnist.load_data()
3
4  # Normalize pixel values to the range [0, 1]
5  x_train = (x_train.astype('float32') /
       255).reshape(x_train.shape[0], 28, 28, 1)
6  x_test = (x_test.astype('float32') /
       255).reshape(x_test.shape[0], 28, 28, 1)
```

3. **Converting Labels to One-hot Encoding:** Convert labels to one-hot encoding using *tf.keras.utils.to_ categorical()* to match the model's output format.

```
1  # Convert labels to one-hot encoding
2  y_train = tf.keras.utils.to_categorical(y_train,
       num_classes=10)
```

4. **Model Definition:** Define the model using the *StochasticSequential* class from *uncertainty_ wizard*. The model architecture consists of convolutional layers, max pooling, dropout regularization, and dense layers. It

is a stochastic model that incorporates uncertainty estimation, which defines a convolutional neural network (CNN) architecture for classifying the *MNIST* dataset. The model starts with convolutional layers for feature extraction, followed by max pooling and dropout for regularization. Then, it flattens the data and passes it through fully connected layers for classification. The final layer outputs probabilities using a softmax activation function.

```
# Create the model
model = uwiz.models.StochasticSequential()
model.add(tf.keras.layers.Conv2D(32, kernel_size=(3, 3),
    activation='relu', input_shape=(28, 28, 1)))
model.add(tf.keras.layers.Conv2D(64, (3, 3),
    activation='relu'))
model.add(tf.keras.layers.MaxPooling2D(pool_size=(2, 2)))
model.add(tf.keras.layers.Dropout(0.5)) # Dropouts !!!
model.add(tf.keras.layers.Flatten())
model.add(tf.keras.layers.Dense(128, activation='relu'))
model.add(tf.keras.layers.Dense(10, activation='softmax'))
```

5. **Model Compilation:** Compile the model by specifying the loss function, optimizer, and evaluation metrics. The function, i.e., *model.compile*, configures the model for training. It requires three arguments: loss, optimizer, and metrics.

```
# Compiling the keras models
model.compile(loss=tf.keras.losses.categorical_crossentropy,
    optimizer='rmsprop', metrics=['accuracy'])
```

6. **Training the Model:** Fit the model to the training data, using a validation split, batch size, and number of epochs. It initiates the training process of the model using the provided training data *(x_ train and y_ train)*. It will run for 5 epochs, with a batch size of 10,000, and 10% of the data will be used for validation. The progress will be displayed with a progress bar due to the *TqdmCallback*.

```
# Fiting the model to the training data
model.fit(x_train, y_train, validation_split=0.1,
    batch_size=10000, epochs=5, verbose=0,
    callbacks=[TqdmCallback(verbose=1)])
```

7. **Making Predictions:** Predict the outputs of the model on the test data while quantifying uncertainty using different quantifiers *'var_ ratio'*,

'pred_entropy', and *'mean_softmax'*. The *predict_quantified* method of
the model from *uncertainty_wizard* is used for this purpose. This code
block applies the trained model to the test data *(x_test)* to make predictions, while also quantifying uncertainty using various methods specified
in quantifiers. The results are stored in the results variable for further
analysis.

```
1 #Predicting the outputs of the model:
2 quantifiers = ['var_ratio', 'pred_entropy', 'mean_softmax']
3 results = model.predict_quantified(x_test,
4                                    quantifier=quantifiers,
5                                    batch_size=64,
6                                    sample_size=32,
7                                    verbose=0)
```

The following code, i.e., Part 2 of the first example, performs additional analysis
and visualization of the uncertainty quantification results obtained from the
stochastic neural network model. The code performs the following steps.

1. **Importing Libraries:** Imports the necessary library *confusion_matrix*
   from *scikit-learn*, *plt* for plotting from *matplotlib.pyplot*, and *np* for numerical computations from *numpy*.

```
1 #=========================================
2 ### Part 2
3 #Imports the necessary library
4 from sklearn.metrics import confusion_matrix
5 import matplotlib.pyplot as plt
6 import numpy as np
```

2. **Initializing the Random Number Generator:** Set the random seed
   to *10* for the *NumPy* random number generator.

```
1 # Initialize the random number generator
2 np.random.seed(10)
```

3. **Calculating Predictions and Prediction Uncertainties:** Extract the
   predictions and prediction uncertainties from the results obtained using
   different quantifiers. It involves the calculation and analysis of predictions
   and uncertainties using different quantifiers like *"pcs"*, *"pred_entropy"*,

and "mean_softmax". The results are stored in separate variables for further processing.

```
1 # Calculate the predictions and prediction uncertainties
2 pcs_predictions, pcs_uncertainties = results[0]
3 pred_entropy_predictions, pred_entropy_uncertainties =
    results[1]
4 mean_softmax_predictions, mean_softmax_uncertainties =
    results[2]
```

4. **Computing the Confusion Matrix:** Compute the confusion matrix using the *confusion_matrix* function from *scikit-learn*, which compares the true labels *(y_test)* with the predictions obtained using the *pcs* quantifier. The confusion matrix is stored in the variable *confusion_mtx*.

```
1 #Calculate the confusion matrix
2 confusion_mtx = confusion_matrix(y_test, pcs_predictions)
```

5. **Creating a Figure with Suplots:** Create a figure with 2 rows and 2 columns to display multiple subplots, i.e., *fig, axs = plt.subplots(2, 2, figsize=(15, 10))*. It utilizes the subplots function from the *matplotlib.pyplot* module to create a grid of subplots, and sets the dimensions of the entire figure and font size to *20*. In this case, the figure will be 15 units wide and *10* units tall.

```
1 # Create a subplot with 2 rows and 2 columns
2 fig, axs = plt.subplots(2, 2, figsize=(15, 10))
3 # Increase the font size for all subplots
4 fontsize = 20
```

6. **Plotting Prediction Uncertainties for VariationRatio:** Plot a histogram of the prediction uncertainties obtained from the *pcs* quantifier in the first subplot for *VariationRatio* and set the x-axis label to *'Variation Ratio'*, the y-axis label to *'Count'*, and giving the plot the title *'Uncertainty - VariationRatio'*. It visualizes the distribution of true labels and predicted labels.

```
1 # Plot a histogram of the prediction uncertainties from pcs
    in the first subplot
2 axs[0, 0].hist(pcs_uncertainties, bins=50)
3 axs[0, 0].set_xlabel('Variation Ratio', fontsize=fontsize)
4 axs[0, 0].set_ylabel('Count', fontsize=fontsize)
5 axs[0, 0].set_title('Uncertainty - VariationRatio',
    fontsize=fontsize)
```

7. **Plotting Prediction Uncertainties for Predictive Entropy:** Plot a histogram of the prediction uncertainties obtained from the *pcs* quantifier in the second subplot. It shows the prediction uncertainty using the metric *PredictiveEntropy*. The x-axis is labeled accordingly, the y-axis is labeled *Count*, and the plot is given the title *Uncertainty - PredictiveEntropy'*.

```
1 # Plot a histogram of the prediction uncertainties from
      pred_entropy in the second subplot
2 axs[0, 1].hist(pred_entropy_uncertainties, bins=50)
3 axs[0, 1].set_xlabel('Prediction uncertainty
      (PredictiveEntropy)', fontsize=fontsize)
4 axs[0, 1].set_ylabel('Count', fontsize=fontsize)
5 axs[0, 1].set_title('Uncertainty - PredictiveEntropy',
      fontsize=fontsize)
```

8. **Plotting Prediction Uncertainties for Mean Softmax:** Plot a histogram of the prediction uncertainties for *Mean Softmax* in the third subplot. It illustrates the prediction uncertainty using the metric *Mean Softmax*. The x-axis is labeled *'Mean Softmax'*, the y-axis is labeled *'Count'*, and the plot is given the title *'Uncertainty - MeanSoftmax'*.

```
1 # Plot a histogram of the prediction uncertainties from
      mean_softmax in the fourth subplot
2 axs[1, 0].hist(mean_softmax_uncertainties, bins=50)
3 axs[1, 0].set_xlabel('Mean Softmax', fontsize=fontsize)
4 axs[1, 0].set_ylabel('Count', fontsize=fontsize)
5 axs[1, 0].set_title('Uncertainty - MeanSoftmax',
      fontsize=fontsize)
```

9. **Plotting the Confusion Matrix:** Plot the confusion matrix in a subplot. The x-axis represents predicted labels, the y-axis represents true labels, and the colors in the matrix indicate the number of instances classified into each class.

```
1 # Plot the confusion matrix in the fifth subplot
2 axs[1, 1].imshow(confusion_mtx, interpolation='nearest',
      cmap=plt.cm.Blues)
3 axs[1, 1].set_xticks(np.arange(10))
4 axs[1, 1].set_yticks(np.arange(10))
5 axs[1, 1].set_xlabel('Predicted label', fontsize=fontsize)
6 axs[1, 1].set_ylabel('True label', fontsize=fontsize)
7 axs[1, 1].set_title('Confusion Matrix', fontsize=fontsize)
```

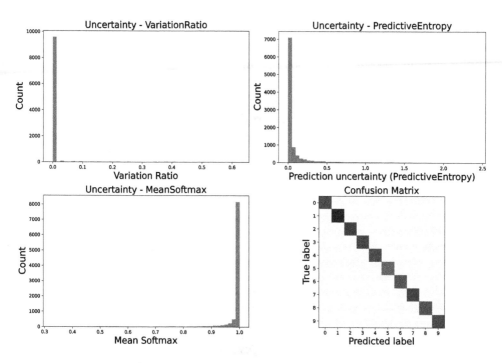

Figure 2.3: This figure displays histograms representing prediction uncertainty measures for different quantifiers (Variation Ratio, Predictive Entropy, and Mean Softmax) along with a Confusion Matrix, providing insights into the model's predictive performance.

10. **Displaying the Results:** Adjust the padding between the subplots for better visualization using *tight_layout* and display results.

```
1  # Adjust the padding between the subplots
2  plt.tight_layout()
3  # Show the plot
4  plt.show()
```

The code helps visualize different aspects of uncertainty in the model's predictions, including the confusion matrix, variation ratio, predictive entropy, and mean softmax values.

The additional code segment, i.e., Part 3 of the first example, sets a threshold to determine highly uncertain instances based on the prediction uncertainties obtained from the *"pred_ entropy"* quantifier. It then identifies the indices of instances that have prediction uncertainties higher than the threshold. Finally, it displays the images corresponding to these highly uncertain instances along with their predicted labels and uncertainties. Each part of the code will be explained below.

1. **Setting the Threshold:** Set a threshold value of 2.5 to determine highly uncertain instances.

```
1  #==========================================
2  # Part 3
3  # Set a threshold to determine highly uncertain instances
4  threshold = 2.5
```

2. **Extracting the Predicted Labels:** Extract the predicted labels *(pred_-labels)* and prediction uncertainties *(pred_ entropy_ uncertainties)* from the *pred_ entropy* quantifier.

```
1  # Get the predictions, prediction uncertainties, and
      predicted labels
2  pred_labels, pred_entropy_uncertainties = results[1][0],
      results[1][1]
```

3. **Finding the Indices:** Finds the indices of instances that have prediction uncertainties greater than the threshold using *np.where.*

```
1  # Find the indices of highly uncertain instances
2  highly_uncertain_indices =
      np.where(pred_entropy_uncertainties > threshold)[0]
```

4. **Seting up the Plotting Layout and Creating Subplots:** Set up the plotting layout based on the number of highly uncertain instances, and calculate the total number of images to display. It does this by finding the length (number of elements) in the list or array *highly_ uncertain_ indices*, and how many rows of subplots are needed to display all the images. It takes into account that you want 5 images in each row. *np.ceil()* rounds up to the nearest integer. Creates a grid of subplots. *fig* is a reference to the entire figure, and *axs* is an array of references to individual subplots.

```
1  # Display the highly uncertain images
```

```
2 num_images = len(highly_uncertain_indices)
3 rows = int(np.ceil(num_images / 5))
4 fig, axs = plt.subplots(rows, 5, figsize=(20, rows*4))
```

5. **Initiating a Loop to Iterate Highly Uncertain Images:** Initiate a loop that iterates over the indices *idx* of highly uncertain images. *i* will keep track of the loop index. The loop is populated with the subplots, their corresponding predicted labels, and uncertainty values. The grid layout ensures that each image is displayed in its respective subplot.

```
1 # Initiate a Loop to Iterate Highly Uncertain Images
2 for i, idx in enumerate(highly_uncertain_indices):
3     row, col = divmod(i, 5)
4     axs[row, col].imshow(x_test[idx, :, :, 0], cmap='gray')
5     axs[row, col].set_title(f'Pred: {pred_labels[idx]},
      Uncertainty: {pred_entropy_uncertainties[idx]:.2f}',
      size=20)
6     axs[row, col].axis('off')
```

6. **Adjust the Padding Between the Subplots and Displaying Results:** Adjusts the padding between the subplots for better visualization using *tight_ layout*, and display results.

```
1 # Adjust the padding between the subplots
2 plt.tight_layout()
3 # Show the plot
4 plt.show()
```

The following code segment, i.e., Part 4 of the first example, enhances the visualization of highly uncertain images by displaying the predicted class probabilities *(softmax values)* for each instance. It uses a bar plot to represent the softmax values of the predicted classes. Each part of the code segment will be explained below.

1. **Displaying the Highly Uncertain Images:** Get the number of highly uncertain images *(num_ images)* based on the length of the *highly_ uncertain_ indices* array, and determine the number of rows needed for the subplot grid by dividing *num_ images* by 5 and taking the ceiling value. Then create a figure and an array of subplots using *plt.subplots* with dimensions (rows, 5) and a specified figure size.

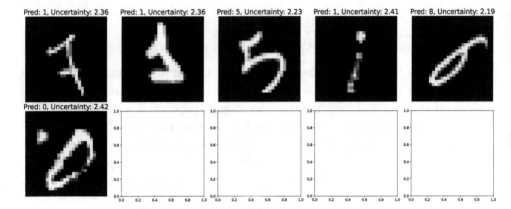

Figure 2.4: In this figure, highly uncertain predictions are visually highlighted. The images with prediction uncertainty exceeding a predefined threshold are displayed, along with their predicted labels and corresponding uncertainty scores.

```
1  #==========================================
2  # Part 4
3  # Display the highly uncertain images
4  num_images = len(highly_uncertain_indices)
5  rows = int(np.ceil(num_images / 5))
6  fig, axs = plt.subplots(rows, 5, figsize=(20, rows*4))
7
8  # Increase the font size for axes labels
9  axes_label_fontsize = 25
```

2. **Initialing a Loop to Iterate Highly Uncertain Indices:** Initiate a loop that iterates over each highly uncertain index and its corresponding position *(i)* in the loop, and calculate the row and column indices (row and col) for the current subplot using divmod based on *(i)* and the number of columns (5). Obtain the predictions *(softmax values)* for the current highly uncertain instance by passing the instance through the model using *model.inner.predict*.

```
1  # Initiate a Loop to Iterate Highly Uncertain Images
2  for i, idx in enumerate(highly_uncertain_indices):
3      row, col = divmod(i, 5)
4      predictions =
```

```
      model.inner.predict(np.expand_dims(x_test[idx], axis=0),
      verbose=0)[0]
5
6     axs[row, col].bar(range(10), predictions, align='center')
7     axs[row, col].set_xticks(range(10))
8     axs[row, col].set_ylabel('Softmax value',
      fontsize=axes_label_fontsize)    # Increase font size
9     axs[row, col].set_xlabel('Classes',
      fontsize=axes_label_fontsize)    # Increase font size
10
11    axs[row, col].set_ylim(0.00, 0.5)
12    axs[row, col].grid()
```

3. **Adjust the Padding Between the Subplots and Displaying Results:** Adjust the padding between the subplots for better visualization using *tight_ layout*, and display results.

```
1 # Adjust the padding between the subplots
2 plt.tight_layout()
3 # Show the plot
4 plt.show()
```

By including the bar plot of softmax values, this code segment provides additional insight into the predicted class probabilities for the highly uncertain images, enabling a better understanding of the model's uncertainty in its predictions.

2.3.5 Practical Example for Ensemble Models

The following code creates an ensemble model, defines each model's architecture and training process, and trains them using a subset of the training data. The resulting ensemble object contains the trained models and their training histories. The code, i.e., Part 1 of the second example, performs the following steps. Each step will be thoroughly explained below.

1. **Importing Libraries:** Import the necessary libraries, including *tensorFlow, uncertainty_ wizard, tqdm, and numpy*.

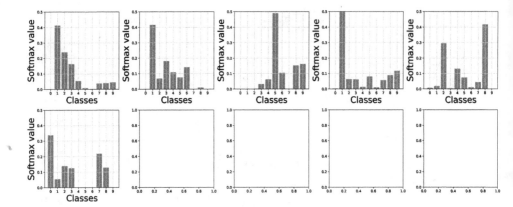

Figure 2.5: In this figure, the softmax prediction probabilities for highly uncertain images are displayed using bar charts. Each bar represents the likelihood of the image belonging to one of the classes. The x-axis represents the classes, while the y-axis represents the softmax values.

```
1  #=============================================
2  ### Part 1
3  import tensorflow as tf
4  import uncertainty_wizard as uwiz
5  from tqdm.keras import TqdmCallback
6  import numpy as np
```

2. **Loading Dataset and Data Preparation:** Load the the MNIST digits dataset, and the dataset is pre-processed by scaling the pixel values and reshaping the input images. This code prepares the MNIST dataset for training a ML model, ensuring the input images are properly formatted and the labels are in the appropriate representation for training.

```
1  # Load the MNIST digits dataset
2  (x_train, y_train), (x_test, y_test) =
       tf.keras.datasets.mnist.load_data()
3
4  # Normalize pixel values to the range [0, 1]
5  x_train = (x_train.astype('float32') /
       255).reshape(x_train.shape[0], 28, 28, 1)
6  x_test = (x_test.astype('float32') /
       255).reshape(x_test.shape[0], 28, 28, 1)
```

3. **Converting Labels to One-hot Encoding:** Convert labels to one-hot encoding using *tf.keras.utils.to_ categorical()* to match the model's output format.

```
1  # Convert labels to one-hot encoding
2  y_train = tf.keras.utils.to_categorical(y_train,
     num_classes=10)
```

4. **Initializing the Random Number Generator:** Set the random seed to *10* for the *NumPy* random number generator.

```
1  #Initialize the random number generator
2  np.random.seed(10)
```

5. **Setting the Total number of Ensembles:** Set the total number of models in the ensemble to *5*.

```
1  #Set the total number of ensembles
2  TOTAL_ENSEMBLES = 5
```

6. **Defining the Model Architecture and the Training Process:** Define the model architecture and the training process for each individual model in the ensemble. The *model_ id* parameter represents the ID of the current model being trained. Inside the *model_ creation_ and_ training* function representing the architecture using the Keras Sequential API. It consists of several layers, such as convolutional, maxpooling, flatten, and dense. The model uses the *ReLU* activation function for intermediate layers and the *Softmax* activation function for the output layer. The model is compiled with the *categorical cross-entropy loss function, the Adam optimizer, and accuracy* as the evaluation metric.

```
1  # Define the Model Architecture and the Training Process
2  def model_creation_and_training(model_id: int):
3      model = tf.keras.models.Sequential()
4      model.add(tf.keras.layers.Conv2D(32, kernel_size=(3, 3),
         activation='relu', input_shape=(28, 28, 1)))
5      model.add(tf.keras.layers.Conv2D(64, (3, 3),
         activation='relu'))
6      model.add(tf.keras.layers.MaxPooling2D(pool_size=(2, 2)))
7      model.add(tf.keras.layers.Flatten())
8      model.add(tf.keras.layers.Dense(128, activation='relu'))
9      model.add(tf.keras.layers.Dense(10,
         activation='softmax'))
```

```
10    model.compile(loss =
      tf.keras.losses.categorical_crossentropy ,
      optimizer='rmsprop', metrics=['accuracy'])
```

Calculate the training subset size for each ensemble model. It divides the total number of training instances *(x_ train.shape[0])* by the number of models in the ensemble *(TOTAL_ ENSEMBLES)*.

```
1 # Calculate the training subset size for each ensemble model
2 sample_size = int(x_train.shape[0] / TOTAL_ENSEMBLES)
```

Randomly select the indices of the training instances for the current model. It uses *np.random.choice* to sample *sample_ size* indices from the total number of training instances without replacement and creates the subset of training images and corresponding labels based on the randomly selected indices.

```
1 # Randomly select the indices of the training instance
2 train_indices = np.random.choice(len(x_train),
      size=sample_size, replace=False)
3 train_images_subset = x_train[train_indices]
4 train_labels_subset = y_train[train_indices]
```

Train the model on the subset of training data by using *model.fit* to train the model with the subset of images and labels. The *validation_ split* parameter specifies the fraction of the training data to be used for validation. The *batch_ size* parameter determines the number of samples per gradient update. The epochs parameter sets the number of times to iterate over the training data. The verbose parameter controls the verbosity mode during training. It also uses the *EarlyStopping* callback to stop training if the validation loss does not improve for 2 consecutive epochs. The *fit_ history* object stores the training history.

```
1 # Train the model
2 # Note that we set the number of epochs to just 1, to be
      able to run this notebook quickly
3 # Set the number of epochs higher if you want to optimally
      train the network
4 fit_history = model.fit(train_images_subset,
      train_labels_subset, validation_split=0.1,
      batch_size=10000, epochs=50, verbose=0,
      callbacks=[tf.keras.callbacks.EarlyStopping(patience=2),
      TqdmCallback(verbose=1)])
```

Return the trained model and the history of the training process.

```
1 # Return the model
2 return model, fit_history.history
```

7. **Initializing the Ensemble Object:** Initialize the ensemble object using the *LazyEnsemble* class from the *uwiz.models* module. It specifies the number of models in the ensemble, the path to save the models, and the number of processes for training. In this case, multiprocessing is disabled *(default_ num_ processes=0)*.

```
1 # Initialize the Ensemble Object
2 ensemble =
      uwiz.models.LazyEnsemble(num_models=TOTAL_ENSEMBLES,
      model_save_path="tmp/ensemble", default_num_processes=0)
```

8. **Creating and Training the Ensemble of Models:** Create and train the ensemble of models with method of the ensemble object and pass the *model_ creation_ and_ training* function as the *create_function* parameter. The method trains the individual models in parallel (if multiprocessing is enabled) or sequentially (in this case, since multiprocessing is disabled) and returns the training histories for each model.

```
1 # Creates, trains and persists atomic models using our
      function defined above
2 training_histories = ensemble.create(create_function =
      model_creation_and_training)
```

The following code, Part 2 of the second example, demonstrates the usage of the predict_quantified method of the ensemble object to obtain predictions and confidences for a given set of input data. Every step will be thoroughly explained below.

1. **Defining a List of Quantifiers:** Define a list of quantifiers that specify the types of information to be extracted from the predictions.

```
1 # ========================================================
2 # Part 2
3 # Get two one-dimensional np arrays: One containing the
      predictions and one containing the confidences
4 # Define a List of Quantifiers
5 quantifiers = ['var_ratio', 'pred_entropy', 'mean_softmax']
```

2. **Predicting the Quantifiers:** Call the *predict_ quantified* method of the ensemble object to obtain the quantified predictions and confidences for the input data *x_ test*. The quantifier parameter is set to the quantifiers list defined earlier, indicating the desired types of information to be extracted. The *batch_ size* parameter specifies the number of samples to be processed in each batch, and the verbose parameter controls the verbosity mode during prediction.

```
1  # Predict the  Quantifiers
2  ensemble_results = ensemble.predict_quantified(x_test,
       quantifier=quantifiers, batch_size=64, verbose=0)
```

The *ensemble_ results* variable will store the output of the *predict_ quantified method*, which will contain the predictions and confidences computed based on the specified quantifiers.

The following code, i.e., Part 3 of the second example, calculates and visualizes various metrics and uncertainties related to the predictions of the ensemble model. The code performs the following steps.

1. **Importing Libraries:** Import the confusion_matrix function to evaluate the performance of a classification algorithm, and the *matplotlib.pyplot* module for creating visualizations in Python.

```
1  #================================
2  # Part 3
3  #Import Libraries
4  from sklearn.metrics import confusion_matrix
5  import matplotlib.pyplot as plt
```

2. **Extracting Predictions and Uncertainties:** Extract predictions and uncertainties from an *ensemble_ results* variable. The code assumes that *ensemble_ results* is a list containing tuples, where each tuple consists of predictions and their associated uncertainties for different uncertainty metrics.

```
1  # Calculate the predictions and prediction uncertainties
       using the pcs and mean_softmax quantifiers
2  pcs_predictions, pcs_uncertainties = ensemble_results[0]
```

```
3 pred_entropy_predictions, pred_entropy_uncertainties =
      ensemble_results[1]
4 mean_softmax_predictions, mean_softmax_uncertainties =
      ensemble_results[2]
```

3. **Computing the Confusion Matrix:** Compute the confusion matrix using the true labels *(y_ test)* and the predicted labels *(pcs_ predictions)* obtained from one of the uncertainty metrics.

```
1 # Calculate the confusion matrix
2 confusion_mtx = confusion_matrix(y_test, pcs_predictions)
```

4. **Creating a Figure with Subplots:** Create a figure with 2 rows and 2 columns of subplots. It also sets the overall size of the figure to *15* inches in width and *10* inches in height, the font size for the axis labels and titles.

```
1 # Create a subplot with 2 rows and 3 columns
2 fig, axs = plt.subplots(2, 3, figsize=(15, 10))
3 # Increase the font size for specified text
4 fontsize = 20
```

5. **Plotting Histograms for Each Uncertainty:** Generate histograms and set their properties for the various uncertainty metrics and the confusion matrix. Each *axs[i, j]* corresponds to a specific subplot in the figure, where *i* is the row and *j* is the column index. The *hist* function creates a histogram of the data provided. *set_ xlabel*, *set_ ylabel*, and *set_ title* set the labels and titles for the respective histograms or plots. The uncertainty metrics include *'Variation Ratio'*, *'Predictive Entropy'*, *and 'Mean Softmax'*. Each has its own histogram.

```
1 # Plot a histogram of the prediction uncertainties from pcs
      in the second subplot
2 axs[0, 0].hist(pcs_uncertainties, bins=50)
3 axs[0, 0].set_xlabel('Variation Ratio', fontsize=fontsize)
4 axs[0, 0].set_ylabel('Count', fontsize=fontsize)
5 axs[0, 0].set_title('Uncertainty - VariationRatio',
      fontsize=fontsize)
6
7 # Plot a histogram of the prediction uncertainties from
      mean_softmax in the third subplot
8 axs[0, 1].hist(pred_entropy_uncertainties, bins=50)
9 axs[0, 1].set_xlabel('Prediction uncertainty
      (PredictiveEntropy)', fontsize=fontsize)
```

```
10 axs[0, 1].set_ylabel('Count', fontsize=fontsize)
11 axs[0, 1].set_title('Uncertainty - PredictiveEntropy',
      fontsize=fontsize)
12
13 # Plot a histogram of the prediction uncertainties from
      mean_softmax in the third subplot
14 axs[1, 0].hist(mean_softmax_predictions, bins=50)
15 axs[1, 0].set_xlabel('Mean Softmax', fontsize=fontsize)
16 axs[1, 0].set_ylabel('Count', fontsize=fontsize)
17 axs[1, 0].set_title('Uncertainty - MeanSoftmax',
      fontsize=fontsize)
```

6. **Plotting the Confusion Matrix:** Plot the confusion matrix, and set ticks, labels, and a title to provide context and information for interpreting the confusion matrix.

```
1 # Plot the confusion matrix in the first subplot (last row)
2 axs[1, 1].imshow(confusion_mtx, interpolation='nearest',
      cmap=plt.cm.Blues)
3 axs[1, 1].set_xticks(np.arange(10))
4 axs[1, 1].set_yticks(np.arange(10))
5 axs[1, 1].set_xlabel('Predicted label', fontsize=fontsize)
6 axs[1, 1].set_ylabel('True label', fontsize=fontsize)
7 axs[1, 1].set_title('Confusion Matrix', fontsize=fontsize)
```

7. **Displaying the Results:** Adjust the spacing between subplots for better aesthetics, and display the entire figure with all the subplots.

```
1 # Adjust the padding between the subplots
2 plt.tight_layout()
3 # Show the plot
4 plt.show()
```

The following code, i.e., Part 4 of the second example, sets a threshold to determine highly uncertain instances based on the prediction uncertainties obtained using the pred_entropy quantifier. It then displays the highly uncertain images along with their predicted labels and corresponding uncertainties. Each part of the code will be explained below.

1. **Setting the Threshold:** Set the threshold value to *2.3*. This threshold will be used to classify predictions with uncertainties above this value as highly uncertain.

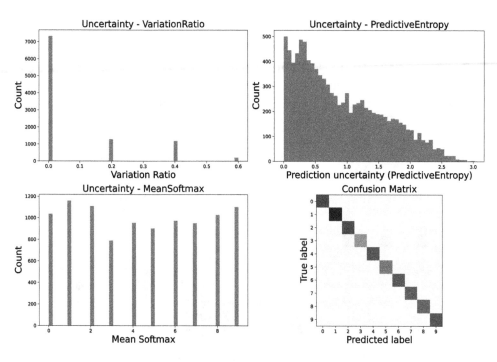

Figure 2.6: This figure illustrates various uncertainty metrics computed for a predictive model, including Variation Ratio, Predictive Entropy, Mutual Information, and Mean Softmax. The histograms in the top row display the distribution of uncertainty values, while the bottom row presents the confusion matrix, providing insights into the model's classification performance.

```
1  # ================================
2  # Part 4
3  # Set a threshold to determine highly uncertain instances
4  threshold = 2.3
```

2. **Extracting the Predicted Labels:** Extract the predicted labels *(pred_ - labels)* and their associated uncertainties *(pred_ entropy_ uncertainties)* from the results of the ensemble. In this case, it uses the *'pred_ entropy'* metric (index 1 in the *ensemble_ results* list).

```
1  # Get the predictions, prediction uncertainties, and
     predicted labels
```

```
2 pred_labels, pred_entropy_uncertainties =
      ensemble_results[1][0], ensemble_results[1][1]
```

3. **Finding the Indices of Highly Uncertain Instances:** Use *NumPy* to find the indices of highly uncertain instances. It checks which predictions have uncertainties above the specified threshold, and calculate the total number of highly uncertain images.

```
1 # Find the indices of highly uncertain instances
2 highly_uncertain_indices =
      np.where(pred_entropy_uncertainties > threshold)[0]
```

4. **Setting up the Plotting Layout and Creating Subplot:** Calculate the number of rows needed to display the highly uncertain images to display *5* images per row and set the font size *20* for figures.

```
1 # Calculate the number of rows
2 rows = int(np.ceil(num_images / 5))
3 fig, axs = plt.subplots(rows, 5, figsize=(20, rows*4))
4
5 # Increase the font size for specified text
6 fontsize = 20
```

5. **Initiating a Loop to Iterate Highly Uncertain Images:** Create a grid of subplots to display the images, iterate over the highly uncertain indices and display the corresponding images, and calculate the row and column indices for placing the image in the grid. *divmod* returns both the quotient and remainder of the division.

```
1 # Initiate a Loop to Iterate Highly Uncertain Images
2 for i, idx in enumerate(highly_uncertain_indices):
3     row, col = divmod(i, 5)
4     axs[row, col].imshow(x_test[idx, :, :, 0], cmap='gray')
5     axs[row, col].set_title(f'Pred: {pred_labels[idx]},
      Uncertainty: {pred_entropy_uncertainties[idx]:.2f}',
6                             fontsize=fontsize)
7     axs[row, col].axis('off')
```

6. **Displaying results:** Adjust the padding between the subplots for better visualization using *tight_ layout*, and display the entire figure with all the subplots.

```
1 # Adjust the padding between the subplots
2 plt.tight_layout()
3 # Show the plot
```

```
plt.show()
```

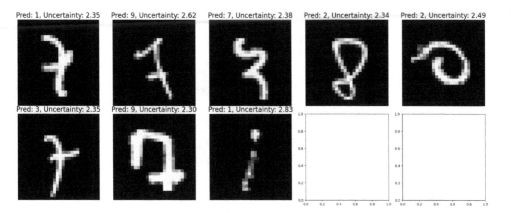

Figure 2.7: This figure displays a set of images representing highly uncertain predictions made by the predictive model. A threshold is applied to identify these instances based on their predictive entropy uncertainties. Each image is accompanied by its predicted label and uncertainty score, enhancing the understanding of instances where the model exhibits uncertainty.

The updated code segment, Part 5 of the second example, loads each individual model from the ensemble and uses them to compute the softmax outputs for the highly uncertain instances. The softmax outputs represent the probabilities assigned to each class by the ensemble members. The updated source code is explained below.

1. **Importing Libraries:** Import the *keras* module from the *tensorflow* library.

```
# =============================
# Part 5

#Import Libraries
from tensorflow import keras
```

2. **Calculating Rows for Highly Uncertain Images and Creating a Figure with Subplots:** Calculate the number of rows needed to display

the highly uncertain images, create a figure for displaying results, and set the font size to *20*.

```
1  # Display the highly uncertain images
2  num_images = len(highly_uncertain_indices)
3
4  # Calculate the number of rows
5  rows = int(np.ceil(num_images / 5))
6
7  # Create a Figure with Subplots
8  fig, axs = plt.subplots(rows, 5, figsize=(20, rows*4))
9
10 # Increase the font size for specified text
11 fontsize = 20
```

3. **Initiating a Loop to Iterate Highly Uncertain Images:** Iterate over the highly uncertain indices and display the softmax outputs for each class, and then create an empty list to store the softmax outputs. Iterate over the ensemble models, load a pre-trained model from a file path based on the *model ID*, make a prediction using the loaded model for the selected test image *(x_ test[idx])*, and append the predictions to the *softmax_ outputs* list. Create a bar chart for visualizing the softmax outputs of a neural network for different classes. It's setting labels, limits, and adding a grid for better visualization. This is done in each subplot of the grid.

```
1  # Initiate a Loop to Iterate Highly Uncertain Images
2  for i, idx in enumerate(highly_uncertain_indices):
3      row, col = divmod(i, 5)
4      softmax_outputs = []
5      for model_id in range(TOTAL_ENSEMBLES):
6          ensemble_local_model =
   keras.models.load_model('tmp/ensemble/' + str(model_id))
7          predictions =
   ensemble_local_model.predict(np.expand_dims(x_test[idx],
   axis=0), verbose=0)[0]
8          softmax_outputs.append(predictions)
9
10     # Store softmax outputs
11     softmax_outputs = np.array(softmax_outputs).mean(axis=0)
12
13     # Plot softmax outputs
14     axs[row, col].bar(range(10), softmax_outputs,
```

```
15   align='center')
     axs[row, col].set_xticks(range(10))
16   axs[row, col].set_ylabel('Softmax value',
     fontsize=fontsize)
17   axs[row, col].set_xlabel('Classes', fontsize=fontsize)
18
19   axs[row, col].set_ylim(0.00, 0.5)
20   axs[row, col].grid()
```

4. **Displaying Results:** Adjust the padding between subplots for better
   aesthetics, and display the entire figure with all the subplots.

```
1   # Adjust the padding between the subplots
2   plt.tight_layout()
3   # Show the plot
4   plt.show()
```

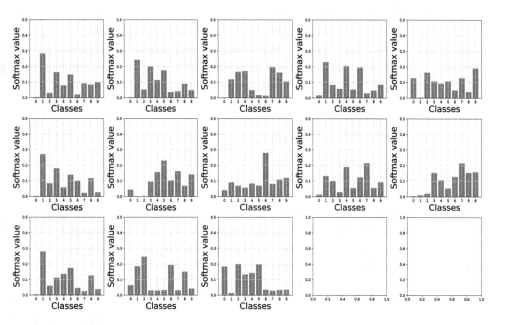

Figure 2.8: In this figure, each subplot represents an image with its corresponding softmax values for highly uncertain predictions. These predictions are made by an ensemble of models, and the softmax values
for each class are displayed in bar plots.

2.4 Unveiling Strategies, Adversarial Challenges, and Robustness in AI

2.4.1 Strategies for Reducing Uncertainty in AI

There are several mitigation methods to reduce uncertainty in AI systems. The first method is *feature engineering*, which is one of essential strategies to reduce uncertainty by providing the model with more informative and discriminative input. It also includes dimensionality reduction, feature selection, and transformation. *Regularization of the model* is another strategy that covers several techniques, such as *regularization L_1 or L_2, dropout*, and *early stopping*. It can help to reduce the reliance on noisy or irrelevant information and overfitting of the model. Model architecture and complexity are one of the strategies which can have an effect on the uncertainty. If a simple model is selected, the number of model parameters can be decreased, or more interpretable models can be employed. *Transfer learning* can also be in these strategies, which is a type of learning method to enable the reuse of a pre-trained model. It can help to improve performance in scenarios with limited data and to minimize uncertainty, especially for complex models. Another strategy is *ensemble methods (such as bagging, boosting, and stacking)*, which involve combining multiple base models to create a single optimal predictive model. Ensemble methods can reduce uncertainty and improve overall AI/ML performance. *Model validation and evaluation* together can provide a more comprehensive understanding of the uncertainty of the model. Model validation is a process to verify model outputs and objectives, while model evaluation measures the overall model performance in terms of accuracy. *Domain expertise and human intervention* are an important combination to be able to reduce uncertainty by guiding the model decision making process and providing additional knowledge, validating predictions, correcting potential errors and biases. *Model calibration* techniques can be used to ensure that the confidence levels of the model accurately reflect the correctness of the predictions. It can improve the reliability of uncertainty estimates. Finally, the *transparency and interpretability of the model* can help identify and understand the sources of uncertainty. They can also help to understand decision making and uncertainties for AI models.

2.4.2 Relation Between Uncertainty and Adversarial Machine Learning

The uncertainty and adversarial ML are closely related topics in the AI/ML concept. Adversarial ML refers to the vulnerabilities in AI models that adversaries can exploit to manipulate or deceive the models. In the scope of adversarial ML, uncertainty in the model's predictions can make it more susceptible to adversarial attacks.

It can start with the primary relationship between *robustness and uncertainty*. As mentioned earlier, the uncertainty in the model's predictions can indicate regions in the input space where the model lacks confidence or is more susceptible to errors. On the other hand, adversarial examples often lie in these uncertain regions, as they exploit the model's vulnerabilities and cause it to make incorrect predictions. Models with higher uncertainty are generally more prone to adversarial attacks. The other relationship is *adversarial examples and uncertainty estimation*. Adversarial attacks rely on generating perturbations of the input designed to be unnoticeable from the original data. However, uncertainty estimation can help to detect adversarial examples. It is assumed that the input might be adversarial or unreliable if the model demonstrates high uncertainty or low confidence in its predictions for a specific input. There is a strong relationship between *adversarial training and uncertainty*. Adversarial training is a defense mechanism to improve the robustness of the model against adversarial attacks, while uncertainty estimation is used in adversarial training to assign higher uncertainty to adversarial examples to make the model more cautious in its predictions.

2.4.3 Robustness and Uncertainty

Robustness in the AI/ML concept refers to the ability of the model to maintain its prediction performance even in perturbations or variations in the input data. It measures the model resistance to errors or adversarial attacks.

For example, an ML model, $f(\mathbf{x}, \theta)$, with input data, $\mathbf{x}$, is considered robust if it satisfies the following condition:

$$\forall \mathbf{x}, \quad \mathbf{x}' \in \mathcal{X} \tag{2.21}$$

where $\mathcal{X}$ is the input space, and $|\mathbf{x} - \mathbf{x}'|$ denotes the distance between $\mathbf{x}$ and $\mathbf{x}'$.

$$|f(\mathbf{x}, \theta) - f(\mathbf{x}', \theta)| \leq \epsilon \tag{2.22}$$

where ϵ represents a small tolerance value.

A robust model ensures that the difference between the predicted outputs for similar inputs (within a certain distance) is limited to a small value. On the other hand, uncertainty in AI/ML refers to the lack of confidence or knowledge about the true label or outcome. It quantifies the degree confidence of the model in its predictions. As mentioned earlier, there are different types of uncertainty, such as aleatoric uncertainty and epistemic uncertainty. In AI/ML, we often focus on epistemic uncertainty, which arises from limited or insufficient training data.

Uncertainty can also be mathematically represented using probability distributions. For example, an AI model predicts the probabilities of the class for a given input $\mathbf{x}$, and the uncertainty associated with the prediction can be represented as a probability distribution over the classes, represented by $(p(y|\mathbf{x}))$, where y represents the class labels.

The uncertainty can be quantified using entropy or variance. Among them, entropy-based uncertainty, given by $H(y|\mathbf{x})$, measures the amount of unpredictability or randomness in a dataset associated with the prediction. It can be calculated using the probability distribution as:

$$H(y|\mathbf{x}) = -\sum_i p(y = i|\mathbf{x}) \log p(y = i|\mathbf{x}) \qquad (2.23)$$

where i represents the class index.

Similarly, variance-based uncertainty measures the variation or spread of the predicted probabilities for different classes. It can be calculated as:

$$Var(y|\mathbf{x}) = \sum_i (p(y = i|\mathbf{x}) - \bar{p}(y|\mathbf{x}))^2 \qquad (2.24)$$

where $\bar{p}(y|\mathbf{x})$ represents the mean or average predicted probability.

Two methods of quantifying uncertainty have been presented. However, there are other techniques that can be used depending on the particular context and needs.

The uncertainty associated with the prediction can be estimated using an uncertainty measure, represented by $U(\mathbf{x})$, which can be calculated using an appropriate uncertainty measure, such as entropy or variance, applied to the probability distribution $p(y|\mathbf{x})$.

After estimating the uncertainty of the model's predictions for a given input, this uncertainty can be used to detect adversarial examples. Adversarial examples are expected to induce higher uncertainty in the model predictions due to their perturbed nature. The common approach is to define a threshold value for the uncertainty, denoted as T. Inputs with uncertainty values exceeding this threshold are considered potentially adversarial. The threshold can be determined based on the desired trade-off between false positives (legitimate inputs mistakenly identified as adversarial) and false negatives (adversarial inputs not detected). Mathematically, the adversarial input detection process can be expressed as follows:

$$\mathbf{x}_{adv} = \mathbf{x} : U(\mathbf{x}) > T \tag{2.25}$$

where $\mathbf{x}_{adv}$ represents the set of potentially adversarial inputs. By comparing the uncertainty estimate of a given input to the threshold, one can determine whether it falls within the range of potentially adversarial examples.

It should be noted that the choice of uncertainty measure and the determination of an appropriate threshold value depend on the specific domain problem, the model architecture, and the desired trade-offs. The uncertainties captured by different uncertainty measures may be different and their effectiveness in detecting adversarial input may vary. Additionally, adversarial input detection is an ongoing research area and various techniques, including ensemble methods, Bayesian approaches, and outlier detection algorithms, have been proposed to improve the detection accuracy.

2.4.4 Practical Example for Detection of Adversarial Examples

In this section, we explore the detection of adversarial examples. The following Python code, Part 1 of the third example, demonstrates how to use a trained model and uncertainty measures to detect highly uncertain adversarial examples. It starts with importing necessary libraries, loading the *MNIST* dataset and creating a *convolutional neural network (CNN)* model. This model will later be used for generating and analyzing adversarial examples. We also set up the model's architecture and compile it with suitable loss and optimization functions. Each step of the source code is explained below.

1. **Importing Libraries:** Import necessary libraries for ML, adversarial attacks, numerical operations, data visualization, and uncertainty estimation, including *tensorflow, numpy, matplotlob, uncertainty_wizard, and cleverhans*. Note that *cleverhans* library is for benchmarking adversarial attacks in ML models.

```
1  #============================================
2  ### Part 1
3  #Import necessary libraries
4  import tensorflow as tf
5  import numpy as np
6  import matplotlib.pyplot as plt
7  import uncertainty_wizard as uwiz
8  from tqdm.keras import TqdmCallback
9  from cleverhans.tf2.attacks.fast_gradient_method import
     fast_gradient_method
```

2. **Loading Dataset and Data Preparation:** Load the *MNIST* dataset, normalize the pixel values to be in the range [0, 1], and reshape the data to match the expected input shape for the model.

```
1  # Load the MNIST digits dataset
2  (x_train, y_train), (x_test, y_test) =
     tf.keras.datasets.mnist.load_data()
3
4  # Normalize pixel values to the range [0, 1]
5  x_train = (x_train.astype('float32') /
     255).reshape(x_train.shape[0], 28, 28, 1)
6  x_test = (x_test.astype('float32') /
     255).reshape(x_test.shape[0], 28, 28, 1)
```

3. **Converting Labels to One-hot Encoding:** Convert labels to one-hot encoding using *tf.keras.utils.to_categorical()* to match the model's output format.

```
1  # Convert labels to one-hot encoding
2  y_train = tf.keras.utils.to_categorical(y_train,
     num_classes=10)
```

4. **Model Definition:** Create a stochastic sequential model. This type of model is likely designed to incorporate stochasticity into its architecture.

Add a flattening layer followed by a fully connected layer with 128 units and *ReLU* activation. Then, a final fully connected layer with 10 units and softmax activation is added. add two convolutional layers followed by a max-pooling layer to the model. Add a dropout layer with a rate of 0.5. Dropout layers are a form of regularization that helps prevent overfitting, and a flattening layer followed by a fully connected layer with 128 units and *ReLU* activation, then a final fully connected layer with 10 units and *softmax* activation.

```
1  # Create the model
2  model = uwiz.models.StochasticSequential()
3  model.add(tf.keras.layers.Conv2D(32, kernel_size=(3, 3),
       activation='relu', input_shape=(28, 28, 1)))
4  model.add(tf.keras.layers.Conv2D(64, (3, 3),
       activation='relu'))
5  model.add(tf.keras.layers.MaxPooling2D(pool_size=(2, 2)))
6
7  # Adding a dropout layer
8  model.add(tf.keras.layers.Dropout(0.5))
9  # Adding a flattening layer and dense layers
10 model.add(tf.keras.layers.Flatten())
11 model.add(tf.keras.layers.Dense(128, activation='relu'))
12 model.add(tf.keras.layers.Dense(10, activation='softmax'))
```

5. **Model Compilation:** Compile the model, specifying the loss function (categorical cross-entropy), optimizer *(RMSprop)*, and evaluation metric *(accuracy)*.

```
1  # Compiling the model
2  model.compile(loss=tf.keras.losses.categorical_crossentropy,
       optimizer='rmsprop', metrics=['accuracy'])
```

6. **Model Training:** Train the model on the training data. It uses a training-validation split of 90% and 10%, a batch size of 10,000, and trains for 50 epochs. The training progress is displayed using the *Tqdm-Callback* to show progress bars. The *verbose* parameter determines the amount of logging output during training. A setting of 0 will not display any progress, while a setting of 1 will provide detailed progress updates.

```
1  # Fitting the model
2  model.fit(x_train, y_train, validation_split=0.1,
       batch_size=10000, epochs=50, verbose=0,
       callbacks=[TqdmCallback(verbose=1)])
```

After setting up the model, we proceed to generate adversarial examples using the Fast Gradient Sign Method (FGSM). FGSM is an attack technique used to craft adversarial examples by perturbing input data slightly. We calculate class probabilities for both the original and adversarial examples and compute prediction uncertainties using various quantifiers. The Python code segment, Part 2 of the third example, along with explanations is given below.

1. **Generating Adversarial Examples:** Generate adversarial examples using the Fast Gradient Sign Method (FGSM). It perturbs the input data *(x_ test)* using the gradient of the loss with respect to the input, with a maximum perturbation of epsilon (ϵ). *np.inf* represents positive infinity in the NumPy library.

```
1  # ============================================
2  ### Part 2
3  # Generate adversarial examples using FGSM
4  epsilon = 0.1
5  adv_x_test = fast_gradient_method(model.inner, x_test,
        epsilon, np.inf)
```

2. **Creating Class Probabilities:** Create class probabilities for both the original *(x_ test)* and adversarial examples *(adv_ x_ test)*. It uses various quantifiers, including *'var_ ratio', 'pred_ entropy', and 'mean_ softmax'*, to calculate uncertainties in the predictions.

```
1  # Class probabilities for original and adversarial examples
2  quantifiers = ['var_ratio', 'pred_entropy', 'mean_softmax']
```

3. **Extracting Predictions and Predicting Uncertainties for Original Examples:** Extract the predictions and prediction uncertainties for the original examples using the *'pred_ entropy'* quantifier, and predict class probabilities for the original examples *(x_ test)*.

```
1  # Predict class probabilities for original examples
2  results = model.predict_quantified(x_test,
3                                      quantifier=quantifiers,
4                                      batch_size=1000,
5                                      sample_size=32,
6                                      verbose=1)
7  # Calculate the predictions and prediction uncertainties
       using the pcs and mean_softmax quantifiers
8  predictions_orig, entropy_orig = results[1]
```

4. **Extracting Predictions and Prediction Uncertainties for Adversarial Samples:** Extract the predictions and prediction uncertainties for the adversarial examples using the *'pred_ entropy'* quantifier. and predict class probabilities for the adversarial examples *(adv_ x_ test)*. It uses the same set of quantifiers as before.

```
1  # Predict class probabilities for adversarial examples
2  results_adv = model.predict_quantified(adv_x_test.numpy(),
3                              quantifier=quantifiers,
4                              batch_size=1000,
5                              sample_size=32,
6                              verbose=1)
7  # Calculate the predictions and prediction uncertainties
       using the pcs and mean_softmax quantifiers
8  predictions_adv, entropy_adv = results_adv[1]
```

To identify highly uncertain adversarial examples, the additional code segment, i.e., Part 3 of the third example, defines a threshold value. Any example with an uncertainty score greater than this threshold is considered highly uncertain. We then sort these examples based on their uncertainty scores and select the top rows for visualization. For each pair of original and adversarial examples, we display the images along with their corresponding predictions and uncertainties. Each part of the code will be explained below.

1. **Setting the Threshold:** Sets a threshold value of 1.95, which will be used to classify adversarial examples with uncertainties above this value as highly uncertain.

```
1  #===================================
2  ### Part 3
3  # Set a threshold to determine highly uncertain instances
4  threshold = 1.95
```

2. **Identifying the Indices of the Highly Uncertain Adversarial Examples:** Identify the indices of the highly uncertain adversarial examples. It uses *np.where* function to find the indices where the uncertainty values *(entropy_ adv)* are greater than the specified threshold.

```
1  # Find the indices of highly uncertain adversarial examples
2  highly_uncertain_indices = np.where(entropy_adv >
       threshold)[0]
```

3. **Arranging Indices of Highly Uncertain Adversarial Examples:** Sort the highly uncertain indices based on the corresponding uncertainty values in ascending order. This ensures that the most uncertain examples come first.

```
# Sort the highly uncertain indices based on uncertainty
    values
sorted_indices = highly_uncertain_indices[ np.argsort(
    entropy_adv[ highly_uncertain_indices ] ) ]
```

4. **Plotting Top 2 Highly Uncertain Adversarial Examples in Rows:** Plot the top 2 highly uncertain adversarial examples per row. For each pair of examples, it displays the original and adversarial images along with their respective predictions and uncertainties.

```
# Plot the top 3 rows of highly uncertain adversarial
    examples
for i in range(0, min(len(sorted_indices), 2), 2):
    plt.figure(figsize=(15, 7))

    for j in range(2):
        if i + j < len(sorted_indices):
            idx = sorted_indices[i + j]
            uncertainty_orig = entropy_orig[idx]
            uncertainty_adv = entropy_adv[idx]
            label_orig = np.argmax(predictions_orig[idx])
            label_adv = np.argmax(predictions_adv[idx])

            plt.subplot(2, 4, j * 2 + 1)
            plt.imshow(x_test[idx].squeeze(), cmap='gray')
            plt.title(f"Image {i+j+1} -
Original\nPrediction: {label_orig} - Uncertainty:
{uncertainty_orig:.2f}")

            plt.subplot(2, 4, j * 2 + 2)
            plt.imshow(adv_x_test[idx], cmap='gray')
            plt.title(f"Image {i+j+1} -
Adversarial\nPrediction: {label_adv} - Uncertainty:
{uncertainty_adv:.2f}")
```

5. **Adjust the Padding Between the Subplots and Displaying Results:** Adjusts the padding between the subplots for better visualization using *tight_ layout*, and display results.

```
1 # Adjust the padding between the subplots
2 plt.tight_layout()
3 # Show the plot
4 plt.show()
```

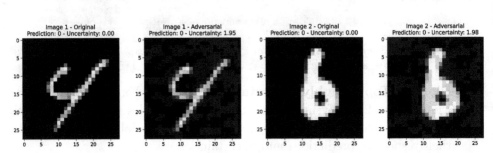

Figure 2.9: Visualization of Highly Uncertain Adversarial Examples: This plot
displays a selection of highly uncertain adversarial examples generated using the Fast Gradient Sign Method (FGSM) on the MNIST
dataset. Each row consists of two images: the left image is the
original digit from the dataset, and the right image is the corresponding adversarial example. For each pair, the predictions and
prediction uncertainties are shown, helping to highlight the model's
uncertainty when dealing with these perturbed inputs.

The following code, Part 4 of the third example, creates a subplot with 1 row
and 2 columns to visualize the distribution of uncertainty values for normal
inputs (original examples) and adversarial inputs.

1. **Creating a Figure:** Create a figure with one row and two columns of
   subplots. The total size of the figure is 10 units in width and 5 units in
   height.

```
1 # ========================================
2 # Part4
3 # Create a subplot with 1 row and 2 columns
4 fig, axs = plt.subplots(1, 2, figsize=(10, 5))
```

2. **Plotting the Histogram of Uncertainty Values for the Orginal
   Examples:** Plot the histogram of uncertainty values for the original examples in the first subplot. It uses 50 bins, sets the color to blue, and

adjust the opacity (alpha) to 0.7 for better visibility. It also sets labels and a title for the subplot.

```
1 # Plot the distribution of uncertainty values for original
    examples in the first subplot
2 axs[0].hist(entropy_orig, bins=50, color='blue', alpha=0.7)
3 axs[0].set_xlabel('Uncertainty')
4 axs[0].set_ylabel('Count')
5 axs[0].set_title('Distribution of Uncertainty for Normal
    Inputs')
```

3. **Plotting Histogram of Uncertainty Values for Adversarial Examples:** Plot the histogram of uncertainty values for the adversarial examples in the second subplot. Similar to the first subplot, it uses 50 bins, sets the color to red, and adjusts the alpha to 0.7. It also sets labels and a title for the subplot.

```
1 # Plot the distribution of uncertainty values for
    adversarial examples in the second subplot
2 axs[1].hist(entropy_adv, bins=50, color='red', alpha=0.7)
3 axs[1].set_xlabel('Uncertainty')
4 axs[1].set_ylabel('Count')
5 axs[1].set_title('Distribution of Uncertainty for
    Adversarial Inputs')
```

4. **Adjust the Padding Between the Subplots and Displaying Results:** Adjusts the padding between the subplots for better visualization using *tight_ layout*, and display results.

```
1 # Adjust the padding between the subplots
2 plt.tight_layout()
3 # Show the plot
4 plt.show()
```

The following Python code segment, i.e., Part 5 of the third example, calculates the success rate of detecting adversarial inputs based on their uncertainty levels. It begins by computing a threshold for uncertainty using the mean uncertainty of known normal inputs. Next, it separates inputs into two groups: those with uncertainty above the threshold (likely adversarial) and those below (normal). The success rate is then determined by comparing the number of correctly identified adversarial inputs to the total number of examples, providing

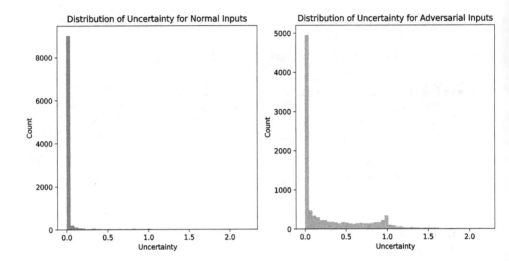

Figure 2.10: Comparison of Uncertainty Distributions: This plot compares the distribution of uncertainty values between normal (blue) and adversarial (red) input examples. It illustrates how the model's prediction uncertainties differ for these two types of inputs, shedding light on the model's response to perturbed data and its robustness to adversarial attacks.

a crucial metric for evaluating the model's ability to detect adversarial attacks and ensuring robustness in ML applications.

1. **Calculating the Threshold for Detection of Adversarial Examples:** Calculate the threshold for detecting adversarial examples. It uses the mean value of the uncertainty scores *(entropy_ orig)* for the original examples, identify the indices of adversarial examples where the uncertainty is greater than the threshold, the indices of normal examples where the uncertainty is less than or equal to the threshold.

```
1  # ===========================================================
2  # Part5
3  # Detect adversarial inputs using uncertainty
4  threshold = entropy_orig.mean()
5  adversarial_indices = np.where(entropy_adv > threshold)[0]
```

```
6 normal_indices = np.where(entropy_orig <= threshold)[0]
```

2. **Calculating Adversarial Examples Detection Success Rate:** Calculate the success rate of detecting adversarial examples based on uncertainty levels. It divides the number of correctly detected adversarial examples by the total number of examples (both adversarial and normal).

```
1 # Calculate success rate of detection
2 success_rate = len(adversarial_indices) /
    (len(adversarial_indices) + len(normal_indices))
```

3. **Printing Results:** Print out the calculated success rate as a percentage with two decimal places.

```
1 print(f"Success rate of detecting adversarial inputs:
    {success_rate:.2%}")
```

According to the results, the success rate in detecting adversarial inputs is *38.67*.

2.5 Summary

This chapter focuses on uncertainty in AI. It begins by introducing uncertainty quantification in the AIML concept. The following sections explore the different types of uncertainty, distinguishing between epistemic and aleatoric uncertainty. It then provides methods for effectively calculating uncertainty methods, including Monte Carlo Dropout, Ensemble Models, and various Quantifiers, with practical Python examples. The chapter also covers strategies for reducing uncertainty and discusses the relationship between uncertainty and adversarial machine learning, as well as between robustness and uncertainty in AI.

Bibliography

[1] Shakeel Ahamad, Ishfaq Hussain Rather, and Ratneshwer Gupta. Uncertainty quantification in advanced machine learning approaches. In *Advanced Applications of NLP and Deep Learning in Social Media Data*, pages 245–258. IGI Global, 2023.

[2] Silvia Seoni, Vicnesh Jahmunah, Massimo Salvi, Prabal Datta Barua, Filippo Molinari, and U Rajendra Acharya. Application of uncertainty quantification to artificial intelligence in healthcare: A review of last decade (2013–2023). *Computers in Biology and Medicine*, page 107441, 2023.

[3] Edmon Begoli, Tanmoy Bhattacharya, and Dimitri Kusnezov. The need for uncertainty quantification in machine-assisted medical decision making. *Nature Machine Intelligence*, 1(1):20–23, 2019.

[4] Zach Cleghern, Keith Rudd, Griffin Thornton, and Alicia Fernandes. Explainable machine learning and uncertainty quantification in robotic lunar surface traversal. In *ASCEND 2023*, page 4719. 2023.

[5] Rhiannon Michelmore, Marta Kwiatkowska, and Yarin Gal. Evaluating uncertainty quantification in end-to-end autonomous driving control. *arXiv preprint arXiv:1811.06817*, 2018.

[6] Christian Gollier. *The economics of risk and uncertainty*. Edward Elgar Publishing Limited, 2018.

[7] Ali K Raz, Paul C Wood, Linas Mockus, and Daniel A DeLaurentis. System of systems uncertainty quantification using machine learning techniques with smart grid application. *Systems Engineering*, 23(6):770–782, 2020.

[8] Talha Siddique, Md Shaad Mahmud, Amy M Keesee, Chigomezyo M Ngwira, and Hyunju Connor. A survey of uncertainty quantification in machine learning for space weather prediction. *Geosciences*, 12(1):27, 2022.

[9] Ferhat Ozgur Catak, Umit Cali, Murat Kuzlu, and Salih Sarp. Uncertainty aware deep learning model for secure and trustworthy channel estimation in 5g networks. In *2023 12th Mediterranean Conference on Embedded Computing (MECO)*, pages 1–4. IEEE, 2023.

[10] Venkat Nemani, Luca Biggio, Xun Huan, Zhen Hu, Olga Fink, Anh Tran, Yan Wang, Xiaoge Zhang, and Chao Hu. Uncertainty quantification in machine learning for engineering design and health prognostics: A tutorial. *Mechanical Systems and Signal Processing*, 205:110796, 2023.

[11] David John Stracuzzi, Michael Christopher Darling, Matthew Gregor Peterson, and Maximillian Gene Chen. Quantifying uncertainty to improve decision making in machine learning. Technical report, Sandia National Lab.(SNL-NM), Albuquerque, NM (United States), 2018.

[12] Brian Jalaian, Michael Lee, and Stephen Russell. Uncertain context: Uncertainty quantification in machine learning. *AI Magazine*, 40(4):40–49, 2019.

[13] Pascal Pernot. Calibration in machine learning uncertainty quantification: Beyond consistency to target adaptivity. *APL Machine Learning*, 1(4), 2023.

[14] Téo Sanchez, Baptiste Caramiaux, Pierre Thiel, and Wendy E Mackay. Deep learning uncertainty in machine teaching. In *27th International Conference on Intelligent User Interfaces*, pages 173–190, 2022.

[15] João Caldeira and Brian Nord. Deeply uncertain: comparing methods of uncertainty quantification in deep learning algorithms. *Machine Learning: Science and Technology*, 2(1):015002, 2020.

[16] Jakob Gawlikowski, Cedrique Rovile Njieutcheu Tassi, Mohsin Ali, Jongseok Lee, Matthias Humt, Jianxiang Feng, Anna Kruspe, Rudolph Triebel, Peter Jung, Ribana Roscher, et al. A survey of uncertainty in deep neural networks. *Artificial Intelligence Review*, 56(Suppl 1):1513–1589, 2023.

[17] Moloud Abdar, Farhad Pourpanah, Sadiq Hussain, Dana Rezazadegan, Li Liu, Mohammad Ghavamzadeh, Paul Fieguth, Xiaochun Cao, Abbas Khosravi, U Rajendra Acharya, et al. A review of uncertainty quantification in deep learning: Techniques, applications and challenges. *Information fusion*, 76:243–297, 2021.

[18] Shiwei Lan, Shuyi Li, and Babak Shahbaba. Scaling up bayesian uncertainty quantification for inverse problems using deep neural networks. *SIAM/ASA Journal on Uncertainty Quantification*, 10(4):1684–1713, 2022.

[19] Francesca Tavazza, Kamal Choudhary, and Brian DeCost. Approaches for uncertainty quantification of ai-predicted material properties: A comparison. *arXiv preprint arXiv:2310.13136*, 2023.

[20] Dimitri P Solomatine and Durga Lal Shrestha. A novel method to estimate model uncertainty using machine learning techniques. *Water Resources Research*, 45(12), 2009.

[21] Eyke Hüllermeier and Willem Waegeman. Aleatoric and epistemic uncertainty in machine learning: An introduction to concepts and methods. *Machine Learning*, 110:457–506, 2021.

[22] Israel Lopez and Nesrin Sarigul-Klijn. A review of uncertainty in flight vehicle structural damage monitoring, diagnosis and control: Challenges and opportunities. *Progress in Aerospace Sciences*, 46(7):247–273, 2010.

[23] Yarin Gal and Zoubin Ghahramani. Dropout as a bayesian approximation: Representing model uncertainty in deep learning. In *international conference on machine learning*, pages 1050–1059. PMLR, 2016.

[24] David Barber and Christopher M Bishop. Ensemble learning in bayesian neural networks. *Nato ASI Series F Computer and Systems Sciences*, 168:215–238, 1998.

[25] Linton C Freeman. Elementary applied statistics: for students in behavioral science. *(No Title)*, 1965.

[26] Lorena Qendro, Alexander Campbell, Pietro Lio, and Cecilia Mascolo. Early exit ensembles for uncertainty quantification. In *Machine Learning for Health*, pages 181–195. PMLR, 2021.

[27] Balaji Lakshminarayanan, Alexander Pritzel, and Charles Blundell. Simple and scalable predictive uncertainty estimation using deep ensembles. *Advances in neural information processing systems*, 30, 2017.

[28] Hussein Al Osman and Shervin Shirmohammadi. Machine learning in measurement part 2: uncertainty quantification. *IEEE Instrumentation & Measurement Magazine*, 24(3):23–27, 2021.

3 Security of Artificial Intelligence: Adversarial Attacks

Let's talk about "adversarial attacks" using our smart traffic sign-reading computer as an example like in Figure 3.1.

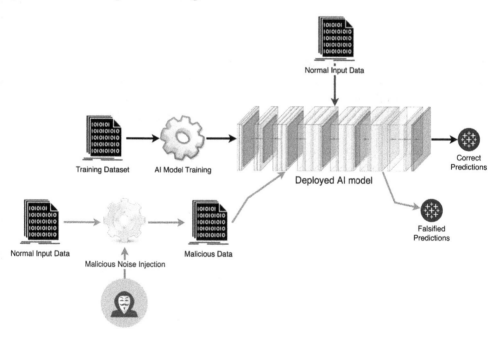

Figure 3.1: Adversarial ML attacks

Imagine you have a friend who knows much about how your computer recognizes traffic signs. They're mischievous and want to play a trick on your computer.

Instead of just putting up a regular stop sign, they stick some weird stickers or draw something funny. Now, to you, it still looks like a stop sign, but your computer needs clarification because you've never seen anything like these stickers before.

That's what we call an adversarial attack. It's like a sneaky attempt to confuse the computer by showing it something different from what it learned. Being super bright but not perfect, the computer might get tricked into thinking the sign means something else, like a yield sign instead of a stop sign.

These attacks happen when someone tries to fool the computer by making small, clever changes to what it sees. It's a bit like giving it an optical illusion - what looks like a stop sign to us might look like something else to the computer because of these tricky changes.

People who build these intelligent systems are constantly working on ways to make them more robust so they can avoid falling for these tricks. It's like giving our computer friend extra lessons to recognize regular signs and signs with funny stickers. This helps it become more resistant to these sneaky attempts to confuse it.

3.1 Introduction

The use of AI technologies has become common in the industry, especially for specific applications such as image classification, object detection, voice control, machine translation, and more advanced areas such as drug composition analysis, etc. However, AI systems are vulnerable to adversarial attacks, restricting the application of AI technologies in essential high-risk areas, such as healthcare [1], finance [2], energy [3], and autonomous driving [4]. Therefore, enhancing the robustness of AI systems against adversarial attacks has become increasingly significant for the further advancement of AI [5] to ensure the security of

AI, which involves measures and practices to protect AI systems from unauthorized access, data breaches, and malicious attacks [6]. These measures are designed to make AI applications and models resilient to any potential threats and vulnerabilities and to ensure that they are running in a secure environment. Attackers can easily generate perturbations by updating theoretical adversarial example generation methods in many ways.

The AI model deployment phase is vulnerable to a variety of security risks throughout the entire process, from the initial data collection and preparation to the training, inference, and eventual deployment. During the data collection and pre-processing phase, AI-based systems are vulnerable to sensor spoofing and scaling attacks. The training and inference phases of the model are susceptible to poisoning and adversarial attacks, respectively. The deployment phase is also vulnerable to model attacks [7]. Perturbations can cause a model to make incorrect predictions with a high degree of accuracy, a phenomenon known as adversarial sample. Adversarial attacks involve manipulating a sample, such as changing a car image to a bird, so that a ML model is trained to classify it differently than a human would. These attacks are divided into white-box, grey-box, and black-box attacks [8]. Each type attack has own objectives, i.e., black box testing provides an attacker's perspective, allowing for a broader scope of security to be examined, grey box testing offers an insider's view with limited access, white box testing provides users with an open access to all applications and systems.

Research on adversarial attacks on AI/ML concept has become significantly growth, and new attack and defense methods are constantly being proposed [9]. The purpose of adversarial attacks can range from causing a misclassification [10] in an image recognition system to bypassing security measures in a natural language processing model. Generally, these attacks can be divided into three categories based on the stage of the target model: attacks during training, attacks during testing, and attacks during deployment. Adversarial attacks are malicious attempts to fool AI systems, resulting in incorrect predictions or classifications through a variety of ways, including adding imperceptible changes to input data (adversarial examples) or manipulating the environment. In the literature, many papers have been published on AI security, adversarial attacks, and their mitigation methods [11, 12, 13, 14, 15]. Researchers have come up with models and methods, i.e., adversarial training and robust optimization, that are resilient to adversarial attacks to enhance the robustness of AI systems against malicious attempts to manipulate them.

This chapter provides an overview of security in AI, focusing on adversarial attacks and mitigation methods, along with practical examples in Python. This is for readers with a background in AI security who have limited experience with adversarial attacks and mitigation methods. If you are already familiar with the security in AI, skip the initial sections and go straight to practical examples.

3.2 Types of Adversarial Attacks

Attacks can be classified into two main types: **targeted attacks** and **untargeted attacks** in the AI / ML concept. These attack types differ in their objectives and strategies for manipulating AI/ML models [16]. In this section, targeted and untargeted attacks will be investigated along with their mathematical formulations and implications for the security and robustness of AI/ML models.

3.2.1 Untargeted Attacks

The main purpose of untargeted attacks is to fool the model by causing misclassification of input data, without a specific target class in mind. An untargeted attack tries to find an adversarial example, i.e., perturbation, that maximizes the model prediction error and to lead to misclassification of the input. In an untargeted attack, the objective can be given as follows:

$$\underset{\mathbf{x}+\delta}{\text{argmax}} \ \mathcal{L}(f(\mathbf{x}+\delta), y) \tag{3.1}$$

where $f(\cdot)$ represents the ML model, $\mathbf{x}$ is the original input, δ is the adversarial perturbation, y is the true label, and $\mathcal{L}(\cdot)$ is a suitable loss function.

Untargeted attacks are particularly concerning, as they can compromise the integrity and reliability of AI/ML systems, and aim to find a perturbation δ that can be added to the original input $\mathbf{x}$ to create a new input $\mathbf{x}' = \mathbf{x} + \delta$, such that the ML model f misclassifies the perturbed input $\mathbf{x}'$. Then the attacker tries to maximize the loss function $\mathcal{L}(f(\mathbf{x}'), y)$, where y is the true label of the original input $\mathbf{x}$.

The untargeted attacks can be defined as an optimization problem. Optimal perturbation, δ^*, can be given as follows:

$$\delta^* = \text{argmax}_\delta \ \mathcal{L}(f(\mathbf{x}+\delta), y)$$
$$\text{subject to } ||\delta||_p \leq \epsilon \tag{3.2}$$

where ϵ is a pre-defined perturbation budget, and $|| \cdot ||_p$, i.e., L_1, L_2 or L_∞, is a norm function, which is used to measure the level of the perturbation.

Some practical examples of untargeted attacks are given as follows:

1. **Adversarial Examples for Image Classification:** In image classification tasks, an attacker can use adversarial examples that appear visually similar to the original images but cause misclassification by the model. For example, an attacker can apply FGSM or PGD to slightly modify the pixel values of an image, leading to misclassification by the model. The perturbed image might look almost identical to the original image to the human eye, but the model makes an incorrect prediction.

77

2. **Speech Recognition Attacks:** Adversarial attacks can also be applied to speech recognition systems. An attacker can cause the speech recognition model to incorrectly transcribe the audio by introducing imperceptible perturbations to the audio waveform.

3. **Text-based Attacks:** Adversarial attacks can be used to target natural language processing (NLP) models by slightly changing the input text. For example, a positive sentence can be modified to a negative one by FGSM or PGD attack generating adversarial text examples. As a result, the selected sentence can be misclassified, i.e., negative, in sentiment analysis using NLP models.

4. **Object Detection Attacks:** AI/ML models have been widely used for object detection applications. An attacker can cause these models to fail to detect certain objects by perturbing the image, i.e., object detection attacks. Please note that object detection applications are very sensitive due to high-risk impact applications, such as autonomous driving.

5. **Malware and Network Intrusion Detection:** Malware and intrusion detection systems have significantly used AI/ML models as an alternative to the existing static approaches for a long time [17]. Adversarial attacks can also lead to misclassification of malware and intrusion detection systems and can cause false alarms or fail to detect and recognize anomaly activity.

These are several examples explaining how untargeted attacks can be applied in various domains. Adversarial attacks are a serious concern, and researchers are actively exploring defense mechanisms to enhance the robustness of AI/ML models against such attacks.

3.2.2 Targeted Attacks

Targeted attacks have a specific target class in contrast to untargeted attacks. An attacker aims to manipulate the model output to lead misclassifying into a pre-determined target class. Mathematically, the objective of a targeted attack can be given as follows:

$$\operatorname*{argmax}_{x+\delta} \mathcal{L}(f(\mathbf{x} + \delta), y_{\text{target}}) \tag{3.3}$$

where y_{target} represents the target class label. The attacker's goal is to find the perturbation δ that maximizes the loss for the target class, causing the model to misclassify the input accordingly.

Targeted attacks can be more challenging to execute compared to untargeted attacks, since they require knowledge of the target class and might need additional optimization strategies. However, they pose serious threats in scenarios where specific outcomes are desired. For example, an attacker attempting to deceive a spam email filter by making legitimate emails appear as malicious could have significant implications for cybersecurity.

Some practical examples of targeted attacks:

1. **Misclassification of Adversarial Images:** In targeted attacks on image classification models, an attacker can craft adversarial examples to cause the model to misclassify the input as a specific target class. The attack is successful when the model confidently predicts the target class despite the input being visually similar to the original class. For example, an attacker could generate a perturbed image of a dog misclassified as a cat by the model.
2. **Identity Theft in Face Recognition Systems:** Face recognition systems can be manipulated to make them think that a particular person is present, even when they are not. An attacker can create a malicious example that is identified as the intended target, resulting in a false positive identification by slightly changing the input face image.
3. **Semantic Manipulation in Natural Language Processing (NLP):** Natural language processing tasks can be categorized into sentiment analysis or text classification. An attacker can slightly alter the text to be misclassified as a particular sentiment, e.g., a positive review of a product could be classified as negative.

4. **Manipulation of Autonomous Vehicles:** Autonomous vehicles applications can be defined as one of the high-risk applications. An attacker can cause the vehicle to misidentify objects or perceive non-existent obstacles by providing carefully designed visual or sensor input. As a result, it will be leading to accidents or disruptions in traffic flow.

5. **Evasion of Intrusion Detection Systems:** Intrusion Detection Systems (IDS) have significantly used AI/ML methods. An attacker can launch targeted attacks against IDS to avoid being detected and create a false alarm. For example, the attacker can create network packets or modify malware code to avoid certain signatures or behaviors that the IDS cannot detect.

3.2.3 L_p Ball

In mathematics, the L_p ball, i.e., $B_p(r)$, is a set of points in a vector space specified by a certain distance metric called the L_p **norm** [18]. It measures the magnitude of a vector, which is defined as follows:

$$\|\mathbf{x}\|_p = \left(\sum_{i=1}^{n} |x_i|^p \right)^{\frac{1}{p}} \tag{3.4}$$

where $\mathbf{x} = (x_1, x_2, ..., x_n)$ is a vector of n elements, and p is a positive real number.

L_p ball represents the collection of all points whose L_p norm is bounded by the radius r, and the L_p norm of $\mathbf{x}$ is less than or equal to a given radius r, i.e., L_p ball $B_p(r)$. It can be defined as follows:

$$B_p(r) = \{\mathbf{x} \in \mathbb{R}^n : \|\mathbf{x}\|_p \leq r\} \tag{3.5}$$

These are the basic definitions and shapes of the Lp balls for L_1, L_2, and L_∞ norms. Depending on the value of p, the L_p ball exhibits different geometrical properties. The shape of the L_p ball depends on the value of p. A few special cases are given below.

■ L_1 **Ball:** The L_1 ball, i.e., Manhattan Ball or taxicab norm or $B_1(r)$, is the collection of all points in the vector space whose L_1 norm is less than or equal to r. $B_1(r)$ is defined as follows:

$$B_1(r) = \{\mathbf{x} \in \mathbb{R}^n : \|\mathbf{x}\|_1 = \sum_{i=1}^{n} |x_i| \leq r\} \tag{3.6}$$

Geometrically, L_1 ball has the shape of a diamond or a hypercube in higher dimensions.

■ L_2 **Ball:** The L_2 ball, i.e., Euclidean Ball or $B_2(r)$, consists of all points in the vector space whose L_2 norm is less than or equal to r. $B_2(r)$ is defined as:

$$B_2(r) = \mathbf{x} \in \mathbb{R}^n : |\mathbf{x}|_2 = \sqrt{\sum i = 1^n |x_i|^2} \leq r \tag{3.7}$$

Geometrically, L_2 is a circle in two dimensions, while it is a regular sphere in three dimensions. In higher dimensions, it forms a hypersphere.

■ L_∞ **Ball:** The L_∞ ball, i.e., Chebyshev ball or supremum norm or $B_\infty(r)$, consists of all points in the vector space. $B_\infty(r)$ is defined as:

$$B_\infty(r) = \mathbf{x} \in \mathbb{R}^n : |\mathbf{x}|_\infty = \max 1 \leq i \leq n \quad |x_i| \leq r \tag{3.8}$$

The L_∞ ball is defined by the maximum absolute value of any component of the vector. Geometrically, it is a square in two dimensions, while it is a cube in three dimensions. In higher dimensions, it forms a hypercube.

Figure 3.2 illustrates unit balls associated with different norms, including the 0.4-norm, 0.8-norm, 1-norm (Manhattan norm), 2-norm (Euclidean norm), 3-

norm, and the 100 norm. Each subplot displays a unit ball scaled according to the respective norm, providing a geometric representation of these mathematical concepts in three-dimensional space.

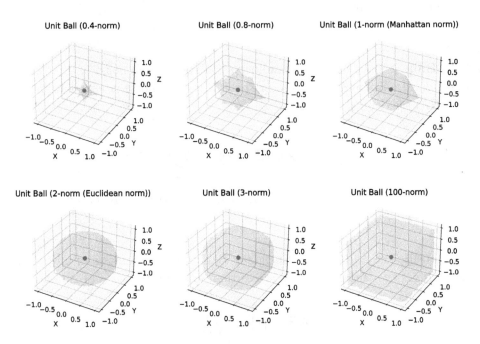

Figure 3.2: Visualization of Unit Balls with Various Norms in Three-Dimensional Space.

3.2.4 Lp Balls and Adversarial Machine Learning

The concept of L_p balls is closely related to adversarial ML because it provides a geometric interpretation of the boundaries within which perturbations can be applied to the input data while remaining imperceptible to humans. Adversarial attacks often utilize small perturbations that are within certain bounds to ensure that the manipulated samples remain visually similar to the original ones.

L_p norms, particularly the L_2 and L_∞, have been used to define adversarial attacks and identify perturbations. Objectivities are to maximize the effect on model output while staying within the specified bounds. For example, when generating adversarial examples for image classification models, the L_2 norm can be used to measure the magnitude of perturbations in pixel space, making sure that the perturbed image remains within a given L_2 ball around the original image. The L_∞ norm can be used to restrict perturbations to be within a prescribed L_∞ ball to limit the maximum allowable change in any single pixel value.

Adversarial attacks typically involve optimization algorithms that search for perturbations within L_p balls to find the optimal perturbation that maximizes the model's vulnerability. To defend against these attacks, techniques such as adversarial training are used, which seek to make the model more resilient to perturbations by augmenting the training data with adversarial examples crafted within the L_p balls. Using L_p balls in adversarial ML provides a mathematical basis for understanding the permitted perturbation regions and is essential for both creating adversarial examples and developing defenses against adversarial attacks.

3.2.5 Cleverhans

Cleverhans is a common Python library of adversarial example toolbox for the implementation of adversarial attacks together with mitigation methods [19]. It makes the implementation and assessment of adversarial attacks and mitigation easier and helps to understand the vulnerabilities of ML models. There are some key features and components of the Cleverhans library, such as adversarial attack algorithms, model wrappers, adversarial training, evaluation metrics, preprocessing and defense mechanisms, and adversarial example datasets. Each key feature is briefly explained below.

The first key feature is **adversarial attack algorithms** to generate adversarial examples for targeted and untargeted attacks. It can be used along with the

Fast Gradient Sign Method (FGSM), Projected Gradient Descent (PGD), Basic Iterative Method (BIM), Carlini and Wagner attack (CW), and others. The second one is **model wrappers** to allow users to be able to easily apply adversarial attacks to their models and assess their robustness against such attacks. The third one is **adversarial training**, which is a model training process with adversarial examples to improve the overall security of AI/ML models against adversarial attacks. The fourth key feature is **evaluation metrics** to evaluate the robustness of ML models against adversarial attacks and provide insights into the model performance and vulnerability. The fifth key feature is **preprocessing and defense mechanisms** for data preprocessing and implementing various defense mechanisms against adversarial attacks. These mechanisms include defensive distillation, feature squeeze, spatial smoothing, and more. The last key feature is **adversarial examples datasets** for collections of adversarial examples, created with different attack techniques, and can be used to evaluate the strength of models.

3.3 Adversarial Machine Learning Attacks

3.3.1 Fast Gradient Sign Method

The Fast Gradient Sign Method (FGSM) is the most popular adversarial attack method [20] in AI/ML content because of its simplicity [21]. The objective of FGSM is to create an adversarial example $\mathbf{x}'$ that model predicts a different label y' than the true label (y) with the constraint, i.e., the perturbation is bounded by a small perturbation value ϵ.

To explain the FGSM method, the first, the perturbation, η, can be defined as follows:

$$\eta = \epsilon \cdot \text{sign}(\nabla_{\mathbf{x}}\mathcal{L}(\theta, \mathbf{x}, y)) \qquad (3.9)$$

where x is an input sample, y is the corresponding true label of $\mathbf{x}$, θ is AI/ML model with parameters, $\nabla_{\mathbf{x}}\mathcal{L}(\theta, \mathbf{x}, y)$ is the gradient of the loss function $\mathcal{L}(\theta, \mathbf{x}, y)$ with respect to $\mathbf{x}$, and the *sign* function computes the sign of each element in the gradient, and the resulting perturbation is scaled by the value of ϵ.

After giving the perturbation, η, the adversarial example is then created by adding the perturbation to the original input as follows:

$$\mathbf{x}' = \mathbf{x} + \eta \qquad (3.10)$$

FGSM is a fast and computationally efficient method for generating adversarial examples, which has made it a popular choice for attacking ML models. However, it has also some limitations, such as being susceptible to gradient masking, where the model's gradient can be intentionally or unintentionally manipulated to prevent the attacker from creating effective adversarial examples.

3.3.2 Practical Example I for Adversarial Attack

The following Python code segment, the first example of adversarial attacks, demonstrates the use of the *Sympy* library to calculate and display symbolic gradients of a multivariate function. The symbolic calculation of the gradients is given as a mathematical function. It defines the variables $w1$ and $w2$ as symbols, computes the gradients of the function with respect to these variables symbolically, and then evaluates the gradients at specific values *(w1 = 5, w2 = 3)*. Each step of the source code is explained below.

1. **Importing Libraries:** Import necessary libraries, such as *sympy, display and Markdown* functions. *sympy* is a powerful symbolic mathematics library in Python to perform symbolic calculations and manipulate mathematical expressions.

```
1  # ================================================
2  # Import libraries
```

```
3 import sympy as sp
4 from IPython.display import display, Markdown
```

2. **Defining Variables and Function:** Define two symbols *w1 and w2* using the sp.symbols function from *Sympy*, the function *f* using the symbolic variables *w1 and w2*.

```
1 # Define the variables w1 and w2 as symbols
2 w1, w2 = sp.symbols('w1 w2')
3
4 # Define the function f(w1, w2)
5 f = 3 * w1**2 + 2 * w1 * w2
```

3. **Calculating the Gradients:** Calculate the gradients of the function *f* with respect to *w1 and w2* using the *sp.diff* function from *Sympy*. The gradients are stored in a list called gradients.

```
1 # Calculate the gradients symbolically
2 gradients = [sp.diff(f, w) for w in [w1, w2]]
```

4. **Displaying the Original Function:** Display the original function *f* and the values of *w1 and w2*. The display function combines with the *Markdown* function.

```
1 # Print the original function f
2 display(Markdown("**Original Function:**"))
3 display(f)
4
5 # Print the values of w1 and w2
6 display(Markdown("**Values:**"))
7 display(Markdown("w1 = 5, w2 = 3"))
```

5. **Displaying the Symbolic Gradients:** Display the symbolic gradients along with their numerical values when *w1 = 5 and w2 = 3*. The display function is used to render the formatted output for each gradient.

```
1 # Print the symbolic gradients with explanations
2 for i, gradient in enumerate(gradients):
3     display(Markdown(f"**Gradient {i+1}:**"))
4     display(gradient)
5     display(gradient.subs([(w1, 5), (w2, 3)]))
```

The gradient of the loss function with respect to x represents the rate of change of the loss function with respect to small changes in the input **x**. In other words, it quantifies how sensitive the model's predictions are to perturbations in the input.

The gradient of the loss function, $\mathcal{L}$ with respect to $\mathbf{x}$, denoted as $\nabla_x \mathcal{L}(\theta, \mathbf{x}, y)$, is a vector that contains the partial derivatives of the loss function with respect to each element of the input $\mathbf{x}$. Each element of the gradient vector represents the direction and magnitude of the change in the loss function when the corresponding element of $\mathbf{x}$ is varied.

In the context of the FGSM attack, the gradient of the loss function with respect to $\mathbf{x}$ is computed to determine the direction in which the loss function increases the most for a given input sample. Attackers can exploit this sensitivity to adversarial examples through the loss function. The attacker can manipulate those features to induce misclassification by the model by identifying the most influential features of the input, as indicated by the gradient.

The gradient of the loss function depends on the model parameters θ, the input $\mathbf{x}$, and the true label y. Therefore, to perform the FGSM attack, the attacker needs access to the model's architecture and parameters and the true label of the input.

3.3.3 Practical Example II for Adversarial Attack

The following source code segment, the second example of adversarial attacks, demonstrates how to define a simple neural network model, perform a forward pass, calculate gradients using automatic differentiation, and print the gradients using *TensorFlow*.

1. **Importing Libraries:** Import the *TensorFlow* library, which is a popular open-source ML framework, and the *NumPy* library, which is used for numerical computations.

```
1  # ===========================================
```

```
2 # Import libraries
3 import tensorflow as tf
4 import numpy as np
```

2. **Creating a Dataset:** Create a small dataset with 3 columns and 3 rows

```
1 # Create a small dataset with 3 columns
2 data = np.array([[1.0, 2.0, 3.0],
3                  [4.0, 5.0, 6.0],
4                  [7.0, 8.0, 9.0]])
```

3. **Defining the Model:** Define a simple sequential model using *Tensor-Flow's Keras* API. It consists of one Dense layer (a single neuron)

```
1 # Define the model
2 model = tf.keras.Sequential([tf.keras.layers.Dense(1)])
```

4. **Setting up Optimizer and Loss Function:** Define the stochastic gradient descent (SGD) optimizer with a learning rate of 0.01, and the *mean squared error (MSE)* loss function.

```
1 # Define the optimizer and loss function
2 optimizer = tf.keras.optimizers.SGD(learning_rate=0.01)
3 loss_fn = tf.keras.losses.MeanSquaredError()
```

5. **Creating TensorFlow Variables:** Create a TensorFlow variable x with the data. This variable will be used as input to the model, a TensorFlow variable y with ones, representing the target values.

```
1 # Create TensorFlow variables for the inputs and targets
2 x = tf.Variable(data, dtype=tf.float32)
3 y = tf.Variable(np.ones((3, 1)), dtype=tf.float32)
```

6. **Performing Forward Pass:** Perform the forward pass and calculate the loss using TensorFlow's automatic differentiation. This starts a context where operations are recorded for automatic differentiation. First, *output = model(x)* computes the output of model given the input x. This is the forward pass. Second, *loss = loss_fn(y, output)* calculates the loss between the predicted output output and the actual target values y using the loss function.

```
1 # Perform the forward pass
2 with tf.GradientTape() as tape:
3     # Forward pass
4     output = model(x)
```

```
5    # Calculate the loss
6    loss = loss_fn(y, output)
```

7. **Calculating Gradients:** Use the recorded operations to compute the gradients of the loss with respect to the input *x*.

```
1  # Calculate the gradients using TensorFlow's automatic
       differentiation
2  gradients = tape.gradient(loss, x)
```

8. **Printing the Gradients:** Print out the gradients that were calculated earlier.

```
1  # Print the gradients
2  print("Gradients:")
3  for i, gradient in enumerate(gradients.numpy()):
4      print(f"Column {i+1}: {gradient}")
```

```
Gradients:
Column 1: [-0.11103031  0.20786518 -0.14710708]
Column 2: [ 0.19241521 -0.36022973  0.25493613]
Column 3: [ 0.49586076 -0.9283247   0.6569794 ]
```

3.3.4 Practical Example for FGSM Adversarial Attack

The following code segment, the third example of adversarial attack, demonstrates an example of training a convolutional neural network (CNN) on the MNIST dataset and generating adversarial examples using the Fast Gradient Sign Method (FGSM). The first part of the third example will be explained below.

1. **Importing Libraries:** Import the necessary libraries and modules, including *random, TensorFlow, NumPy, Keras, MNIST dataset, Clever-Hans, Matplotlib, Scikit-learn and Tqdm*.

```
1  #==========================================
```

```
 2 # Import libraries
 3 import random
 4 import numpy as np
 5 import tensorflow as tf
 6 from tensorflow import keras
 7 from tensorflow.keras import layers
 8 from tensorflow.keras.datasets import mnist
 9 from cleverhans.tf2.attacks.fast_gradient_method import
       fast_gradient_method
10 import matplotlib.pyplot as plt
11 from sklearn.metrics import confusion_matrix
12 from tqdm.keras import TqdmCallback
```

2. **Loading Dataset and Preparation:** Load the MNIST dataset using
   mnist.load_ data(), and prepare the MNIST dataset for training a ML
   model, ensuring the input images are properly formatted and the labels
   are in the appropriate representation for training, and normalizes pixel
   values to the range [0, 1].

```
 1 # Load the MNIST dataset
 2 (x_train, y_train), (x_test, y_test) = mnist.load_data()
 3
 4 # Normalize pixel values to the range [0, 1]
 5 x_train = x_train.astype("float32") / 255.0
 6 x_test = x_test.astype("float32") / 255.0
```

3. **Converting Labels to One-hot Encoding:** Convert labels to one-hot
   encoding using *tf.keras.utils.to_ categorical()* to match the model's output
   format.

```
 1 # Convert labels to one-hot encoding
 2 y_train = tf.keras.utils.to_categorical(y_train, 10)
 3 y_test = tf.keras.utils.to_categorical(y_test, 10)
```

4. **Model Definition:** Define the CNN model using the Keras Sequential
   API. It consists of several layers, including convolutional layers, max-
   pooling layers, flattening layer, dropout layer, and a dense (fully connected) layer with softmax activation for multiclass classification.

```
 1 # Define the pre-trained MNIST model
 2 model = keras.Sequential([
 3     layers.Input(shape=(28, 28)),
 4     layers.Reshape(target_shape=(28, 28, 1)),
 5     layers.Conv2D(32, kernel_size=(3, 3), activation="relu"),
 6     layers.MaxPooling2D(pool_size=(2, 2)),
```

```
7    layers.Conv2D(64, kernel_size=(3, 3), activation="relu"),
8    layers.MaxPooling2D(pool_size=(2, 2)),
9    layers.Flatten(),
10   layers.Dropout(0.5),
11   layers.Dense(10, activation="softmax")
12 ])
```

5. **Model Compilation:** Compile the model with the *categorical cross entropy loss* function, the *Adam* optimizer, and *accuracy* as the metric.

```
1 # Compile the model
2 model.compile(loss="categorical_crossentropy",
     optimizer="rmsprop", metrics=["accuracy"])
```

6. **Training the Model:** Train the model on the training dataset using *model.fit()*. The batch size is set to 2000, and the training is performed for 10 epochs with a validation split of 0.1. The TqdmCallback is used to display a progress bar during training.

```
1 # Train the model on the training set
2 model.fit(x_train, y_train, batch_size=2000, epochs=10,
     validation_split=0.1, verbose=0,
     callbacks=[TqdmCallback(verbose=1)])
```

7. **Saving the Model:** Save the mode to a file named *'model.h5'* using *model.save()*.

```
1 # Save the model
2 model.save('model.h5')
```

The following code segment, Part 2 of the third example for FGSM adversarial attach, focuses on generating adversarial examples using the FGSM with untargeted values and visualizing the effects on the model's predictions. Each part of the Python code will be explained below.

1. **Generating Adversarial Examples (FGSM):** Generate adversarial examples using the FGSM attack by calling *fast_gradient_method()*. The model is the target model, *x_test* is the original test data, epsilon controls the magnitude of the perturbation, and *np.inf* indicates that the perturbation is bounded by the maximum distortion (i.e. L_∞) allowed.

```
1 # ===========================================
```

```
2 ### Part 2
3 # Generate adversarial examples using FGSM with untargeted
    values
4 epsilon = 0.2
5 adv_x_test = fast_gradient_method(model, x_test, epsilon,
    np.inf)
```

2. **Predicting Labels:** Predict labels for the original and adversarial test sets obtained using *model.predict()* function.

```
1 # Get predicted labels for the test set
2 y_pred = model.predict(x_test, verbose=0).argmax(axis=1)
3 adv_y_pred = model.predict(adv_x_test,
    verbose=0).argmax(axis=1)
```

3. **Computing Confusion Matrices:** Compute confusion matrices using *confusion_ matrix()* to evaluate the model's performance before and after the attack.

```
1 # Get predicted labels for the test set after the attack
2 confusion_mtx_adv = confusion_matrix(y_test.argmax(axis=1),
    adv_y_pred)
3
4 # Get predicted labels for the test set after the attack
5 confusion_mtx_adv = confusion_matrix(y_test.argmax(axis=1),
    adv_y_pred)
```

4. **Plotting Confusion Matrices:** Plot confusion matrices using *Matplotlib*, display the true and predicted labels on the y-axis and the predicted labels on the x-axis. Two subplots are created, one for the confusion matrix before and one for the confusion matrix after the attack.

```
1 # Plot the confusion matrices in the same subplot
2 fig, axs = plt.subplots(1, 2, figsize=(8, 4))
3 axs[0].imshow(confusion_mtx, interpolation='nearest',
    cmap=plt.cm.Blues)
4 axs[0].set_xticks(range(10))
5 axs[0].set_yticks(range(10))
6 axs[0].set_xlabel('Predicted label')
7 axs[0].set_ylabel('True label')
8 axs[0].set_title('Confusion Matrix (Before Attack)')
9
10 axs[1].imshow(confusion_mtx_adv, interpolation='nearest',
    cmap=plt.cm.Blues)
11 axs[1].set_xticks(range(10))
```

```
12  axs[1].set_yticks(range(10))
13  axs[1].set_xlabel('Predicted label')
14  axs[1].set_ylabel('True label')
15  axs[1].set_title('Confusion Matrix (After Attack)')
```

5. **Displaying the Results:** Adjust the padding between the subplots for better visualization using *tight_layout* and display results.

```
1  # Adjust the padding between the subplots
2  plt.tight_layout()
3  # Show the plot
4  plt.show()
```

6. **Visualizing Example Images:** Visualize examples of original images and their corresponding adversarial examples. Random samples from the test set are chosen, and the images and their predicted labels are displayed using *Matplotlib*.

```
1   # Plot some examples with predicted labels as titles
2   fig, axs = plt.subplots(2, 10, figsize=(10, 3))
3   axs = axs.flatten()
4   sample_indices = random.sample(range(len(x_test)), 10)
5   for i, sample_index in enumerate(sample_indices):
6       axs[i].imshow(x_test[sample_index], cmap="gray")
7       axs[i].set_title(f"Label: {y_pred[sample_index]}")
8       axs[i].axis("off")
9       axs[i + 10].imshow(adv_x_test[sample_index], cmap="gray")
10      axs[i + 10].set_title(f"Label:
        {adv_y_pred[sample_index]}")
11      axs[i + 10].axis("off")
```

7. **Displaying the Results:** Adjust the padding between the subplots for better visualization using *tight_layout* and display results.

```
1  # Adjust the padding between the subplots
2  plt.tight_layout()
3  # Show the plot
4  plt.show()
```

The following code segment, Part 3 of the third example for FGSM adversarial attack, provides a complete pipeline for training a CNN model on the MNIST dataset, generating adversarial examples using FGSM, and visualizing the model's performance and the perturbed images. The additional code builds

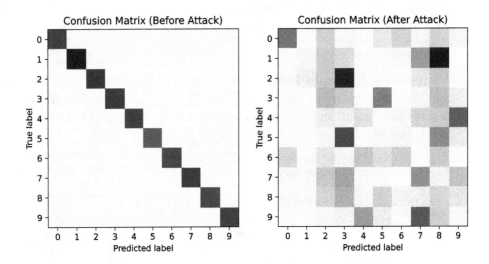

Figure 3.3: Confusion Matrix (Before Attack): This figure visualizes the confusion matrix representing the model's performance on the original test data before any adversarial attack. It provides insights into how well the model's predictions match the true labels. Confusion Matrix (After Attack): This figure presents the confusion matrix for the model's performance on the test data after the adversarial attack using FGSM. It shows how the model's predictions change when subjected to adversarial perturbations.

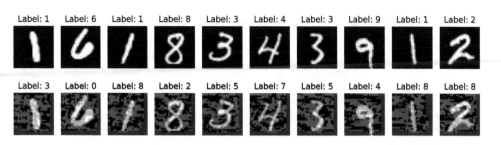

Figure 3.4: Example Predictions with Adversarial Perturbations. This figure showcases a set of sample images from the test dataset. The top row displays the original images, while the bottom row shows the same images after being subjected to adversarial perturbations using the Fast Gradient Sign Method (FGSM). The titles indicate the predicted labels by the model for each image, both before and after the adversarial attack.

upon the previous code and introduces targeted adversarial examples using the FGSM. In this section of the code, a targeted adversarial attack is performed using the FGSM with a specified epsilon value. The goal is to perturb the original images in a way that the model misclassifies them as a specific target class (in this case, class 5). The resulting adversarial images is generated and their predicted labels are compared to the original labels. Additionally, the code generates confusion matrices before and after the attack to evaluate the model's performance. Finally, it selects and displays ten examples where the original prediction was the target class but the adversarial prediction is different. The following Python code will be explained step by step below.

1. **Defining Variables and Setting up a Target Class:** Define variables and set up a target class. The variable epsilon is set to 0.5, which controls the magnitude of the perturbation in the FGSM attack. The variable *target_ adv* is created as an array of zeros with the same shape as *y_ test*. The target class for the attack is set to 5 *(TARGET_ CLASS = 5)*, and the corresponding elements in *target_ adv* are set to 1. This creates a targeted attack where the goal is to misclassify the examples as class 5. The *target_ adv* array is converted into a one-dimensional array containing

the indices of the target classes using *argmax(axis=1)*.

```
1 #===================================
2 ## PART 3
3 # Generate adversarial examples using FGSM with targeted
      values
4 # Define variables and set up a target class
5 epsilon = 0.5
6 target_adv = np.zeros_like(y_test)
7 TARGET_CLASS = 5
8 target_adv[:, TARGET_CLASS] = 1
9 target_adv = target_adv.argmax(axis=1)
```

2. **Generating Adversarial Examples with Targeted Values:** Generate adversarial examples using FGSM with targeted values by calling *fast_gradient_method()* with the *target_adv* array provided as the y parameter. This ensures that the attack is targeted towards the specified class.

```
1 adv_x_test = fast_gradient_method(model, x_test, epsilon,
      np.inf, y = target_adv)
```

3. **Predicting Labels:** Predict labels for the original and adversarial test sets obtained using *model.predict()* function.

```
1 # Get predicted labels for the test set
2 y_pred = model.predict(x_test, verbose=1).argmax(axis=1)
3 adv_y_pred = model.predict(adv_x_test,
      verbose=1).argmax(axis=1)
```

4. **Computing Confusion Matrices:** Compute confusion matrices using *confusion_matrix()* to evaluate the model's performance before and after the attack.

```
1 # Get predicted labels for the test set before the attack
2 confusion_mtx = confusion_matrix(y_test.argmax(axis=1),
      y_pred)
3
4 # Get predicted labels for the test set after the attack
5 confusion_mtx_adv = confusion_matrix(y_test.argmax(axis=1),
      adv_y_pred)
```

5. **Finding Indices:** Find indices where the original input's prediction is not 0 (indicating that the original prediction is the target class) but the adversarial version's prediction is not the target class are identified using *np.where()*. The first 10 indices are selected *([:10])*.

```
1 # Find indices where original input prediction is not 0 but
    adversarial version's prediction is 0
2 indices = np.where((y_pred == TARGET_CLASS) & (adv_y_pred !=
    TARGET_CLASS))[0][:10]
```

6. **Plotting Selected Examples:** Create a figure to plot the selected examples. The original images corresponding to the selected indices are displayed along with their predicted and adversarial labels.

```
1 # Plot the selected examples
2 fig, axs = plt.subplots(2, 5, figsize=(10, 4))
3 axs = axs.flatten()
4 for i, index in enumerate(indices):
5     axs[i].imshow(x_test[index], cmap="gray")
6     axs[i].set_title(f"Label: {y_pred[index]}\nAdv Label:
    {adv_y_pred[index]}")
7     axs[i].axis("off")
```

7. **Displaying the Results:** Adjust the padding between the subplots for better visualization using *tight_ layout* and display results.

```
1 # Adjust the padding between the subplots
2 plt.tight_layout()
3 # Show the plot
4 plt.show()
```

8. **Plotting Confusion Matrices:** Similar to the previous code, another plot is created to visualize the confusion matrices before and after the attack. The additional code demonstrates how to generate targeted adversarial examples using FGSM, evaluate the model's performance, and visualize the selected examples and confusion matrices.

```
1  # Plot the confusion matrices in the same subplot
2  fig, axs = plt.subplots(1, 2, figsize=(8, 4))
3  axs[0].imshow(confusion_mtx, interpolation='nearest',
    cmap=plt.cm.Blues)
4  axs[0].set_xticks(range(10))
5  axs[0].set_yticks(range(10))
6  axs[0].set_xlabel('Predicted label')
7  axs[0].set_ylabel('True label')
8  axs[0].set_title('Confusion Matrix (Before Attack)')
9
10 axs[1].imshow(confusion_mtx_adv, interpolation='nearest',
    cmap=plt.cm.Blues)
11 axs[1].set_xticks(range(10))
```

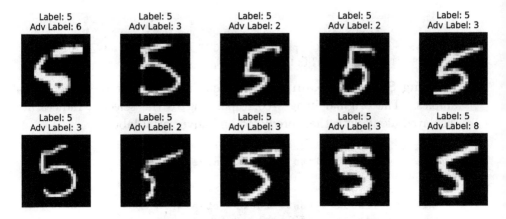

Figure 3.5: Targeted Adversarial Examples: This plot displays a set of ten selected examples where a targeted adversarial attack was performed
using the FGSM with the goal of misclassifying the images as a specific target class (class 5). The original labels and the adversarial
labels are shown for each example.

```
12  axs[1].set_yticks(range(10))
13  axs[1].set_xlabel('Predicted label')
14  axs[1].set_ylabel('True label')
15  axs[1].set_title('Confusion Matrix (After Attack)')
```

9. **Displaying the Results:** Adjust the padding between the subplots for
   better visualization using *tight_layout* and display results.

```
1  # Adjust the padding between the subplots
2  plt.tight_layout()
3  # Show the plot
4  plt.show()
```

3.3.5 Basic Iterative Method

The Basic Iterative Method (BIM) attack is an iterative variant of the FGSM
attack that aims to generate stronger adversarial examples by taking multiple

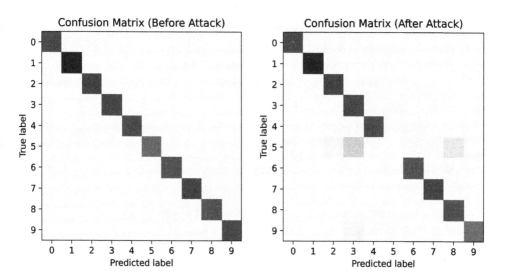

Figure 3.6: Confusion Matrices. This plot shows two confusion matrices, one before the adversarial attack and one after. Each matrix illustrates the true labels versus the predicted labels for the MNIST dataset. The matrix on the left represents the classification performance before the attack, while the matrix on the right demonstrates the impact of the adversarial attack on the model's predictions.

small steps in the direction of the gradient [22]. It follows a similar approach as FGSM, but instead of making a single update to the input, it performs multiple iterations to refine the adversarial perturbation.

Here's a step-by-step breakdown of the BIM attack using math notation:

1. Given an input image $\mathbf{x}$, its true label y_{true}, a targeted class y_{target} (optional), and a maximum perturbation size ϵ.
2. Initialize the adversarial example $\mathbf{x}_{\text{adv}}$ as a copy of the original input $\mathbf{x}$.
3. Repeat for a fixed number of iterations T:
   - Compute the gradient of the loss function $\mathcal{L}(\theta, \mathbf{x}_{\text{adv}}, y_{\text{true}})$ with respect to the input: $\nabla_{\mathbf{x}_{\text{adv}}} \mathcal{L}(\theta, \mathbf{x}_{\text{adv}}, y_{\text{true}})$

   - Compute the perturbation by taking a small step in the direction of the gradient: $\delta = \epsilon \cdot \text{sign}(\nabla_{\mathbf{x}_{\text{adv}}} \mathcal{L}(\theta, \mathbf{x}_{\text{adv}}, y_{\text{true}}))$

   - Update the adversarial example by adding the perturbation: $\mathbf{x}_{\text{adv}} = \mathbf{x}_{\text{adv}} + \delta$

   - Clip the adversarial example to ensure it stays within the ϵ-ball around the original input: $\mathbf{x}_{\text{adv}} = \text{clip}(\mathbf{x}_{\text{adv}}, \mathbf{x} - \epsilon, \mathbf{x} + \epsilon)$
4. Return the final adversarial example $\mathbf{x}_{\text{adv}}$.

The main differences between FGSM and BIM can be summarized, namely iteration, strength, defense detection, and computational cost. Each difference will briefly be explained. Regarding the iteration, FGSM performs a single update to the input using the sign of the gradient, while BIM iteratively updates the adversarial example using multiple small steps in the direction of the gradient. In terms of strength, BIM generates more effective adversarial examples than FGSM by refining the perturbation over multiple iterations. BIM can also explore the input space more effectively and find perturbations that can lead to misclassification. For defense detection, BIM is more likely to be detected by certain defense mechanisms this is because they can detect repeated patterns or multiple modifications to the input. In addition, FGSM may produce less noticeable perturbations. The last difference is the computational cost. BIM requires more computational resources than FGSM due to its iterative nature.

Each iteration involves computing the gradient and updating the adversarial example, which can increase the overall run-time.

3.3.6 Practical Example for BIM Adversarial Attack

The following Python source code provides a practical example of how to train a convolutional neural network (CNN) on the MNIST dataset and generate adversarial examples using the Basic Iterative Method (BIM) attack. It also includes a visualization of adversarial examples and a comparison of the confusion matrices before and after the attack. Each part of Python code is explained as follows:

1. **Importing Libraries:** Import the necessary libraries and modules, including *TensorFlow, NumPy, Keras, MNIST dataset, CleverHans, Matplotlib, Scikit-learn.*

```
1  # Import libraries
2  import numpy as np
3  import tensorflow as tf
4  from tensorflow.keras.datasets import mnist
5  from cleverhans.tf2.attacks.basic_iterative_method import
       basic_iterative_method
6  import matplotlib.pyplot as plt
7  from tensorflow.keras.models import load_model
8  from sklearn.metrics import confusion_matrix
```

2. **Data Loading and Preprocessing**: Load the the MNIST dataset, containing training and testing images and labels, then reshape the image data to (batch_size, 28, 28, 1) and normalized to values between 0 and 1.

```
1  # Load the MNIST dataset
2  (x_train, y_train), (x_test, y_test) = mnist.load_data()
3
4  # Normalize pixel values to the range [0, 1]
5  x_train = x_train.astype("float32") / 255.0
6  x_test = x_test.astype("float32") / 255.
```

3. **Converting Labels to One-hot Encoding:** Convert labels to one-hot encoding using *tf.keras.utils.to_ categorical()* to match the model's output format.

```
1 # Convert labels to one-hot encoding
2 y_train = tf.keras.utils.to_categorical(y_train, 10)
3 y_test = tf.keras.utils.to_categorical(y_test, 10)
```

4. **Loading Pre-trained Model:** A pre-trained deep learning model, saved as *model.h5*, is loaded. This model was likely trained on the MNIST dataset for image classification tasks.

```
1 # Load the pre-trained model
2 model = load_model('model.h5')
```

5. **Generating Adversarial Examples (BIM):** Generate adversarial examples using the Basic Iterative Method (BIM). Key parameters include the *epsilon* value, determining the perturbation magnitude applied to input images, the *TARGET_ CLASS*, set to class 5 for targeting, and *y_ - attack_target*, a binary vector specifying the target class for the attack. BIM iteratively perturbs input images, attempting to force the model to classify them as the targeted class (class 5). The generated adversarial examples are stored in *adv_ x_ test*.

```
1  # Generate adversarial examples using BIM
2  epsilon = 0.1
3  target_adv = np.zeros_like(y_test)
4  TARGET_CLASS = 5
5  target_adv[:, TARGET_CLASS] = 1
6  target_adv = target_adv.argmax(axis=1)
7
8  y_attack_target = (np.ones((y_test.shape[0],)) *
       1).astype(int)
9
10 adv_x_test = basic_iterative_method(model, x_test,
       eps=epsilon, eps_iter=0.01, nb_iter=100, clip_min=0.0,
       clip_max=1.0, norm=np.inf, y=target_adv, targeted=True,
       sanity_checks=False)
```

6. **Predicting Labels:** Predict labels for the original and adversarial test sets obtained using *model.predict()* function. The code computes predictions on both the original test set (*x_ test*) and the adversarial test set (*adv_ x_ test*) using the pre-trained model. These predictions are used to generate two sets of images for visualization.

```
1 # Get predicted labels for the test set
2 y_pred = model.predict(x_test, verbose=0).argmax(axis=1)
3 adv_y_pred = model.predict(adv_x_test,
     verbose=0).argmax(axis=1)
```

7. **Finding Indices:** Find indices where the original input's prediction is not 0 (indicating that the original prediction is the target class) but the adversarial version's prediction is not the target class are identified using *np.where()*. The first 10 indices are selected *([:10])*.

```
1 # Find indices where original input prediction is not 0 but
     adversarial version's prediction is 0
2 indices = np.where((y_pred != TARGET_CLASS) & (adv_y_pred ==
     TARGET_CLASS))[0][:10]
```

8. **Plotting Examples:** Plot the examples generated two sets of images for visualization. The top row displays a selection of original test examples and their predicted labels, while the bottom row shows corresponding adversarial examples and their predicted labels.

```
1  # Plot the examples
2  fig, axs = plt.subplots(2, 10, figsize=(10, 3))
3  axs = axs.flatten()
4  for i in range(10):
5      axs[i].imshow(x_test[indices[i]], cmap="gray")
6      axs[i].set_title(f"Label: {y_pred[indices[i]]}")
7      axs[i].axis("off")
8      axs[i + 10].imshow(adv_x_test[indices[i]], cmap="gray")
9      axs[i + 10].set_title(f"Label: {adv_y_pred[indices[i]]}")
10     axs[i + 10].axis("off")
```

9. **Displaying the Results:** Adjust the padding between the subplots for better visualization using *tight_layout* and display results.

```
1 # Adjust the padding between the subplots
2 plt.tight_layout()
3 # Show the plot
4 plt.show()
```

10. **Computing Confusion Matrices:** Compute confusion matrices using *confusion_matrix()* to evaluate the model's performance before and after the attack.

```
1 # Get predicted labels for the test set before the attack
2 confusion_mtx = confusion_matrix(y_test.argmax(axis=1),
     y_pred)
```

```
3
4 # Get predicted labels for the test set after the attack
5 confusion_mtx_adv = confusion_matrix(y_test.argmax(axis=1),
    adv_y_pred)
```

11. **Plotting Confusion Matrices** Plot two confusion matrices side by side, i.e., model predictions before and after the adversarial attack.

```
1 # Plot the confusion matrices in the same subplot
2 fig, axs = plt.subplots(1, 2, figsize=(8, 4))
3 axs[0].imshow(confusion_mtx, interpolation='nearest',
    cmap=plt.cm.Blues)
4 axs[0].set_xticks(range(10))
5 axs[0].set_yticks(range(10))
6 axs[0].set_xlabel('Predicted label')
7 axs[0].set_ylabel('True label')
8 axs[0].set_title('Confusion Matrix (Before Attack)')
9
10 axs[1].imshow(confusion_mtx_adv, interpolation='nearest',
    cmap=plt.cm.Blues)
11 axs[1].set_xticks(range(10))
12 axs[1].set_yticks(range(10))
13 axs[1].set_xlabel('Predicted label')
14 axs[1].set_ylabel('True label')
15 axs[1].set_title('Confusion Matrix (After Attack)')
```

12. **Displaying the Results:** Adjust the padding between the subplots for better visualization using *tight_ layout* and display results.

```
1 # Adjust the padding between the subplots
2 plt.tight_layout()
3 # Show the plot
4 plt.show()
```

3.3.7 Projected Gradient Descent

Projected Gradient Descent (PGD) is another iterative method used for generating adversarial examples in ML [23]. It is an extension of the Basic Iterative Method (BIM) and further enhances the strength of the attack by incorporating a projection step.

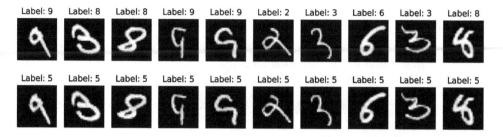

Figure 3.7: This figure showcases pairs of original MNIST images and their corresponding adversarial examples generated using the Basic Iterative Method (BIM) attack. Each row contains an original image (top row) and its adversarial counterpart (bottom row), with labels indicating the predicted classes.

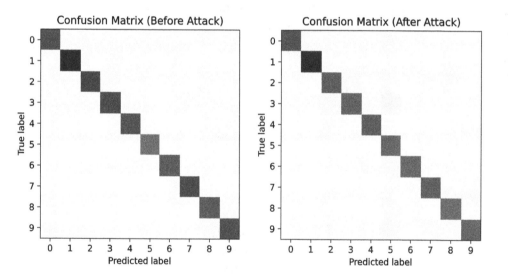

Figure 3.8: This figure shows two confusion matrices side by side. The left matrix represents the confusion matrix before the adversarial attack, showing the relationship between true labels and predicted labels. The right matrix, on the other hand, represents the confusion matrix after the attack, illustrating how the attack impacts the model's classification performance on the MNIST dataset.

Similar to BIM, PGD starts with an initial adversarial example and performs multiple iterations to refine the perturbation. However, PGD incorporates an additional step that ensures the adversarial example remains within a certain range of the original input, called the epsilon-ball.

A step-by-step breakdown of the PGD attack utilizing mathematical notation will be explained as follows:

1. Given an input image $\mathbf{x}$, its true label y_{true}, a targeted class y_{target} (optional), a maximum perturbation size ϵ, and a maximum number of iterations T:
2. Initialize the adversarial example $\mathbf{x}_{\text{adv}}$ as a copy of the original input $\mathbf{x}$.
3. Repeat for T iterations:
   - Compute the gradient of the loss function $\mathcal{L}(\theta, \mathbf{x}_{\text{adv}}, y_{\text{true}})$ with respect to the input: $\nabla_{x_{\text{adv}}} \mathcal{L}(\theta, \mathbf{x}_{\text{adv}}, y_{\text{true}})$
   - Compute the perturbation by taking a small step in the direction of the gradient: $\delta = \epsilon \cdot \text{sign}(\nabla_{\mathbf{x}_{\text{adv}}} \mathcal{L}(\theta, \mathbf{x}_{\text{adv}}, y_{\text{true}}))$
   - Update the adversarial example by adding the perturbation: $\mathbf{x}_{\text{adv}} = \mathbf{x}_{\text{adv}} + \delta$
   - Project the adversarial example onto the epsilon-ball to ensure it stays within the range of the original input: $\mathbf{x}_{\text{adv}} = \text{proj}_{\mathbf{x},\epsilon}(\mathbf{x}_{\text{adv}})$
4. Return the final adversarial example $\mathbf{x}_{\text{adv}}$.

The projection step, represented by $\text{proj}_{x,\epsilon}$, constrains the adversarial example to the epsilon-ball centered around the original input $\mathbf{x}$. This means that if the perturbation pushes the adversarial example outside the allowed range, it will be adjusted to fall back within the boundary.

Compared to BIM, PGD offers several advantages in terms of Robustness, Attack strength, Detection resilience, and Computational cost. The first advantage is **Robustness** to develop more robust adversarial examples. The robustness can make the attack more effective against defense mechanisms that rely on input constraints. The second one is **Attack strength** to generate stronger adversarial examples by performing multiple iterations and incorporating the projection step. It explores the input space more thoroughly and can find perturbations that lead to higher misclassification rates. The third advantage is **Detection resilience** to make PGD more susceptible to detection by certain defense mechanisms. The last advantage is **Computational cost**, which requires more computational resources compared to BIM due to the additional projection step.

3.3.8 Practical Example for PGD Adversarial Attack

The provided code segment showcases the process of training a convolutional neural network (CNN) on the MNIST dataset and generating adversarial examples using the Projected Gradient Descent (PGD) attack. Additionally, it includes a visualization of the adversarial examples and a comparison of the confusion matrices before and after the attack. Below, the purpose and functionality of each part of the Python code will be explained:

1. **Importing Libraries:** Import the necessary libraries and modules, including *TensorFlow, NumPy, Keras, MNIST dataset, CleverHans, Matplotlib, Scikit-learn.*

```
1 # Import libraries
2 import numpy as np
3 import tensorflow as tf
4 from tensorflow.keras.datasets import mnist
5 from cleverhans.tf2.attacks.projected_gradient_descent
       import projected_gradient_descent
6 import matplotlib.pyplot as plt
7 from tensorflow.keras.models import load_model
8 from sklearn.metrics import confusion_matrix
```

2. **Data Loading and Preprocessing**: Load the the MNIST dataset, containing training and testing images and labels, then reshape the image data to (batch_size, 28, 28, 1) and normalized to values between 0 and 1.

```
1 # Load the MNIST dataset
2 (x_train, y_train), (x_test, y_test) = mnist.load_data()
```

```
3
4  # Normalize pixel values to the range [0, 1]
5  x_train = x_train.astype("float32") / 255.0
6  x_test = x_test.astype("float32") / 255.
```

3. **Converting Labels to One-hot Encoding:** Convert labels to one-hot encoding using *tf.keras.utils.to_ categorical()* to match the model's output format.

```
1  # Convert labels to one-hot encoding
2  y_train = tf.keras.utils.to_categorical(y_train, 10)
3  y_test = tf.keras.utils.to_categorical(y_test, 10)
```

4. **Loading Pre-trained Model:** Load the pre-trained deep learning model, saved as *model.h5*. This model was likely trained on the MNIST dataset for image classification tasks.

```
1  # Load the pre-trained model
2  model = load_model('model.h5')
```

5. **Generating Adversarial Examples (PDG):** Generate adversarial examples using the Projected Gradient Descent (PGD). The main parameters are the *epsilon* value, which determines the size of the perturbation applied to input images, the *TARGET_ CLASS*, which is set to class 5 for the purpose of targeting, and *y_ attack_ target*, a binary vector that specifies the desired target class for the attack. The PGD method iteratively perturbs input images in an attempt to make the model classify them as the targeted class (class 5). The resulting adversarial examples are saved in the variable *adv_ x_ test*.

```
1  # Generate adversarial examples using PGD
2  epsilon = 0.1
3  target_adv = np.zeros_like(y_test)
4  TARGET_CLASS = 5
5  target_adv[:, TARGET_CLASS] = 1
6  target_adv = target_adv.argmax(axis=1)
7
8  y_attack_target = (np.ones((y_test.shape[0],)) *
       1).astype(int)
9
10 adv_x_test = projected_gradient_descent(model, x_test,
       eps=epsilon, eps_iter=0.01, nb_iter=100,
11                                     clip_min=0.0,
       clip_max=1.0, norm=np.inf, y=target_adv,
```

```
12                                    targeted=True,
   sanity_checks=False)
```

6. **Predicting Labels:** Predict labels for the original and adversarial test sets obtained using *model.predict()* function.

```
1 # Get predicted labels for the test set
2 y_pred = model.predict(x_test, verbose=0).argmax(axis=1)
3 adv_y_pred = model.predict(adv_x_test,
   verbose=0).argmax(axis=1)
```

7. **Finding Indices:** Find indices where the original input's prediction is not 0 (indicating that the original prediction is the target class) but the adversarial version's prediction is not the target class identified using *np.where()*. The first 10 indices are selected *([:10])*.

```
1 # Find indices where original input prediction is not 0 but
   adversarial version's prediction is 0
2 indices = np.where((y_pred != TARGET_CLASS) & (adv_y_pred ==
   TARGET_CLASS))[0][:10]
```

8. **Plotting Selected Examples:** Plot the selected examples generated two sets of images for visualization. The upper row exhibits a variety of initial test examples and their predicted labels, whereas the lower row presents corresponding adversarial examples and their predicted labels. The images are displayed in a 2x10 grid for visual comparison.

```
1  # Plot the examples
2  fig, axs = plt.subplots(2, 10, figsize=(10, 3))
3  axs = axs.flatten()
4  for i in range(10):
5      axs[i].imshow(x_test[indices[i]], cmap="gray")
6      axs[i].set_title(f"Label: {y_pred[indices[i]]}")
7      axs[i].axis("off")
8      axs[i + 10].imshow(adv_x_test[indices[i]], cmap="gray")
9      axs[i + 10].set_title(f"Label: {adv_y_pred[indices[i]]}")
10     axs[i + 10].axis("off")
```

9. **Displaying the Results:** Adjust the padding between the subplots for better visualization using *tight_layout* and display results.

```
1  # Adjust the padding between the subplots
2  plt.tight_layout()
3  # Show the plot
4  plt.show()
```

10. **Computing Confusion Matrices:** Compute confusion matrices using *confusion_ matrix()* to evaluate the model's performance before and after the attack.

```
1 # Get predicted labels for the test set before the attack
2 confusion_mtx = confusion_matrix(y_test.argmax(axis=1),
     y_pred)
3
4 # Get predicted labels for the test set after the attack
5 confusion_mtx_adv = confusion_matrix(y_test.argmax(axis=1),
     adv_y_pred)
```

11. **Plotting Confusion Matrices:** Plot confusion matrices to evaluate the model's performance for PGD adversarial attacks, and visualize the selected examples and confusion matrices.

```
1  # Plot the confusion matrices in the same subplot
2  fig, axs = plt.subplots(1, 2, figsize=(8, 4))
3  axs[0].imshow(confusion_mtx, interpolation='nearest',
      cmap=plt.cm.Blues)
4  axs[0].set_xticks(range(10))
5  axs[0].set_yticks(range(10))
6  axs[0].set_xlabel('Predicted label')
7  axs[0].set_ylabel('True label')
8  axs[0].set_title('Confusion Matrix (Before Attack)')
9
10 axs[1].imshow(confusion_mtx_adv, interpolation='nearest',
      cmap=plt.cm.Blues)
11 axs[1].set_xticks(range(10))
12 axs[1].set_yticks(range(10))
13 axs[1].set_xlabel('Predicted label')
14 axs[1].set_ylabel('True label')
15 axs[1].set_title('Confusion Matrix (After Attack)')
```

12. **Displaying the Results:** Adjust the padding between the subplots for better visualization using *tight_ layout* and display results.

```
1 # Adjust the padding between the subplots
2 plt.tight_layout()
3 # Show the plot
4 plt.show()
```

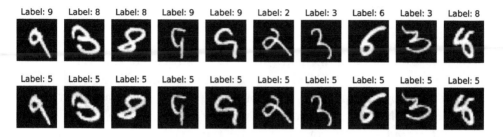

Figure 3.9: This figure showcases pairs of original MNIST images and their corresponding adversarial examples generated using the Basic Iterative Method (BIM) attack. Each row contains an original image (top row) and its adversarial counterpart (bottom row), with labels indicating the predicted classes.

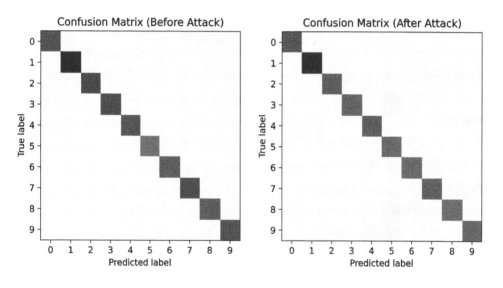

Figure 3.10: This figure shows two confusion matrices side by side. The left matrix represents the confusion matrix before the adversarial attack, showing the relationship between true labels and predicted labels. The right matrix, on the other hand, represents the confusion matrix after the attack, illustrating how the attack impacts the model's classification performance on the MNIST dataset.

3.3.9 Momentum Iterative Method

The momentum iterative method (MIM) is an advance of the basic iterative method (BIM) attack [24]. MIM can provide a better attack effectiveness compared to BIM by incorporating the momentum term. The momentum term is used to accumulate gradients from previous iterations to create a smoother and more stable gradient direction. This makes the attack more effective in finding the adversarial perturbation leading to misclassification.

It can be explained with the math notations. Suppose there is a neural network model f with parameters θ, input image $\mathbf{x}$, true label y, and target label t. The goal of the adversarial attack is to find an adversarial perturbation δ such that the perturbed image $\mathbf{x}' = \mathbf{x} + \delta$ maximizes the loss function $\mathcal{L}(\theta, \mathbf{x}', t)$, where $\mathcal{L}$ is a suitable loss function that penalizes misclassification. The MIM attack achieves this by iteratively updating the perturbation as follows:

$$\delta^{(0)} = 0$$

$$g^{(i)} = \frac{\partial \delta^{(i-1)}}{\partial \mathcal{L}(\theta, \mathbf{x}^{(i)} + \delta^{(i-1)}, t)} \tag{3.11}$$

$$m^{(i)} = \mu m^{(i-1)} + |g^{(i)}|_1 \cdot \text{sign}(g^{(i)})$$

The above equations show the MIM attack with momentum. The iterative process starts with $\delta^{(0)} = 0$. In each iteration i, the gradient of the loss function with respect to the perturbation $g^{(i)}$ is calculated using the current perturbed image $\mathbf{x}^{(i)} + \delta^{(i-1)}$. Then, the momentum term $m^{(i)}$ is updated using the previous momentum $m^{(i-1)}$ and the normalized gradient $g^{(i)}$. Finally, the perturbation is updated by taking the sign of the momentum and scaling it by the maximum perturbation allowed ϵ. This ensures that the perturbation remains within the specified bounds.

As mentioned earlier, MIM incorporates the concept of momentum to improve the efficiency and effectiveness of attack against AI/ML models. A step-by-step breakdown of the MIM attack using math notation can given as follows:

1. Give an input image $\mathbf{x}$, its true label y_{true}, a targeted class y_{target} (optional), a maximum perturbation size ϵ, a momentum factor μ, and a decay factor α:
2. Initialize the adversarial example $\mathbf{x}_{\text{adv}}$ as a copy of the original input $\mathbf{x}$.
3. Initialize the momentum term v as zero, representing the accumulated gradient direction.
4. Repeat for a fixed number of iterations T:
   ◼ Compute the gradient of the loss function $\mathcal{L}(\theta, \mathbf{x}_{\text{adv}}, y_{\text{true}})$ with respect to the input: $\nabla_{x_{\text{adv}}}\mathcal{L}(\theta, \mathbf{x}_{\text{adv}}, y_{\text{true}})$

   ◼ Update the momentum term: $v = \mu \cdot v + \dfrac{\nabla_{\mathbf{x}_{\text{adv}}}\mathcal{L}(\theta,\mathbf{x}_{\text{adv}},y_{\text{true}})}{|\nabla_{\mathbf{x}_{\text{adv}}}\mathcal{L}(\theta,\mathbf{x}_{\text{adv}},y_{\text{true}})|_1}$

   ◼ Compute the perturbation by scaling the momentum term: $\delta = \epsilon \cdot \text{sign}(v)$

   ◼ Update the adversarial example by adding the perturbation: $\mathbf{x}_{\text{adv}} = \mathbf{x}_{\text{adv}} + \delta$

   ◼ Clip the adversarial example to ensure it stays within the ϵ-ball around the original input: $\mathbf{x}_{\text{adv}} = \text{clip}(\mathbf{x}_{\text{adv}}, \mathbf{x} - \epsilon, \mathbf{x} + \epsilon)$

   ◼ Decay the momentum term to gradually reduce the influence of past gradients: $v = \alpha \cdot v$
5. Return the final adversarial example $\mathbf{x}_{\text{adv}}$.

The main differences between FGSM and MIM can include Momentum, Iterative refinement, Efficiency, Defense detection, and Computational cost. The first difference is *Momentum*, which is utilized by MIM. The momentum accumulates the gradient information over iterations so that the attack can maintain a sense of direction and exploit more information from the gradient landscape, potentially leading to more effective perturbations. The second one is *Iterative refinement*. MIM performs multiple iterations to refine the adversarial perturbation, like BIM. This iterative refinement enables MIM to explore the input space more comprehensively and potentially find stronger perturbations. The third main difference is *Efficiency*. MIM can reduce the number of iterations required to achieve a similar level of perturbation as FGSM. This offers a better efficiency than the other method, i.e., FGSM and BIM. The other main difference is *Defense detection*. The iterative nature of MIM can make it more susceptible to detection by certain defense mechanisms, i.e., identification of repeated patterns or multiple modifications. The last one is *Computational cost.* The MIM's computational cost is higher than FGSM due to the iterative nature of the attack.

3.3.10 Practical Example for MIM Adversarial Attack

The following Python code demonstrates the training of a convolutional neural network (CNN) model on the MNIST dataset and generates adversarial examples using the MIM attack. The code includes adversarial example visualization and confusion matrices before and after the attack. Each the Python code section is explained below:

1. **Importing Libraries:** Import the necessary libraries and modules are imported, including *TensorFlow, NumPy, Keras, MNIST dataset, CleverHans, Matplotlib, Scikit-learn.*

```
1 # Import libraries
2 import numpy as np
3 import tensorflow as tf
4 from tensorflow.keras.datasets import mnist
5 from cleverhans.tf2.attacks.momentum_iterative_method import
      momentum_iterative_method
6 import matplotlib.pyplot as plt
7 from tensorflow.keras.models import load_model
8 from sklearn.metrics import confusion_matrix
```

2. **Data Loading and Preprocessing:** First, the MNIST dataset, including the training and test sets, is loaded. Pixel values in the images are normalized to the range [0, 1].

```
1 # Load the MNIST dataset
2 (x_train, y_train), (x_test, y_test) = mnist.load_data()
3
4 # Normalize pixel values to the range [0, 1]
5 x_train = x_train.astype("float32") / 255.0
6 x_test = x_test.astype("float32") / 255.0
```

3. **Converting Labels to One-hot Encoding:** Convert labels to one-hot encoding using *tf.keras.utils.to_ categorical()* to match the model's output format.

```
1  # Convert labels to one-hot encoding
2  y_train = tf.keras.utils.to_categorical(y_train, 10)
3  y_test = tf.keras.utils.to_categorical(y_test, 10)
```

4. **Loading Pre-trained Model:** Load the pre-trained deep learning model, saved as *model.h5*. This model was likely trained on the MNIST dataset for image classification tasks.

```
1  # Load the pre-trained model
2  model = load_model('model.h5')
```

5. **Generating Adversarial Examples (BIM):** Generate adversarial examples using the Momentum Iterative Method (MIM). It starts with setting the key parameters. The variable *epsilon* is set to 0.1, which controls the magnitude of the perturbation in the MIM attack. The variable *target_ adv* is created as an array of zeros with the same shape as *y_ test*. The target class for the attack is set to 5 *(TARGET_ CLASS = 5)*, and the corresponding elements in target_adv are set to 1. This creates a targeted attack where the goal is to misclassify the examples as class 5. Then, the *target_ adv* array is converted into a one-dimensional array containing the indices of the target classes using argmax(axis=1). Adversarial examples are generated using the targeted MIM attack by calling *momentum_ iterative_ method()* with the *target_ adv* array provided as the y parameter. This ensures that the attack is targeted towards the specified class.

```
1   # Generate adversarial examples using MIM
2   epsilon = 0.1
3   target_adv = np.zeros_like(y_test)
4   TARGET_CLASS = 5
5   target_adv[:, TARGET_CLASS] = 1
6   target_adv = target_adv.argmax(axis=1)
7
8   y_attack_target = (np.ones((y_test.shape[0],)) *
        1).astype(int)
9
10  adv_x_test = momentum_iterative_method(model, x_test,
        eps=epsilon, eps_iter=0.01, nb_iter=100,
11                                        decay_factor=1.0,
        clip_min=0.0, clip_max=1.0, y=target_adv,
```

```
12                                            targeted=True,
            sanity_checks=False)
```

6. **Predicting Labels:** Predict the labels for the original and adversarial test sets using *model.predict().argmax(axis=1)*.

```
1 # Get predicted labels for the test set
2 y_pred = model.predict(x_test, verbose=0).argmax(axis=1)
3 adv_y_pred = model.predict(adv_x_test,
       verbose=0).argmax(axis=1)
```

7. **Finding Indices:** Find indices where the original input's prediction is not 0 (indicating that the original prediction is the target class) but the adversarial version's prediction is not the target class are identified using *np.where()*. The first 10 indices are selected *([:10])*.

```
1 # Find indices where original input prediction is not 0 but
      adversarial version's prediction is 0
2 indices = np.where((y_pred != TARGET_CLASS) & (adv_y_pred ==
      TARGET_CLASS))[0][:10]
```

8. **Plotting Examples:** Create a figure with 2 rows and 2 columns to display multiple subplots. It utilizes the subplots function from the *matplotlib.pyplot* module to create a grid of subplots. Plot the selected examples. The original images corresponding to the selected indices are displayed along with their predicted and adversarial labels.

```
1  # Plot the examples
2  fig, axs = plt.subplots(2, 10, figsize=(10, 3))
3  axs = axs.flatten()
4  for i in range(10):
5      axs[i].imshow(x_test[indices[i]], cmap="gray")
6      axs[i].set_title(f"Label: {y_pred[indices[i]]}")
7      axs[i].axis("off")
8      axs[i + 10].imshow(adv_x_test[indices[i]], cmap="gray")
9      axs[i + 10].set_title(f"Label: {adv_y_pred[indices[i]]}")
10     axs[i + 10].axis("off")
```

9. **Displaying the Results:** Adjust the padding between the subplots for better visualization using *tight_layout* and display results.

```
1 # Adjust the padding between the subplots
2 plt.tight_layout()
3 # Show the plot
4 plt.show()
```

10. **Computing Confusion Matrix:** Compute the confusion matrices using confusion_matrix() to evaluate the model's performance before and after the attack.

```
1 # Get predicted labels for the test set before the attack
2 confusion_mtx = confusion_matrix(y_test.argmax(axis=1),
    y_pred)
3
4 # Get predicted labels for the test set after the attack
5 confusion_mtx_adv = confusion_matrix(y_test.argmax(axis=1),
    adv_y_pred)
```

11. **Plotting Confusion Matrix:** Plot the confusion matrices before and after the attack. The additional code demonstrates how to generate targeted adversarial examples using MIM, evaluate the model's performance, and visualize the selected examples and confusion matrices.

```
1 # Plot the confusion matrices in the same subplot
2 fig, axs = plt.subplots(1, 2, figsize=(8, 4))
3 axs[0].imshow(confusion_mtx, interpolation='nearest',
    cmap=plt.cm.Blues)
4 axs[0].set_xticks(range(10))
5 axs[0].set_yticks(range(10))
6 axs[0].set_xlabel('Predicted label')
7 axs[0].set_ylabel('True label')
8 axs[0].set_title('Confusion Matrix (Before Attack)')
9
10 axs[1].imshow(confusion_mtx_adv, interpolation='nearest',
    cmap=plt.cm.Blues)
11 axs[1].set_xticks(range(10))
12 axs[1].set_yticks(range(10))
13 axs[1].set_xlabel('Predicted label')
14 axs[1].set_ylabel('True label')
15 axs[1].set_title('Confusion Matrix (After Attack)')
```

12. **Displaying the Results:** Adjust the padding between the subplots for better visualization using *tight_layout* and display results.

```
1 # Adjust the padding between the subplots
2 plt.tight_layout()
3 # Show the plot
4 plt.show()
```

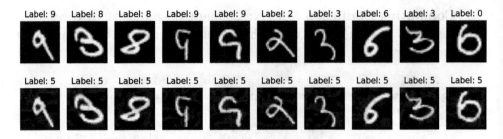

Figure 3.11: Original vs. Adversarial Examples (MIM Attack): This plot displays pairs of original MNIST digit images on the top row and their corresponding adversarial examples generated using the Momentum Iterative Method (MIM) attack on the bottom row. The titles indicate the true labels of the original images.

3.3.11 Carlini-Wagner

The Carlini-Wagner (CW) attack is a state-of-the-art optimization-based adversarial attack that aims to find the smallest possible perturbation to the input image that will cause the model to misclassify it [25]. The CW attack is unique in that it is capable of producing adversarial examples that are specifically designed to target a certain misclassification, as opposed to simply finding any misclassification.

The CW attack formulates the problem of finding an adversarial example as an optimization problem. Specifically, given an input image $\mathbf{x}$, the attack aims to find a perturbation δ that minimizes the distance between the perturbed image $\mathbf{x}+\delta$ and the original image $\mathbf{x}$ subject to the constraint that the perturbed image is misclassified by the model. The optimization problem can be formulated as:

$$\min_{\delta} \|\delta\|_p + c \cdot f(\mathbf{x} + \delta) \tag{3.12}$$

where $\| \cdot \|_p$ is a norm used to measure the size of the perturbation, $f(\mathbf{x}+\delta)$ is a function that measures the model's confidence in its prediction for the perturbed

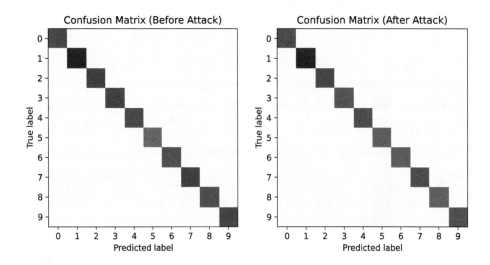

Figure 3.12: Confusion Matrix (Left - Before Attack): This plot shows the confusion matrix of the model's predictions on the MNIST dataset before the adversarial attack. It provides insight into the model's classification performance on the original data. Confusion Matrix (Right - After Attack): This plot displays the confusion matrix of the model's predictions on the MNIST dataset after applying the Momentum Iterative Method (MIM) adversarial attack. It illustrates the impact of adversarial perturbations on the model's classification accuracy.

image, and c is a trade-off parameter that controls the importance of the two terms in the objective function. The $f(\mathbf{x} + \delta)$ term in the objective function is designed to encourage the perturbed image to be classified as the target class, or to be misclassified if targeted attacks are not used.

Here's a step-by-step breakdown of the CW attack using math notation:

1. Given an input image $\mathbf{x}$, its true label y_{true}, a targeted class y_{target} (optional), and a constant c controlling the trade-off between perturbation magnitude and misclassification confidence:
2. Initialize the adversarial example $\mathbf{x}_{\text{adv}}$ as a copy of the original input $\mathbf{x}$.
3. Initialize a binary search range for the perturbation magnitude:

$$[0, \text{upper\_bound}]$$

   The upper bound can be set based on the desired maximum perturbation.
4. Repeat until convergence (e.g., the maximum number of iterations reached or desired confidence achieved):

   ■ Perform a change of variables to ensure the perturbation lies within the valid range. For example, use $w = \frac{1}{2}(\tanh^{-1}(2\mathbf{x}_{\text{adv}} - 1) + 1)$ to map $\mathbf{x}_{\text{adv}}$ to the range $[0, 1]$.

   ■ Define the objective function that must be minimized to generate the adversarial example. It typically consists of two components: the magnitude of the perturbation and the misclassification confidence. The objective function is formulated as follows: minimize $|w - \frac{1}{2}(\tanh^{-1}(2\mathbf{x} - 1) + 1)|2^2 + c \cdot f(\mathbf{x}_{\text{adv}}, y_{\text{true}})$

   ■ Solve the optimization problem using an optimization algorithm (e.g., gradient descent) to find the adversarial example $\mathbf{x}_{\text{adv}}$ that minimizes the objective function.

   ■ Perform the inverse change of variables to map w back to the original input space.

   ■ Clip the adversarial example to ensure it stays within a valid range (e.g., pixel range of $[0, 1]$ for images).

   ■ If the adversarial example is misclassified, update the binary search range to explore smaller perturbation magnitudes.

▪ If a targeted attack is desired and the adversarial example is classified as the targeted class, update the binary search range to explore larger perturbation magnitudes.

5. Return the final adversarial example x_{adv}.

Now, let's discuss the main characteristics and differences of the CW attack:

1. Optimization-based approach: CW attack formulates the generation of adversarial examples as an optimization problem. Optimizing the objective function, it finds perturbations that result in misclassification while keeping the perturbation magnitude low.

2. Trade-off parameter: The constant c controls the trade-off between the perturbation magnitude and the misclassification confidence. Higher values of c prioritize smaller perturbations, while lower values prioritize higher misclassification confidence.

3. Binary search: CW attack employs a binary search to find the smallest perturbation that achieves misclassification. This ensures that the adversarial example is generated with the smallest possible perturbation.

4. Misclassification confidence: CW attack maximizes the misclassification confidence , aiming to generate adversarial examples that are highly likely to be classified as the target class.

5. Perturbation magnitude: CW attack focuses on minimizing the perturbation amount, aiming to generate adversarial examples visually similar to the original input.

6. Computational cost: CW attack is expensive in terms of computational demand due to its complex optimization process consisting of iterative optimization algorithms and multiple evaluations of objective functions.

3.3.12 Practical Example for CW Adversarial Attack

In the following code segment, it will be performed an adversarial attack on a pre-trained deep learning model using the Carlini-Wagner L_2 attack method. The execution time of the CW method is very high. It will take some time to finish the code execution. The goal is to generate adversarial examples that the model misclassifies while maintaining visual similarity to the original input images, and to evaluate the impact on the model's predictions and confusion matrices. Each part of the Python code segment, i.e., Part 1 of the example for CW adversarial attack, will be explained as follows:

1. **Importing Libraries:** Import the necessary libraries and modules are imported, including *TensorFlow, NumPy, Keras, MNIST dataset, CleverHans, Matplotlib, Scikit-learn, and Tdqm.*

```
1  #=================================
2  ### Part 1
3  #Import Libraries
4  import random
5  import numpy as np
6  import tensorflow as tf
7  from tensorflow import keras
8  from tensorflow.keras import layers
9  from tensorflow.keras.datasets import mnist
10 from cleverhans.tf2.attacks.carlini_wagner_l2 import
      carlini_wagner_l2
11 import matplotlib.pyplot as plt
12 from tqdm.notebook import tqdm
13 from tensorflow.keras.models import load_model
14 from sklearn.metrics import confusion_matrix
15 from tqdm.keras import TqdmCallback
```

2. **Data Loading and Preprocessing:** Load the MNIST dataset consisting of hand-written digit images. The pixel values of these images are normalized to the range $[0, 1]$.

```
1  # Load the MNIST dataset
2  (x_train, y_train), (x_test, y_test) = mnist.load_data()
3
4  # Normalize pixel values to the range [0, 1]
5  x_train = x_train.astype("float32") / 255.0
```

```
6  x_test = x_test.astype("float32") / 255.0
```

3. **Converting Labels to One-hot Encoding:** Convert labels to one-hot encoding using *tf.keras.utils.to_ categorical()* to match the model's output format.

```
1  # Convert labels to one-hot encoding
2  y_train = tf.keras.utils.to_categorical(y_train, 10)
3  y_test = tf.keras.utils.to_categorical(y_test, 10)
```

4. **Loading Pre-trained Model:** Load the pre-trained deep learning model from the *model.h5*. This model has been previously trained on the MNIST dataset.

```
1  # Load the pre-trained model
2  model = load_model('model.h5')
```

5. **Fine-tuning Model:** Fine-tune the loaded model on the training set before launching the adversarial attack. The model is trained for ten epochs using a batch size of 5000 and a validation split 0.1. The training progress is displayed using a tqdm callback.

```
1  # Train the model on the training set
2  model.fit(x_train, y_train, batch_size=5000, epochs=10,
       validation_split=0.1,
3               verbose=0, callbacks=[TqdmCallback(verbose=1)])
```

6. **Creating Variables and Setting up Key Parameters:** Create the variables *adv_ x_ test, adv_ y_ org, rand_ idx_ list, and TARGET_ CLASS* are initialized for use in generating adversarial examples using the *Carlini-Wagner L2* attack, a one-hot encoded target label *(y_ tmp_ target)* for the target class.

```
1  # Create variables and set up key parameters
2  adv_x_test = []
3  adv_y_org = []
4  rand_idx_list = []
5
6  TARGET_CLASS = 5
7  y_tmp_target = np.zeros((1, 10))
8  y_tmp_target[:, TARGET_CLASS] = 1
```

7. **Generating Adversarial Examples (CW):** Generate adversarial examples using the *Carlini-Wagner L2* attack by the following steps. It iterates 150 times and adds the perturbed images to *adv_ x_ test.*

■ Randomly select an index *rand_idx* from the test dataset *x_test*.

■ Extract the corresponding test image and its original class label *adv_-y_org*.

■ Use the Carlini-Wagner L_2 attack method to generate an adversarial example *adv_x_test_tmp* for the selected image. This attack is targeted towards the specified target class *TARGET_CLASS* and aims to maximize the confidence of misclassification. It runs with various parameters, including batch size, confidence, maximum iterations, and clipping values.

■ Append the generated adversarial example *adv_x_test_tmp* to the list of adversarial examples *adv_x_test*.

■ Repeat the process for 150 random test images.

```
1  # Generate adversarial examples using Carlini-Wagner L2
     attack
2  for _ in tqdm(range(150)):
3      rand_idx = np.random.randint(0, x_test.shape[0])
4      rand_idx_list.append(rand_idx)
5
6      tmp_input = x_test[rand_idx:rand_idx + 1, :]
7      adv_y_org.append(y_test[rand_idx])
8
9      logits_model = tf.keras.Model(model.input,
     model.layers[-1].output)
10
11     adv_x_test_tmp = carlini_wagner_l2(model,
     tmp_input.reshape((1, 28, 28, 1)), targeted=True,
     y=[TARGET_CLASS], batch_size=128, confidence=100.0,
     abort_early=True, max_iterations=500, clip_min=0.0,
     clip_max=1.0)
12
13     adv_x_test.append(adv_x_test_tmp.reshape(28, 28))
```

The generated adversarial examples will be visually similar to the original images but will cause the model to misclassify them into the target class *TARGET_CLASS*.

In Part 2, the effectiveness of the *Carlini-Wagner L2* adversarial attack on the pre-trained model will be evaluated along with how the attack affects the model's predictions and analyze the confusion matrices. Each part of the code segment will be explained as follows:

1. **Importing Libraries:** Import the necessary libraries and modules for visualization and confusion matrix computation, such as *Matplotlib and Scikit-learn.*

```
# =============================================
### PART 2
import matplotlib.pyplot as plt
from sklearn.metrics import confusion_matrix
```

2. **Predicting Labels:** Predict labels for the original and adversarial test sets obtained using *model.predict()* function. It consists of several steps as follows:

   ■ *Predictions Before Attack:* Predict the test dataset before the adversarial attack. The predicted labels are stored in *y_pred.*

```
# Get predicted labels for the test set
y_pred = model.predict(x_test[rand_idx_list,:],
    verbose=0).argmax(axis=1)
y_org = y_test[rand_idx_list].argmax(axis=1)
```

   ■ *Predictions After Attack:* Predict labels for the test dataset after applying the *Carlini-Wagner L2* attack. The predicted labels are stored in *adv_y_pred.*

```
adv_y_pred = model.predict(np.array(adv_x_test),
    verbose=0).argmax(axis=1)
y_org_pred = model.predict(x_test, verbose=0).argmax(axis=1)
```

3. **Finding Indices:** To analyze the impact of the attack, it is selected examples where the original labels *adv_y_org* were not equal to the target class *TARGET_CLASS* but became equal to the target class after the attack. We choose the first 10 examples and store them in *indices.*

```
# Find indices where original input prediction is not 0 but
    adversarial version's prediction is 0
indices = np.where((adv_y_org != TARGET_CLASS) & (adv_y_pred
    == TARGET_CLASS))[0][:10]
```

4. **Creating Lists for Analysis:** Create three lists for analysis: *y_list* contains the true labels of the selected textit, *y_pred_cw_list* contains

125

the predicted labels before the attack, and *y_adv_cw_list* contains the predicted labels after the attack.

```
1  # Create lists for analysis
2  y_list = []
3  y_pred_cw_list = []
4  y_adv_cw_list = []
```

5. **Plotting Examples:** Plot the selected examples in a 2x10 grid. The top row displays the original images with their predicted labels before the attack, while the bottom row shows the corresponding adversarial examples with their predicted labels after the attack.

```
1  # Plot the examples
2  fig, axs = plt.subplots(2, 10, figsize=(10, 3))
3  axs = axs.flatten()
4  for i in range(10):
5      idx_val = indices[i]
6      idx_val = rand_idx_list[idx_val]
7      axs[i].imshow(x_test[idx_val], cmap="gray")
8      axs[i].set_title(f"Label: {y_pred[indices[i]]}")
9      axs[i].axis("off")
10     axs[i + 10].imshow(adv_x_test[indices[i]], cmap="gray")
11     axs[i + 10].set_title(f"Label: {adv_y_pred[indices[i]]}")
12     axs[i + 10].axis("off")
13
14     y_pred_cw_list.append(y_pred[indices[i]])
15     y_adv_cw_list.append(adv_y_pred[indices[i]])
16     y_list.append(y_test[indices[i]].argmax(axis=0))
```

6. **Displaying the Results:** Adjust the padding between the subplots for better visualization using *tight_layout* and display results.

```
1  # Adjust the padding between the subplots
2  plt.tight_layout()
3  # Show the plot
4  plt.show()
```

7. **Computing Confusion Matrix Before Attack:** Compute the confusion matrix *confusion_mtx* for the test dataset's true labels *y_test* and the predicted labels before the attack *y_org_pred*. This matrix provides insights into the model's performance before the attack.

```
1  # Get predicted labels for the test set before the attack
2  confusion_mtx = confusion_matrix(y_test.argmax(axis=1),
       y_org_pred)
```

8. **Computing Confusion Matrix After Attack:** Compute another confusion matrix *confusion_ mtx_ adv* for the true labels *y_ list* of the selected examples and their predicted labels after the attack *y_ adv_ cw_list*. This matrix helps us assess the attack's impact on model predictions for the specific examples of the attack targets.

```
1  # Get predicted labels for the test set after the attack
2  confusion_mtx_adv = confusion_matrix(y_list, y_adv_cw_list)
```

9. **Plotting Confusion Matrices:** Plot the confusion matrices. It visualizes two confusion matrices, one labeled *Before Attack* and the other *After Attack*. The matrices represent the performance of a ML model on a classification task. Each subplot is customized with appropriate axis labels and titles.

```
1  # Plot the confusion matrices in the same subplot
2  fig, axs = plt.subplots(1, 2, figsize=(8, 4))
3  axs[0].imshow(confusion_mtx, interpolation='nearest',
       cmap=plt.cm.Blues)
4  axs[0].set_xticks(range(10))
5  axs[0].set_yticks(range(10))
6  axs[0].set_xlabel('Predicted label')
7  axs[0].set_ylabel('True label')
8  axs[0].set_title('Confusion Matrix (Before Attack)')
9
10 axs[1].imshow(confusion_mtx_adv, interpolation='nearest',
       cmap=plt.cm.Blues)
11 axs[1].set_xticks(range(10))
12 axs[1].set_yticks(range(10))
13 axs[1].set_xlabel('Predicted label')
14 axs[1].set_ylabel('True label')
15 axs[1].set_title('Confusion Matrix (After Attack)')
```

10. **Displaying the Results:** Adjust the padding between the subplots for better visualization using *tight_ layout* and display results.

```
1  # Adjust the padding between the subplots
2  plt.tight_layout()
3  # Show the plot
4  plt.show()
```

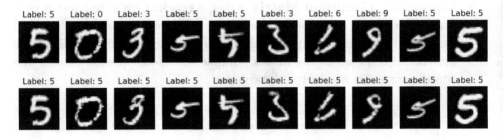

Figure 3.13: Original test set images and their predicted labels before the attack (Top). Adversarial examples generated by the Carlini-Wagner L2 attack and their predicted labels after the attack (Bottom).

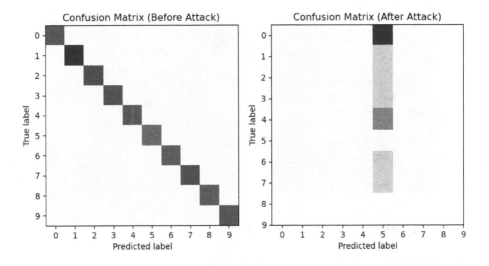

Figure 3.14: (Confusion Matrix Before Attack - Left): Confusion matrix showing the distribution of predicted labels versus true labels before the Carlini-Wagner L_2 attack. This matrix reflects the model's performance on the original test set. (Confusion Matrix After Attack - Right): Confusion matrix illustrating the distribution of predicted labels versus true labels after applying the Carlini-Wagner L_2 attack. It reveals how the attack affects the model's classification accuracy, particularly in the presence of adversarial examples.

3.4 Other Adversarial Machine Learning Attacks

This section briefly discusses the other adversarial ML attacks used in the AI/ML concept. Note that practical examples are not provided for these adversarial attacks in this section.

3.4.1 Deepfool

DeepFool attack is a type of adversarial attack on AI/ML models, introduced by Moosavi-Dezfooli et al. in 2016 [26]. The attack is based on the observation that many deep neural networks are linearly separable, i.e., the decision boundary between different classes in the input space can be approximated by a hyperplane. The basic idea of the DeepFool Attack is to find the closest hyperplane to the input that separates it from the correct class, and to move the input along the normal vector to that hyperplane, in order to cross the decision boundary and be classified as a different class.

The working principle of DeepFool algorithm consists of several steps. It starts with a given input image $\mathbf{x}$, then the DeepFool algorithm computes the linearized approximation of the decision boundary of the classifier f, and finds the distance d between $\mathbf{x}$ and the decision boundary. The algorithm changes the input image by a small amount δ in the direction of the decision boundary. New image is slightly closer to the decision boundary, i.e., $\mathbf{x}' = \mathbf{x} + \delta$. This process is repeated until the new image is misclassified or the maximum number of iterations is reached. The amount of perturbation δ is computed by solving a linear optimization problem that minimizes the distance to the decision boundary subject to the constraint that the image is misclassified.

The DeepFool attack can be given as follows:

$$\min_{\delta}\|\delta\|_2 \quad \text{subject to} \quad f(\mathbf{x}+\delta) \neq y, \qquad (3.13)$$

where $\mathbf{x}$ is the original input, f is the target model, y is the correct label, and δ is the adversarial perturbation to be added to $\mathbf{x}$. The objective is to minimize the L_2 norm of δ subject to the constraint that the adversarial example $\mathbf{x} \times \delta$ is misclassified by the model.

3.4.2 Spatial Transformation Attack

Spatial Transformation Attack (STA) is another type of adversarial attack [27]. The goal of this attack is to fool, i.e., misclassification or change the model prediction, an AI/ML model by applying spatial transformations to the input image.

The process of the Spatial Transformation Attack process consists of the following steps. The first step is *Image Transformation*, appling geometric transformations to the input image, such as translation, rotation, scaling, and shearing. The transformations are usually small in magnitude to ensure that the perturbed image remains visually similar to the original image. The second step is *Prediction* through the target deep learning model, and the model predicts a class label. The third step is *Adversarial Objective* to find the optimal set of transformation parameters that maximize the model loss or mislead the model prediction. The fourth step is *Optimization* to adjust the transformation parameters iteratively using optimization techniques and to minimize the adversarial objective function. The optimization process aims to find the optimal set of transformation parameters that lead to the desired misclassification or change in the prediction of the model.

The objective of the Spatial Transformation attack can be given as follows:

$$\text{maximize } \mathcal{L}(f(T(\mathbf{x})), y_{\text{target}}) \qquad (3.14)$$

where $f(\cdot)$ is the target deep learning model, which takes an image as input and produces a prediction, $T(\cdot)$ isnthe spatial transformation function, which applies geometric transformations to the input image, x is the original input image, y_{target} is the desired target label or class, $\mathcal{L}(\cdot)$ is the loss function, which quantifies the discrepancy between the predicted label and the desired target label.

STA attacks concentrate on altering the input image through geometric transformations instead of directly changing the pixel values or introducing perturbations compared to other attacks, such as FGSM, BIM, MIM, and C&W. This attack takes advantage of the model susceptibility to spatial transformations to generate adversarial examples that can fool the model without considerable modifications in the pixel values or visible perturbations.

3.4.3 Universal Adversarial Perturbation

Universal Adversarial Perturbation (UAP) is another type of adversarial attack [28]. The main objective of UAP is to generate a single perturbation to be added to any input image to cause misclassification or misprediction. UAP aims to find a perturbation that has a universal effect across a wide range of images unlike other attacks that generate perturbations specific to individual images.

The working principle of generating a Universal Adversarial Perturbation consisting of the following steps. The first step is *Initialization*, which start the process by initializing a perturbation vector. This perturbation vector is usually small and initialized randomly or with zero values. The second step is *Iterative Update*, which updated iteratively the perturbation vector to maximize its adversarial effect. The third step is *Adversarial Objective* to find a perturbation vector, when added to any input image. This is usually accomplished by creating a hostile objective function that measures the difference between the forecasted label and the desired target label. The last step is *Optimization* to minimize the adversarial objective function and to find the optimal perturbation vector that consistently leads to misclassification across a wide range of input images.

The objective of the Universal Adversarial Perturbation can be given as follows:

$$\text{maximize} \quad \frac{1}{N} \sum_{i=1}^{N} \mathcal{L}(f(x_i + \delta), y_{\text{target}}) + \lambda \cdot |\delta|_p \tag{3.15}$$

where $f(\cdot)$: the target deep learning model, which takes an image as input and produces a prediction, x_i: an input image from the dataset, δ: the universal perturbation vector, y_{target}: the desired target label or class, $\mathcal{L}(\cdot)$: the loss function, which quantifies the discrepancy between the predicted label and the desired target label, N: the number of images in the dataset, λ: a regularization parameter that balances the adversarial objective and the magnitude of the perturbation.

3.4.4 Zeroth Order Optimization

Zeroth Order Optimization (ZOO) is a family of optimization-based adversarial attack algorithms that do not require explicit access to the target model's gradient information [29]. Instead, ZOO methods estimate the gradients using black-box optimization techniques, such as finite differences, random directions, or coordinate-wise optimization.

The basic idea of ZOO is to construct an adversarial example by iteratively perturbing the original input in the direction that maximizes the target loss. The perturbation is restricted by a norm constraint to ensure that the perturbed input is still perceptually similar to the original input. The optimization problem can be formulated as follows:

$$\min_{\delta}, \mathcal{L}(f(\mathbf{x} + \delta), y) \quad \text{subject to} \quad |\delta|_p \leq \epsilon, \tag{3.16}$$

where $\mathbf{x}$ is the original input, y is the true label, f is the target model, $\mathcal{L}$ is the loss function, δ is the perturbation, ϵ is the maximum allowed perturbation size, and $|\cdot|_p$ is the p-norm.

ZOO methods differ in the way they estimate the gradients of the loss function with respect to the perturbation. For example, the coordinate-wise ZOO (CW-ZOO) algorithm estimates the gradient by perturbing each pixel independently, while the zeroth order coordinate descent (ZO-CD) algorithm estimates the gradient by perturbing each pixel sequentially.

Compared to other attack methods, ZOO has the advantage of being model-agnostic and not requiring access to the target model's gradient information. However, it may require more iterations and function evaluations to find an effective perturbation, and the resulting adversarial examples may be less transferable to other models than those generated by gradient-based attacks.

3.5 Mitigation Methods

Mitigation methods for adversarial ML attacks are very crucial in AI/ML concept. There are several methods and ways to achieve it. Common methods can include *Adversarial Training, Test Loss and Test Accuracy, Interpretation, Defensive Distillation, Randomization, and Gradient Masking*. Each selected method will be explained below.

3.5.1 Adversarial Training

Adversarial training is a widely used method to improve the robustness of AI/ML models against adversarial attacks [30]. It augments the training set with adversarial examples to make the model more robust to these examples during testing.

The working principle of adversarial training is simple. It starts with a given dataset $\mathcal{D} = \{(\mathbf{x}_1, y_1), (\mathbf{x}_2, y_2), \cdots, (\mathbf{x}_n, y_n)\}$ of n training examples, where $\mathbf{x}_i$ represents the input image and y_i represents the true label of the image. The main purpose is to train a classifier $f(\mathbf{x}; \theta)$ with parameters θ that minimizes the following objective function:

$$\min_{\theta} \frac{1}{n} \sum_{i=1}^{n} \mathcal{L}\left(f(\mathbf{x}_i + \delta; \theta), y_i\right) \qquad (3.17)$$

where $\mathcal{L}$ is the loss function used for training, and δ is a small perturbation added to the input image $\mathbf{x}_i$ to create an adversarial example.

The perturbation δ is computed by solving the following optimization problem:

$$\delta = \operatorname{argmax}|\delta|_{\infty \leq \epsilon} \quad \mathcal{L}(f(\mathbf{x}_i + \delta; \theta), y_i) \qquad (3.18)$$

where ϵ is a small hyperparameter that controls the magnitude of the perturbation.

During training, the adversarial examples are generated using a variety of techniques, such as FGSM, BIM, or PGD. The resulting augmented dataset is used to train the classifier $f(\mathbf{x}; \theta)$ using standard backpropagation algorithms.

The intuition behind adversarial training is that by training the model with adversarial examples, it learns to become more robust to small perturbations in the input space, thus improving its generalization performance on both clean and adversarial examples.

3.5.2 Practical Example for Adversarial Training

The following Python code provides a practical example of the adversarial training process using CleverHans to enhance the robustness of a pre-trained model against adversarial attacks. Through the training process, the model learns to defend against perturbations and improve its overall performance in the presence of adversarial examples. Each part of the source code is given as follows:

1. **Importing Libraries:** Import the necessary libraries and modules, including *TensorFlow, NumPy, Keras, MNIST dataset, CleverHans, Matplotlib, Scikit-learn, and Tdqm.*

```
1 #Import Libraries
2 import tensorflow as tf
3 import numpy as np
4 from tensorflow.keras.datasets import mnist
5 from tensorflow.keras.models import load_model
6 from cleverhans.tf2.attacks.fast_gradient_method import
    fast_gradient_method
7 from cleverhans.tf2.attacks.basic_iterative_method import
    basic_iterative_method
8 import matplotlib.pyplot as plt
9 from tqdm.notebook import tqdm
```

2. **Loading Dataset and Data Preparation:** Load the *MNIST* digits dataset, and prepare the *MNIST* dataset for training a ML model, ensuring the input images are properly formatted and the labels are in the appropriate representation for training. The pixel values of the images are normalized to the range [0, 1].

```
1 # Load the MNIST dataset
2 (x_train, y_train), (x_test, y_test) = mnist.load_data()
3
4 # Normalize pixel values to the range [0, 1]
```

```
5 x_train = x_train.astype("float32") / 255.0
6 x_test = x_test.astype("float32") / 255.0
```

3. **Converting Labels to One-hot Encoding:** Convert labels to one-hot encoding using *tf.keras.utils.to_ categorical()* to match the model's output format.

```
1 # Convert labels to one-hot encoding
2 y_train = tf.keras.utils.to_categorical(y_train, 10)
3 y_test = tf.keras.utils.to_categorical(y_test, 10)
```

4. **Loading Pre-trained Model:** A pre-trained deep learning model is loaded from *model.h5*. This model has been previously trained on the MNIST dataset.

```
1 # Load the pre-trained model
2 model = load_model('model.h5')
```

5. **Creating Variables and Empty Lists for Metrics:** Create the variable *epsilon* assigned a value of 0.1. This typically represents the magnitude of perturbation applied during adversarial attacks, and empty lists for metrics, such as *test_ loss, test_ accuracy, test_ loss_fgsm, test_ accuracy_fgsm, test_ loss_ bim, test_ accuracy_ bim*. These lists are used to keep track of loss and accuracy values for different scenarios or attack methods during model evaluation.

```
1  # Epsilon value
2  epsilon = 0.1
3
4  # Define empty lists to store the metrics
5  test_loss = []
6  test_accuracy = []
7  test_loss_fgsm = []
8  test_accuracy_fgsm = []
9  test_loss_bim = []
10 test_accuracy_bim = []
```

6. **Evaluating the Model Before Adversarial Training:** Evaluate the performance of the pre-trained model on the test set before applying adversarial training. It calculates and stores the test loss and accuracy.

```
1 # Evaluate the model on the test set before adversarial
      training
2 score = model.evaluate(x_test, y_test, verbose=0)
```

```
3  test_loss.append(score[0])
4  test_accuracy.append(score[1])
```

7. **Applying Adversarial Attacks and Evaluating the Model:** Apply two types of adversarial attacks, i.e., FGSM and BIM, and evaluate the model performance. Adversarial examples are generated by applying these attacks to the test set. For FGSM, the *fast_ gradient_ method* function is used, while BIM utilizes the *basic_ iterative_ method* function from *CleverHans*. It calculates and stores the test loss and accuracy.

```
1  # Evaluate the model on the test set before adversarial
       training with FGSM attack
2  x_test_fgsm = fast_gradient_method(model, x_test,
       eps=epsilon, norm=np.inf, targeted=False)
3  score_fgsm = model.evaluate(x_test_fgsm, y_test, verbose=0)
4  test_loss_fgsm.append(score_fgsm[0])
5  test_accuracy_fgsm.append(score_fgsm[1])
6
7  # Evaluate the model on the test set before adversarial
       training with BIM attack
8  x_test_bim = basic_iterative_method(model, x_test,
       eps=epsilon, eps_iter=0.01, nb_iter=10, norm=np.inf,
       targeted=False, sanity_checks=False)
9  score_bim = model.evaluate(x_test_bim, y_test, verbose=0)
10 test_loss_bim.append(score_bim[0])
11 test_accuracy_bim.append(score_bim[1])
```

8. **Defining Adversarial Training Function:** Define the adversarial training function. The adversarial training function begins by iterating through a specified number of epochs. Within each epoch, the training data is divided into batches. For each batch, adversarial perturbations are generated using FGSM and BIM attacks. These perturbations are combined with the original images to create adversarial examples. The model is then trained on both the original images and their corresponding adversarial examples from the batch.

```
1  # Define the adversarial training method
2  def adversarial_training(x, y, model, epochs, epsilon,
       batch_size):
3      for epoch in tqdm(range(epochs)):
4          for batch in tqdm(range(0, len(x), batch_size),
           leave=False):
5              x_batch = x[batch:batch+batch_size]
```

```
6        y_batch = y[batch:batch+batch_size]
7          # Generate adversarial examples using FGSM and
   BIM attacks
8          perturbation_fgsm = fast_gradient_method(model,
   x_batch, eps=epsilon, norm=np.inf, targeted=False)
9          perturbation_bim = basic_iterative_method(model,
   x_batch, eps=epsilon, eps_iter=0.01, nb_iter=10,
10
   norm=np.inf, targeted=False,
11
   sanity_checks=False)
12
13         # Combine the original image with the
   adversarial perturbation
14         x_batch_fgsm = x_batch + perturbation_fgsm
15         x_batch_bim = x_batch + perturbation_bim
16
17       # Train the model on the original image and the
   adversarial example
18         loss_fgsm = model.train_on_batch(x_batch_fgsm,
   y_batch)
19         loss_bim = model.train_on_batch(x_batch_bim, y_batch)
```

Then, evaluate the model the model performance on the test set using
adversarial examples generated with FGSM and BIM attacks after each
epoch of adversarial training. It calculates and stores the test loss and
accuracy for each evaluation.

```
1        # Evaluate the model on the test set with FGSM attack
2        perturbation_fgsm = fast_gradient_method(model,
   x_test, eps=epsilon, norm=np.inf, targeted=False)
3        x_test_fgsm = x_test + perturbation_fgsm
4        score_fgsm = model.evaluate(x_test_fgsm, y_test,
   verbose=0)
5        test_loss_fgsm.append(score_fgsm[0])
6        test_accuracy_fgsm.append(score_fgsm[1])
7
8        # Evaluate the model on the test set with BIM attack
9        perturbation_bim = basic_iterative_method(model,
   x_test, eps=epsilon, eps_iter=0.01, nb_iter=10,
10
   norm=np.inf, targeted=False,
11
   sanity_checks=False)
```

```
12      x_test_bim = x_test + perturbation_bim
13      score_bim = model.evaluate(x_test_bim, y_test,
        verbose=0)
14      test_loss_bim.append(score_bim[0])
15      test_accuracy_bim.append(score_bim[1])
16
17      # Evaluate the model on the test set
18      score = model.evaluate(x_test, y_test, verbose=0)
19
20      test_loss.append(score[0])
21      test_accuracy.append(score[1])
22
23      print('Epoch:', epoch, '- Test loss:', score[0], '-
        Test accuracy:', score[1])
```

9. **Defining Hyperparameters:** Define hyper parameters for adversarial training, including the perturbation amount *epsilon*, the number of *epochs*, and the *batch size*.

```
1  # Set the hyperparameters for adversarial training
2  epsilon = 0.1
3  epochs = 10
4  batch_size = 4096
```

10. **Running Adversarial Training:** Run the adversarial training loop with the specified hyperparameters, i.e., the final step.

```
1  # Run adversarial training
2  adversarial_training(x_train, y_train, model, epochs,
     epsilon, batch_size)
```

11. **Plotting the Prediction Performance Metrics:** Plot various prediction performance metrics for a machine-learning model. These metrics are evaluated over a range of epochs, including both the performance before and after adversarial training.

```
1  # Plot the prediction performance metrics
2  epochs_range = range(epochs + 1)  # Add 1 to include the
     evaluation before adversarial training
3
4  plt.figure(figsize=(12, 4))
5
6  plt.subplot(1, 2, 1)
7  plt.plot(epochs_range, test_loss, label='Test Loss')
8  plt.plot(epochs_range, test_loss_fgsm, label='Test Loss with
     FGSM attack')
```

```
 9  plt.plot(epochs_range, test_loss_bim, label='Test Loss with
        BIM attack')
10  plt.xlabel('Epochs')
11  plt.ylabel('Loss')
12  plt.legend()
13
14  plt.subplot(1, 2, 2)
15  plt.plot(epochs_range, test_accuracy, label='Test Accuracy')
16  plt.plot(epochs_range, test_accuracy_fgsm, label='Test
        Accuracy with FGSM attack')
17  plt.plot(epochs_range, test_accuracy_bim, label='Test
        Accuracy with BIM attack')
18  plt.xlabel('Epochs')
19  plt.ylabel('Accuracy')
20  plt.legend()
```

12. **Displaying the Results:** Adjust the padding between the subplots for better visualization using *tight_ layout* and display results.

```
1  # Adjust the padding between the subplots
2  plt.tight_layout()
3  # Show the plot
4  plt.show()
```

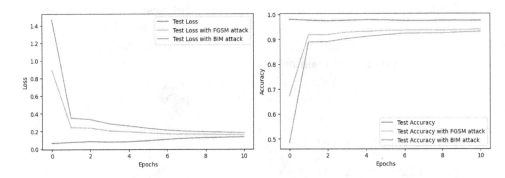

Figure 3.15: Comparison of Test Loss and Test Accuracy

3.5.3 Defensive Distillation

Defensive distillation is a mitigation method for protecting AI/ML models from adversarial attacks [31]. The basic idea is to train a distilled model that is less sensitive to small changes in its inputs, which can be caused by an adversary attempting to fool the model.

The algorithm for defensive distillation involves training two models, i.e., a regular model and a distilled model. The regular model is trained on the original training data, while the distilled model is trained on the outputs of the regular model. The distilled model will learn to approximate the function computed by the regular model but with a smoother decision boundary that is less susceptible to adversarial examples.

Let $\mathcal{X}$ be the input space and $\mathcal{Y}$ be the output space. Let $f : \mathcal{X} \rightarrow \mathcal{Y}$ be the original model we want to defend, and let $\hat{f} : \mathcal{X} \rightarrow \mathcal{Y}$ be the distilled model. Let $\mathcal{D}$ be the training data and $\mathcal{L}$ be the loss function. Then, the algorithm for defensive distillation can be summarized as follows:

1. Train the regular model f on the training data $\mathcal{D}$, using the loss function $L(f(\mathbf{x}_i), y_i)$, where $\mathbf{x}_i$ is the ith input, and y_i is the corresponding output.
2. Generate a new training set $\mathcal{D}'$ by passing each input $\mathbf{x}_i$ in $\mathcal{D}$ through the regular model f and using the output $\tilde{y}_i = f(\mathbf{x}_i)$ as the new training label.
3. Train the distilled model $\hat{f}$ on the training data $\mathcal{D}'$, using the loss function $\mathcal{L}(\hat{f}(\mathbf{x}_i), \tilde{y}_i)$.
4. Use the distilled model $\hat{f}$ to infer new inputs.

By training the distilled model on the outputs of the regular model, we hope to smooth out the decision boundary of the distilled model, making it more robust to small perturbations in the input. Additionally, since the distilled model is trained on the outputs of the regular model, it is less likely to make errors on adversarial examples crafted to fool the regular model.

Defensive distillation is not foolproof and can be bypassed by clever adversaries. However, it is effective against many attacks and can be a helpful tool in a defence-in-depth strategy for protecting ML models.

A description of Defensive Distillation can be provided in a series of steps:

1. **Training the Teacher Model:**
   - Given a dataset consisting of input samples x and their corresponding true labels y_true.
   - Train a *teacher model* utilizing the original training dataset and standard AI/ML methods.
   - The objective is to construct a model that performs well and can accurately forecast the training data.

2. **Softening the Output Probabilities:**
   - Apply a temperature parameter T to the output probabilities of the teacher model after training.
   - Soften the output probabilities by applying the softmax function to the logits of the teacher model divided by the temperature T.
   - Smoothing the probabilities can reduce the strictness of the model decision boundaries to make it more uncertain about its predictions.

3. **Training the Student Model:**
   - Generate a new dataset with *soft labels* utilizing the softened output probabilities of the teacher model.
   - Train a *student model* using the new dataset and standard AI/ML methods.
   - It is expected that the student model can be simpler than the teacher model and to mimic the behavior of the teacher model in terms of its softened predictions.

4. **Evaluating the Trained Student Model:**
   - Evaluate the performance of the trained student model on a separate test set or deployment scenarios.
   - Evaluate the model accuracy and robustness against both original in-

puts and adversarial examples.

■ Compare the performance of the student model and the teacher model and evaluate the effectiveness of the defense.

3.5.4 Practical Example for Defensive Distillation

The following Python code demonstrates the implementation of defensive distillation. The code is divided into different parts, and Part 1 of the practical example will now be explained in detail.

1. **Importing Libraries:** Import the necessary libraries and modules, including *TensorFlow, NumPy, Keras, MNIST dataset, CleverHans, Matplotlib, Scikit-learn, and Tdqm.*

```
1  #================================
2  ### Part 1
3  #Import Libraries
4  import tensorflow as tf
5  from tqdm.keras import TqdmCallback
6  from tensorflow.keras.datasets import mnist
7  import keras
8  from keras import layers
9  import numpy as np
```

2. **Data Loading and Preparation:** Load the MNIST dataset, which consists of handwritten digit images and their corresponding labels. The pixel values of the images are normalised to the range [0, 1].

```
1  # Load the MNIST dataset
2  (x_train, y_train), (x_test, y_test) = mnist.load_data()
3
4  # Normalize pixel values to the range [0, 1]
5  x_train = x_train.astype("float32") / 255.0
6  x_test = x_test.astype("float32") / 255.0
```

3. **Converting Labels to One-hot Encoding:** Convert labels to one-hot encoding using *tf.keras.utils.to_ categorical()* to match the model's output format.

```
1  # Convert labels to one-hot encoding
2  y_train = tf.keras.utils.to_categorical(y_train, 10)
3  y_test = tf.keras.utils.to_categorical(y_test, 10)
```

4. **Creating Empty Lists for Metrics:** Create empty lists for metrics, such as *test_loss, test_accuracy, test_loss_fgsm, test_accuracy_fgsm, test_loss_bim, test_accuracy_bim.* These lists are used to keep track of loss and accuracy values for different scenarios or attack methods during model evaluation.

```
1  # Define empty lists to store the metrics
2  test_loss = []
3  test_accuracy = []
4  test_loss_fgsm = []
5  test_accuracy_fgsm = []
6  test_loss_bim = []
7  test_accuracy_bim = []
```

5. **Defining and Compiling Original Model:** Define and compile the original model. The original neural network model is defined with convolutional and pooling layers, followed by dropout and a softmax output layer, and compiled with the *categorical cross-entropy loss function, the Adam optimizer, and accuracy* as the metric.

```
1  # Defining the original model
2  def get_model():
3      model = keras.Sequential([
4          layers.Input(shape=(28, 28)),
5          layers.Reshape(target_shape=(28, 28, 1)),
6          layers.Conv2D(32, kernel_size=(3, 3),
   activation="relu"),
7          layers.MaxPooling2D(pool_size=(2, 2)),
8          layers.Conv2D(64, kernel_size=(3, 3),
   activation="relu"),
9          layers.MaxPooling2D(pool_size=(2, 2)),
10         layers.Flatten(),
11         layers.Dropout(0.5),
12         layers.Dense(10, activation="softmax")
13     ])
14
15     # Train the original model on the training data
16     model.compile(loss="categorical_crossentropy",
17                   optimizer="adam",
18                   metrics=["accuracy"])
```

```
19
20      return model
```

6. **Defining, Compiling and Training Distilled and Original Models:**
Define, compile and train a defensively distilled and original models given
training data and hyperparameters. Defensive distillation involves training a new distilled model using softened labels of the original model. The
softmax outputs of the original model are scaled by a temperature parameter T to create softened labels. The distilled model is then trained on
these softened labels, incorporating a Kullback-Leibler divergence term as
a regularization to match the original model's predictions. This function
consists of several parts as follows:

■ *Defining Defensive Distillation:* Define the distilled model architecture.
It consists of convolutional layers followed by max-pooling layers, a flatten
layer, temperature scaling, and a dense layer for classification.

```
1  def train_defense_model(x_train, y_train, T=100, alpha=0.1):
2      """
3      Trains a defensively distilled model given training data
       and hyperparameters.
4      Args:
5      x_train (numpy.ndarray): Training data input.
6      y_train (numpy.ndarray): Training data labels.
7      T (int): Temperature parameter for softened labels.
8      alpha (float): Strength of the KL regularization term.
9
10     Returns:
11     The defensively distilled model.
12     """
13     # Define the distilled model
14     distilled_model = keras.Sequential([
15         layers.Input(shape=(28, 28)),
16         layers.Reshape(target_shape=(28, 28, 1)),
17         layers.Conv2D(32, kernel_size=(3, 3),
       activation="relu"),
18         layers.MaxPooling2D(pool_size=(2, 2)),
19         layers.Conv2D(64, kernel_size=(3, 3),
       activation="relu"),
20         layers.MaxPooling2D(pool_size=(2, 2)),
21         layers.Flatten(),
22         layers.Lambda(lambda x: x / T),  # Softmax
       temperature scaling
23         layers.Dense(10, activation="softmax")
```

145

```
24     ])
```

■ *Training the Original Model:* Train the original model with training data and a conventional categorical cross-entropy loss. After this training, it is ready to generate softened labels.

```
1 # Define the original model
2 model = get_model()
3 model.fit(x_train, y_train, epochs=10, batch_size=2000,
      verbose=0, callbacks=[TqdmCallback(verbose=1)])
```

■ *Generating Softened Labels:* Generate the softmax outputs of the original model scaled by the temperature parameter T and re-normalized. These softened labels represent the probabilities associated with each class.

```
1 # Generate softened labels for the training data using the
      original model
2 y_train_soft = model.predict(x_train)
3 y_train_soft = np.exp(np.log(y_train_soft) / T)
4 y_train_soft = y_train_soft / np.sum(y_train_soft, axis=1,
      keepdims=True)
```

■ *Training the Distilled Model:* Train the distilled model, which is identical to the original model. However, it is trained on the softened labels generated by the original model. The training process minimizes the categorical cross-entropy loss with an additional regularization term using the Kullback-Leibler (KL) divergence between the softened labels and the distilled model's predictions. The code provides flexibility in specifying hyperparameters such as the temperature parameter T and the strength of the KL regularization term α. These hyperparameters can be adjusted to control the trade-off between accuracy and robustness.

```
1 # Train the distilled model on the softened labels
2 def kl_divergence(y_true, y_pred):
3     return keras.losses.kullback_leibler_divergence(y_true,
      y_pred) * alpha
```

■ *Compiling the Distilled Model:* Compile the distilled model with the specified loss function, optimizer, and evaluation metric.

```
1 distilled_model.compile(loss="categorical_crossentropy",
      optimizer="adam", metrics=["accuracy"])
```

■ *Training the Distilled Model:* Train the distilled model on the specified soft labels, monitoring progress with a *TQDM* progress bar and using the training data as validation data.

```
distilled_model.fit(x_train, y_train_soft, epochs=10,
    batch_size=2000,
callbacks=[TqdmCallback(verbose=1)], verbose=0,
validation_data=(x_train, y_train))
# Use training data as validation data for distillation
```

■ *Returning the model:* Return the defensive distillation model.

```
return distilled_model
```

The second part of the code segment contains plotting functions to illustrate the training and evaluation outcomes, demonstrating how the model's performance develops during training and its resistance to adversarial attacks. Each part of the code segment, i.e., Part 2 of the example, is explained as follows:

1. **Importing Libraries:** Import the necessary libraries and modules, including *CleverHans*.

```
# Import libraries
from cleverhans.tf2.attacks.fast_gradient_method import
    fast_gradient_method
from cleverhans.tf2.attacks.basic_iterative_method import
    basic_iterative_method
```

2. **Defining Adversarial Attack Parameter:** Define the adversarial attack parameter. An epsilon value (ϵ) is set to 0.1, determining the magnitude of perturbations added to the input data during adversarial attacks.

```
# Define the attack parameter
epsilon = 0.1
```

3. **Defining Empty Lists to Store the Metrics:** Define empty lists to store the metrics, i.e., *test_loss and test_accuracy*.

```
# Define empty lists to store the metrics
test_loss = []
test_accuracy = []
```

4. **Initializing and Training the Model:** Initialize and train the original model (*org_ model*) on the clean training data for 10 epochs. After training its performance is evaluated on the clean test data and record the test loss and accuracy. Subsequently, we apply FGSM and BIM attacks to the test data and evaluate the model's performance after these attacks. The results are recorded in the *test_ loss* and *test_ accuracy* lists.

```
1  # Initialize the odel
2  org_model = get_model()
3
4  # Train the model
5  org_model.fit(x_train, y_train, epochs=10, batch_size=2000,
       verbose=0,
6              callbacks=[TqdmCallback(verbose=1)])
```

5. **Evaluating the Model on the Test Set Before Applying Defense Model:** Evaluate the performance of the *org_ model* on the test set before adversarial training. The score variable contains the evaluation results, where *score[0]* is the test loss, and *score[1]* is the test accuracy.

```
1  # Evaluate the model on the test set before defensive
       distillation
2  score = org_model.evaluate(x_test, y_test, verbose=0)
3  test_loss.append(score[0])
4  test_accuracy.append(score[1])
```

6. **Evaluating the Model on the Test Set Before Applying Defense Model with FGSM Attack:** Evaluate the performance of the *org_ - model* on the test set after applying the Fast Gradient Sign Method (FGSM) attack. The obtained test loss and accuracy scores after the FGSM attack are appended to the respective lists *test_ loss and test_ accuracy.*

```
1  # Evaluate the model on the test set before defensive
       distillation with FGSM attack
2  x_test_fgsm = fast_gradient_method(org_model, x_test,
       eps=epsilon, norm=np.inf, targeted=False)
3  score = org_model.evaluate(x_test_fgsm, y_test, verbose=0)
4  test_loss.append(score[0])
5  test_accuracy.append(score[1])
```

7. **Evaluating the Model on the Test Set Before Applying Defense Model with BIM Attack:** Evaluate the performance of the *org_ model*

on the test set after applying the Basic Iterative Method (BIM) attack. The obtained test loss and accuracy scores after the BIM attack are appended to the respective lists *test_loss and test_accuracy.*

```
1 # Evaluate the model on the test set before defensive
    distillation with BIM attack
2 x_test_bim = basic_iterative_method(org_model, x_test,
    eps=epsilon, eps_iter=0.01, nb_iter=10,
3                                   norm=np.inf,
    targeted=False,
4                                   sanity_checks=False)
5 score = org_model.evaluate(x_test_bim, y_test, verbose=0)
6 test_loss.append(score[0])
7 test_accuracy.append(score[1])
```

8. **Training Defense Model:** Train the defense model *(distilled_model)* using the function *train_defense_model* with a temperature parameter T set to 100. The use of a temperature parameter is often associated with knowledge distillation.

```
1 # Train distilled model
2 distilled_model = train_defense_model(x_train, y_train,
    T=100)
```

9. **Evaluating the Model on the Test Set with Defense Model:** Evaluate the performance of the *distilled_model* on the test set. The obtained test loss and accuracy scores are appended to the respective lists *(test_loss and test_accuracy).*

```
1 # Evaluate the model on the test set before defensive
    distillation
2 score = distilled_model.evaluate(x_test, y_test, verbose=0)
3 test_loss.append(score[0])
4 test_accuracy.append(score[1])
```

10. **Evaluating the Model on the Test Set with Defense Model and FGSM attack:** Evaluate the performance of the *distilled_model* on the test set after applying the FGSM attack. The obtained test loss and accuracy scores after the FGSM attack are appended to the respective lists *(test_loss and test_accuracy).*

```
1 # Evaluate the model on the test set before defensive
    distillation with FGSM attack
2 x_test_fgsm = fast_gradient_method(distilled_model, x_test,
    eps=epsilon, norm=np.inf, targeted=False)
```

```
3 score = distilled_model.evaluate(x_test_fgsm, y_test,
      verbose=0)
4 test_loss.append(score[0])
5 test_accuracy.append(score[1])
```

11. **Evaluating the Model on the Test Set with Defense Model and BIM attack:** Evaluate the performance of the *distilled_ model* on the test set after applying the BIM attack. The obtained test loss and accuracy scores after the BIM attack are appended to the respective lists*(test_ loss and test_ accuracy)*.

```
1 # Evaluate the model on the test set before defensive
      distillation with BIM attack
2 x_test_bim = basic_iterative_method(distilled_model, x_test,
      eps=epsilon, eps_iter=0.01, nb_iter=10,
3                                       norm=np.inf,
      targeted=False,
4                                       sanity_checks=False)
5 score = distilled_model.evaluate(x_test_bim, y_test,
      verbose=0)
6 test_loss.append(score[0])
7 test_accuracy.append(score[1])
```

The last part of the code segment, i.e., Part 3 of the example, displays the analysis and visualization process to compare the performance of a ML model under different defense scenarios, including various adversarial attacks and a distilled model. It generates two bar plots to visualize the model's robustness metrics under various conditions. The two plots display the test accuracy and test loss for different scenarios, including no defence, Fast Gradient Sign Method (FGSM) attack, Basic Iterative Method (BIM) attack, and the same attacks applied to a defensively distilled model. The results are presented in terms of test accuracy and test loss. Each part of the code segment will be explained as follows:

1. **Importing Libraries:** Import the necessary library, i.e., *Matplotlib*.

```
1 #==============================
2 ### PART 3
3 # Import libraries
4 import matplotlib.pyplot as plt
```

2. **Creating Subplots:** Create a figure with two subplots arranged horizontally. The figure size is set to (10, 4).

```
1 # Create subplots
2 fig, axes = plt.subplots(1, 2, figsize=(10, 4))
```

3. **Plotting Test Accuracy:** Plot the test accuracy. The first plot shows the test accuracy for different scenarios. The x-axis represents the defence configurations, including *"No Defense," "FGSM," "BIM," "Distilled," "Distilled+FGSM,"* and *"Distilled+BIM"*. The y-axis represents the test accuracy. The second plot visualizes the test loss for the same defence scenarios. Again, the x-axis represents the defence configurations, and the y-axis represents the test loss. Both plots help evaluate and compare the robustness of the original and defensively distilled models against adversarial attacks, providing insights into their performance under different conditions.

```
1 # Plot test accuracy
2 axes[0].bar(['No Defense', 'FGSM', 'BIM', 'Distilled',
      'Distilled+FGSM', 'Distilled+BIM'], test_accuracy)
3 axes[0].set_title('Test Accuracy')
4 axes[0].tick_params(axis='x', rotation=90)  # rotate xtick
      labels by 90 degrees
5
6 # Plot test loss
7 axes[1].bar(['No Defense', 'FGSM', 'BIM', 'Distilled',
      'Distilled+FGSM', 'Distilled+BIM'], test_loss)
8 axes[1].set_title('Test Loss')
9 axes[1].tick_params(axis='x', rotation=90)  # rotate xtick
      labels by 90 degrees
```

4. **Displaying the Results:** Adjust the padding between the subplots for better visualization using *tight_layout* and display results.

```
1 # Adjust the padding between the subplots
2 plt.tight_layout()
3 # Show the plot
4 plt.show()
```

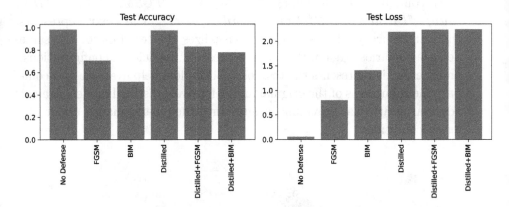

Figure 3.16: Bar plots illustrates the test accuracy and test loss metrics for various defense scenarios, including "No Defense," "FGSM," "BIM," "Distilled," "Distilled+FGSM," and "Distilled+BIM." The x-axis represents the defense configurations, while the y-axis represents the corresponding metric values. These plots provide insights into model robustness against adversarial attacks and the impact of defensive distillation.

3.5.5 Randomization

Randomization-based mitigation methods protect ML models from adversarial attacks [32]. They work by adding some randomness to the input data or model parameters during training or inference, which can make it harder for an attacker to create compelling adversarial examples.

Let us consider a dataset $\mathcal{D} = \{(\mathbf{x}_1, y_1), (\mathbf{x}_2, y_2), \ldots, (\mathbf{x}_n, y_n)\}$, where $\mathbf{x}_i \in \mathbb{R}^d$ is a data point and $y_i \in \mathcal{Y}$ is the corresponding label. The goal is to learn a function $f : \mathbb{R}^d \to \mathcal{Y}$ that accurately maps inputs to their labels. Let us assume we can access a classifier g that approximates f using some learning algorithm.

In a typical adversarial attack scenario, an attacker tries to craft an adversarial example $\mathbf{x}'$ by adding a small perturbation δ to the original input $\mathbf{x}$, such that $\mathbf{x}' = \mathbf{x} + \delta$ and $g(\mathbf{x}') \neq f(\mathbf{x})$. The perturbation δ is usually constrained to have a small ℓ_p-norm, where ℓ_p is a measure of distance, such as the Euclidean distance (ℓ_2) or the maximum absolute difference (ℓ_∞).

Randomization-based methods add random noise to the input data or the model parameters. For example, during training time, we can add random noise to the input data $\mathbf{x}_i$, such that $\mathbf{x}'_i = x_i + \epsilon$, where $\epsilon \sim \mathcal{N}(0, \sigma^2)$ is a random vector sampled from a Gaussian distribution with mean 0 and variance σ^2. Alternatively, it can be added random noise to the model parameters θ themselves, such that $\theta' = \theta + \epsilon$, where $\epsilon \sim \mathcal{N}(0, \sigma^2)$.

Formally, let $\hat{g}$ be a randomized classifier that maps an input $\mathbf{x}$ to a label y by adding some random noise ϵ, such that $\hat{g}(\mathbf{x}) = \arg\max_{y \in \mathcal{Y}} f(\mathbf{x}, \theta + \epsilon)$, where $f(\mathbf{x}, \theta)$ is the deterministic classifier that maps $\mathbf{x}$ to y using the model parameters θ. Then, we can train $\hat{g}$ using the following objective:

$$L(\hat{g}) = \frac{1}{n} \sum_{i=1}^{n} E_{\epsilon_i \sim N(0,\sigma^2)}[\ell(\hat{g}(\mathbf{x}_i + \epsilon_i), y_i)] + \lambda R(g^*) \tag{3.19}$$

Here, ℓ is a loss function that measures the discrepancy between the predicted label and the true label, $R(\hat{g})$ is a regularization termcontaining some prior knowledge about the distribution of the added noise, and λ is a hyperparameter that controls the strength of the regularization.

The first term in the objective encourages the classifier to make accurate predictions on the original data points $\mathbf{x}_i$, while the second term encourages it to be robust to small perturbations by penalizing large changes in the model parameters θ. By training the classifier with this objective, we can effectively balance the trade-off between accuracy and robustness.

Randomization-based mitigation methods are a powerful tool for improving the robustness of ML models to adversarial attacks. By adding random noise to either the input data or the model parameters, we can make it harder for an attacker to create effective adversarial examples, while also encouraging the model to be more robust to small perturbations.

3.5.6 Practical Example for Randomization

The following Pyhtin code segment trains a neural network model for image classification on the MNIST dataset, incorporating randomization-based mitigation techniques to enhance robustness against adversarial attacks. Each part of the code segment, i.e., Part 1 of the example, will explained as follows:

1. **Importing Libraries:** Import the necessary libraries and modules, including *Numpy, Tensorflow, and tqdm.*

```
1  #======================================
2  ### Part 1
3  #Import Libraries
4  import numpy as np
5  import tensorflow as tf
6  from tensorflow import keras
7  import matplotlib.pyplot as plt
```

```
8  from tqdm import tqdm
```

2. **Data Loading and Preprocessing:** Loading the MNIST dataset, which contains images of handwritten digits. The pixel values of the images are normalized to the range [0, 1].

```
1  # Load the MNIST dataset
2  (x_train, y_train), (x_test, y_test) =
       keras.datasets.mnist.load_data()
3
4  # Normalize pixel values
5  x_train = x_train.astype('float32') / 255.0
6  x_test = x_test.astype('float32') / 255.0
```

3. **Converting Labels to One-hot Encoding:** Convert labels to one-hot encoding using *tf.keras.utils.to_ categorical()* to match the model's output format.

```
1  # Convert labels to one-hot encoding
2  y_train = tf.keras.utils.to_categorical(y_train, 10)
3  y_test = tf.keras.utils.to_categorical(y_test, 10)
```

4. **Defining Model Architecture:** Define the neural network model consisting of a flattened input layer, a hidden layer with *ReLU* activation, and an output layer with softmax activation for classifying digits.

```
1  # Define the model
2  model = keras.models.Sequential([
3      keras.layers.Flatten(input_shape=(28, 28)),
4      keras.layers.Dense(128, activation='relu'),
5      keras.layers.Dense(10, activation='softmax')
6  ])
```

5. **Defining Custom Loss Function:** Define a custom loss function, *loss_-fn*. The custom loss function also applies gradient masking, which involves calculating the gradients of the KL divergence concerning model parameters and applying these gradients to the model's trainable variables. It is introduced to combine two components:

■ *Cross-Entropy Loss (CE Loss):* The standard categorical cross-entropy loss measures the dissimilarity between true labels and model predictions.

■ *Kullback-Leibler (KL) Divergence Loss:* The KL divergence quantifies the difference between the original model predictions and the predictions when evaluated with perturbed input data.

```
1  # Define the loss function
2  def loss_fn(y_true, y_pred):
3      # Calculate the cross-entropy loss
4      ce_loss = keras.losses.categorical_crossentropy(y_true,
       y_pred)
5      # Calculate the KL divergence between the original and
       perturbed predictions
6      kl_div = keras.losses.kl_divergence(y_true, y_pred)
7      # Apply gradient masking
8      masked_grads = tape.gradient(kl_div,
       model.trainable_variables)
9      # Return the combined loss and masked gradients
10     return tf.reduce_mean(ce_loss + kl_div), masked_grads
```

6. **Model Compilation:** Compile the model, specifying the loss function (categorical cross-entropy), optimizer *(Adam)*, and evaluation metric *(accuracy)*.

```
1  # Define the optimizer
2  optimizer = keras.optimizers.Adam()
3
4  # Compile the model
5  model.compile(optimizer=optimizer,
       loss='categorical_crossentropy', metrics=['accuracy'])
```

7. **Defining Training Parameters and Creating a Training Loop:** Define training parameters, and create a training loop. The training loop continues for the specified number of epochs, i.e., *range(epochs)*. Within each epoch, it iterates over batches *(steps_per_epoch)* of training data and records operations for automatic differentiation, *tf.GradientTape()*. The forward pass is performed, and the loss and masked gradients are computed using a loss function *(loss_fn)*. The masked gradients are then applied to the model variables using the optimizer (optimizer). The epoch loss and accuracy are updated based on the batch statistics. After the completion of each epoch in the training loop, the average loss and accuracy for that epoch are computed and printed at intervals (every 25 epochs).

```
1  # Training parameters
2  batch_size = 2000
3  epochs = 500
4  steps_per_epoch = x_train.shape[0] // batch_size
5
```

```
6  # Training loop
7  for epoch in tqdm(range(epochs)):
8      epoch_loss = 0.0
9      epoch_accuracy = 0.0
10
11     for step in range(steps_per_epoch):
12         # Get a batch of training data
13         batch_x = x_train[step * batch_size : (step + 1) *
           batch_size]
14         batch_y = y_train[step * batch_size : (step + 1) *
           batch_size]
15
16         with tf.GradientTape() as tape:
17             # Forward pass
18             y_pred = model(batch_x)
19             # Compute the loss and masked gradients on the
           batch
20             loss, masked_grads = loss_fn(batch_y, y_pred)
21
22         # Apply the masked gradients to the model variables
           optimizer.apply_gradients(zip(masked_grads,
           model.trainable_variables))
23
24         # Update the epoch loss and accuracy
25         epoch_loss += loss.numpy()
26         epoch_accuracy += np.mean(np.argmax(batch_y,
           axis=-1) == np.argmax(y_pred, axis=-1))
27
28     epoch_loss /= steps_per_epoch
29     epoch_accuracy /= steps_per_epoch
30     if epoch % 25 == 0:
31         print(f'Epoch {epoch+1}/{epochs}:
           Loss={epoch_loss:.4f}, Accuracy={epoch_accuracy:.4f}')
```

8. **Evaluating the Model:** Evaluate the model's performance on the test data, and display the test loss and accuracy. This implementation demonstrates how incorporating randomization-based mitigation techniques in the loss function can enhance a model's robustness against adversarial attacks.

```
1  # Evaluate the model on the test data
2  test_loss, test_accuracy = model.evaluate(x_test, y_test,
       verbose=0)
3  print(f'Test Loss={test_loss:.4f}, Test
```

```
Accuracy={test_accuracy:.4f}')
```

3.5.7 Gradient Masking

The Gradient Masking method is a type of adversarial defense method to mitigate adversarial examples by *masking* the gradients of the model with respect to the input [33]. It is also known as Gradient Obfuscation or Jacobian Masking. The idea behind this method is to add random noise to the gradients of the model during the training phase to make it harder for an attacker to construct adversarial examples. The objective of this section is to give a brief idea about the Gradient Masking, which can simply be calculated as follows:

$$\nabla_{\mathbf{x}}\mathcal{L}(\theta) = J(\mathbf{x})^T \cdot g + r \tag{3.20}$$

where $\mathbf{x}$ is input, y is output, f_θ is the model, $\mathcal{L}(\theta)$ is the loss function of the model, $J(\mathbf{x})$ is the Jacobian matrix of model, g is the gradient of the loss function, and r is the random noise.

3.5.8 Practical Example for Gradient Masking

The following code snippet demonstrates the gradients for a given input data and applies masking to the gradients by perturbing the input tensor. This shows the gradient manipulation process for applying gradient masking techniques in defensive mechanisms. Part 2 of the previous example will be explained as follows:

1. **Computing Gradients:** Compute the model output gradients with respect to the input data for a sample batch. This process is common in many ML tasks consisting of following steps:

■ It is selected a sample input data batch *(sample_batch_x)* and corresponding labels *(sample_batch_y)* from the training set.

■ The input data *(sample_batch_x)* is converted to a TensorFlow tensor *(sample_batch_x_tensor)* of type float32.

■ A *GradientTape* is initiated using *tf.GradientTape()* to record operations for gradient computation.

■ The input tensor *(sample_batch_x_tensor)* is watched by the tape using *tape.watch(sample_batch_x_tensor)* to track its operations.

■ The model predictions *(sample_batch_y_pred)* are computed by passing the input tensor through the model.

■ The categorical cross-entropy loss between the true labels *(sample_-batch_y)* and predicted labels *(sample_batch_y_pred)* is calculated using *keras.losses.categorical_crossentropy.*

■ The tape is used to compute the gradients of the loss with respect to the input tensor *(sample_batch_x_tensor)* using *tape.gradient(sample_loss, sample_batch_x_tensor).*

■ The gradients are stored in the variable *sample_gradients.*

```
1  #==========================================
2  ### PART 2
3  # Compute gradients for a sample batch
4  sample_batch_x = x_train[:batch_size]
5  sample_batch_y = y_train[:batch_size]
6
7  sample_batch_x_tensor = tf.convert_to_tensor(sample_batch_x,
       dtype=tf.float32)
8
9  with tf.GradientTape() as tape:
10     tape.watch(sample_batch_x_tensor)
11     sample_batch_y_pred = model(sample_batch_x_tensor)
12     sample_loss =
       keras.losses.categorical_crossentropy(sample_batch_y,
       sample_batch_y_pred)
13
14  sample_gradients = tape.gradient(sample_loss,
       sample_batch_x_tensor)
```

2. **Appling Masking to Gradients:** Apply masking to gradients by adding

random noise to the input data and then computing the gradients with respect to the perturbed input. This can be used, for example, in adversarial training or to investigate the model's sensitivity to small changes in the input data. This process consists of several steps as follows:

■ The input tensor *(sample_ batch_ x_ tensor)* is perturbed by adding random noise using *tf.random.normal.*

■ Another *GradientTape* is initiated to record operations for gradient computation.

■ The perturbed input tensor *(sample_ batch_ x_ perturbed)* is watched by the tape using *tape.watch(sample_ batch_ x_ perturbed).*

■ The model predictions *(sample_ batch_ y_ pred_ perturbed)* are computed by passing the perturbed input tensor through the model.

■ The categorical cross-entropy loss between the true labels *(sample_ - batch_ y)* and perturbed predictions *(sample_ batch_ y_ pred_ perturbed)* is calculated.

■ The tape is used to compute the gradients of the perturbed loss with respect to the perturbed input tensor using *tape.gradient(sample_ loss_ - perturbed, sample_ batch_ x_ perturbed).*

■ The gradients are stored in the variable *sample_ gradients_ perturbed.*

```
1  # Apply masking to gradients
2  sample_batch_x_perturbed = sample_batch_x_tensor
3        + tf.random.normal( shape =
    sample_batch_x_tensor.shape, mean = 0.0, stddev = 0.01)
4  with tf.GradientTape() as tape:
5      tape.watch(sample_batch_x_perturbed)
6      sample_batch_y_pred_perturbed =
    model(sample_batch_x_perturbed)
7      sample_loss_perturbed =
    keras.losses.categorical_crossentropy( sample_batch_y,
    sample_batch_y_pred_perturbed )
8
9  sample_gradients_perturbed = tape.gradient(
    sample_loss_perturbed, sample_batch_x_perturbed)
```

The following code, i.e., Part 3 of the example, allows to visualize the gradients before and after masking, as well as their difference, for a specific image. This can help in understanding the impact of gradient masking and how it modifies the gradients of the model with respect to the input data. Each part of the code segment will be explained as follows:

1. **Computing Gradients Difference:** Compute the difference between gradients before and after masking.

```
# Compute the difference between gradients before and after
   masking
sample_gradients_diff = sample_gradients_perturbed -
   sample_gradients
```

2. **Selecting Image Index for Visualization:** Select an image index (img_ind) for visualization through a random index or a specific one, and set the image index to 882.

```
# img_ind = np.random.randint(sample_batch_x.shape[0])
img_ind = 882
```

3. **Determining Axis Limits:** Determine the maximum and minimum values of gradients for consistent axis limits in the 3D plot.

```
# Determine the maximum and minimum values of gradients for
   consistent axis limits
z_min = min(np.min(sample_gradients[img_ind].numpy()),
   np.min(sample_gradients_perturbed[img_ind].numpy()),
   np.min(sample_gradients_diff[img_ind].numpy()))
z_max = max(np.max(sample_gradients[img_ind].numpy()),
   np.max(sample_gradients_perturbed[img_ind].numpy()),
   np.max(sample_gradients_diff[img_ind].numpy()))
```

4. **Creating 3D Plot:** Creare a 3D figure with three subplots *(ax1, ax2, ax3)* arranged horizontally.

```
# Create 3G Plot
fig = plt.figure(figsize=(15, 5))

ax1 = fig.add_subplot(131, projection='3d')
ax2 = fig.add_subplot(132, projection='3d')
ax3 = fig.add_subplot(133, projection='3d')
```

5. **Plotting Gradients Before Masking:** Plot, i.e., *ax1*, the surface of gradients before masking.

```
1  # Plot Gradients Before Masking
2  Z = sample_gradients[img_ind].numpy()
3  ax1.plot_surface(X, Y, Z, cmap='viridis')
4  ax1.set_title('Gradients Before Masking')
5  ax1.set_xlim([0, 28])
6  ax1.set_ylim([0, 28])
7  ax1.set_zlim([z_min, z_max])
```

6. **Plotting Gradients After Masking:** Plot, i.e., *ax2*, the surface of gradients after masking.

```
1  # Plot Gradients After Masking
2  Z_perturbed = sample_gradients_perturbed[img_ind].numpy()
3  ax2.plot_surface(X, Y, Z_perturbed, cmap='viridis')
4  ax2.set_title('Gradients After Masking')
5  ax2.set_xlim([0, 28])
6  ax2.set_ylim([0, 28])
7  ax2.set_zlim([z_min, z_max])
```

7. **Plotting Gradients Difference:** Plot, i.e., *ax3*, the surface of the difference between gradients.

```
1  # Plot Gradients Difference
2  Z_diff = sample_gradients_diff[img_ind].numpy()
3  ax3.plot_surface(X, Y, Z_diff, cmap='viridis')
4  ax3.set_title('Gradients Difference')
5  ax3.set_xlim([0, 28])
6  ax3.set_ylim([0, 28])
7  ax3.set_zlim([z_min, z_max])
```

8. **Displaying the Results:** Adjust the padding between the subplots for better visualization using *tight_ layout* and display results.

```
1  # Adjust the padding between the subplots
2  plt.tight_layout()
3  # Show the plot
4  plt.show()
```

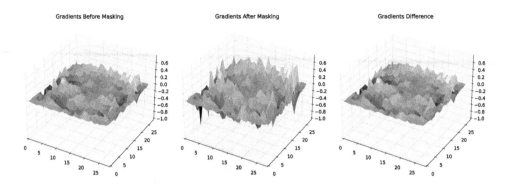

Figure 3.17: Comparison of Gradients: The 3D plot showcases the gradients before and after masking, highlighting the difference. This visualization aids in understanding how gradient masking impacts the neural network's training process and its resistance to adversarial attacks.

3.6 Summary

This chapter provides an extensive overview of security in AI, focusing on adversarial attacks and their mitigation methods. It begins by classifying adversarial attacks into two categories: untargeted and targeted. It then introduces the concept of *Lp balls* used to define regions where adversarial examples can be found. This chapter also discusses a variety of adversarial ML attacks, such as *Fast Gradient Sign Method, Basic Iterative Method, Projected Gradient Descent, Momentum Iterative Method, Carlini-Wagner, DeepFool, Spatial Transformation Attack, Universal Adversarial Perturbation, and Zeroth Order Optimization*. In addition, it covers mitigation methods to defend against these attacks. These include *Adversarial Training, Defensive Distillation, Randomization*, and *Gradient Masking*. These methods are designed to increase the robustness of AI models against adversarial attempts.

Bibliography

[1] AKM Iqtidar Newaz, Nur Imtiazul Haque, Amit Kumar Sikder, Moham-mad Ashiqur Rahman, and A Selcuk Uluagac. Adversarial attacks to ma-chine learning-based smart healthcare systems. In *GLOBECOM 2020-2020 IEEE Global Communications Conference*, pages 1–6. IEEE, 2020.

[2] Ivan Fursov, Matvey Morozov, Nina Kaploukhaya, Elizaveta Kovtun, Ro-drigo Rivera-Castro, Gleb Gusev, Dmitry Babaev, Ivan Kireev, Alexey Zaytsev, and Evgeny Burnaev. Adversarial attacks on deep models for fi-nancial transaction records. In *Proceedings of the 27th ACM SIGKDD Con-ference on Knowledge Discovery & Data Mining*, pages 2868–2878, 2021.

[3] Murat Kuzlu, Salih Sarp, Ferhat Ozgur Catak, Umit Cali, Yanxiao Zhao, Onur Elma, and Ozgur Guler. Analysis of deceptive data attacks with adversarial machine learning for solar photovoltaic power generation fore-casting. *Electrical Engineering*, pages 1–9, 2022.

[4] Yao Deng, Xi Zheng, Tianyi Zhang, Chen Chen, Guannan Lou, and Miryung Kim. An analysis of adversarial attacks and defenses on au-tonomous driving models. In *2020 IEEE international conference on per-vasive computing and communications (PerCom)*, pages 1–10. IEEE, 2020.

[5] Yupeng Hu, Wenxin Kuang, Zheng Qin, Kenli Li, Jiliang Zhang, Yansong Gao, Wenjia Li, and Keqin Li. Artificial intelligence security: Threats and countermeasures. *ACM Computing Surveys (CSUR)*, 55(1):1–36, 2021.

[6] Ayodeji Oseni, Nour Moustafa, Helge Janicke, Peng Liu, Zahir Tari, and Athanasios Vasilakos. Security and privacy for artificial intelligence: Op-portunities and challenges. *arXiv preprint arXiv:2102.04661*, 2021.

[7] Mingfu Xue, Chengxiang Yuan, Heyi Wu, Yushu Zhang, and Weiqiang Liu. Machine learning security: Threats, countermeasures, and evaluations. *IEEE Access*, 8:74720–74742, 2020.

[8] Muhammad Maaz Irfan, Sheraz Ali, Irfan Yaqoob, and Numan Zafar. To-wards deep learning: A review on adversarial attacks. In *2021 Interna-tional Conference on Artificial Intelligence (ICAI)*, pages 91–96, 2021. doi: 10.1109/ICAI52203.2021.9445247.

[9] Shilin Qiu, Qihe Liu, Shijie Zhou, and Chunjiang Wu. Review of artificial intelligence adversarial attack and defense technologies. *Applied Sciences*, 9(5):909, 2019.

[10] Ishai Rosenberg, Asaf Shabtai, Yuval Elovici, and Lior Rokach. Adversarial machine learning attacks and defense methods in the cyber security domain. *ACM Computing Surveys (CSUR)*, 54(5):1–36, 2021.

[11] Tong Chen, Jiqiang Liu, Yingxiao Xiang, Wenjia Niu, Endong Tong, and Zhen Han. Adversarial attack and defense in reinforcement learning-from ai security view. *Cybersecurity*, 2:1–22, 2019.

[12] Giovanni Apruzzese, Michele Colajanni, Luca Ferretti, and Mirco Marchetti. Addressing adversarial attacks against security systems based on machine learning. In *2019 11th international conference on cyber conflict (CyCon)*, volume 900, pages 1–18. IEEE, 2019.

[13] Samuel G Finlayson, John D Bowers, Joichi Ito, Jonathan L Zittrain, Andrew L Beam, and Isaac S Kohane. Adversarial attacks on medical machine learning. *Science*, 363(6433):1287–1289, 2019.

[14] Shuai Zhou, Chi Liu, Dayong Ye, Tianqing Zhu, Wanlei Zhou, and Philip S Yu. Adversarial attacks and defenses in deep learning: From a perspective of cybersecurity. *ACM Computing Surveys*, 55(8):1–39, 2022.

[15] Huali Ren, Teng Huang, and Hongyang Yan. Adversarial examples: attacks and defenses in the physical world. *International Journal of Machine Learning and Cybernetics*, pages 1–12, 2021.

[16] Pradeep Rathore, Arghya Basak, Sri Harsha Nistala, and Venkataramana Runkana. Untargeted, targeted and universal adversarial attacks and defenses on time series. In *2020 International Joint Conference on Neural Networks (IJCNN)*, pages 1–8, 2020. doi: 10.1109/IJCNN48605.2020. 9207272.

[17] Vladimir Golovko, Sergei Bezobrazov, Pavel Kachurka, and Leanid Vaitsekhovich. Neural network and artificial immune systems for malware and network intrusion detection. In *Advances in Machine Learning II: Dedicated to the Memory of Professor Ryszard S. Michalski*, pages 485–513. Springer, 2010.

[18] Jing Lin, Long Dang, Mohamed Rahouti, and Kaiqi Xiong. Ml attack models: adversarial attacks and data poisoning attacks. *arXiv preprint arXiv:2112.02797*, 2021.

[19] Qingyuan Hu. A survey of adversarial example toolboxes. In *2021 2nd International Conference on Computing and Data Science (CDS)*, pages 603–608. IEEE, 2021.

[20] Alexey Kurakin, Ian Goodfellow, and Samy Bengio. Adversarial machine learning at scale. *arXiv preprint arXiv:1611.01236*, 2016.

[21] Haolin Tang, Ferhat Ozgur Catak, Murat Kuzlu, Evren Catak, and Yanxiao Zhao. Defending ai-based automatic modulation recognition models against adversarial attacks. *IEEE Access*, 2023.

[22] Shuming Shi, Fengyang Weng, Yicheng Zhang, and Yunquan Zhang. Adversarial attacks with the use of different gradient-based methods. *International Core Journal of Engineering*, 8(2):303–312, 2022.

[23] Yingpeng Deng and Lina J Karam. Universal adversarial attack via enhanced projected gradient descent. In *2020 IEEE International Conference on Image Processing (ICIP)*, pages 1241–1245. IEEE, 2020.

[24] Yinpeng Dong, Fangzhou Liao, Tianyu Pang, Hang Su, Jun Zhu, Xiaolin Hu, and Jianguo Li. Boosting adversarial attacks with momentum. In *Proceedings of the IEEE conference on computer vision and pattern recognition*, pages 9185–9193, 2018.

[25] Nicholas Carlini and David Wagner. Towards evaluating the robustness of neural networks. In *2017 ieee symposium on security and privacy (sp)*, pages 39–57. Ieee, 2017.

[26] Seyed-Mohsen Moosavi-Dezfooli, Alhussein Fawzi, and Pascal Frossard. Deepfool: a simple and accurate method to fool deep neural networks. In *Proceedings of the IEEE conference on computer vision and pattern recognition*, pages 2574–2582, 2016.

[27] Chaowei Xiao, Jun-Yan Zhu, Bo Li, Warren He, Mingyan Liu, and Dawn Song. Spatially transformed adversarial examples. *arXiv preprint arXiv:1801.02612*, 2018.

[28] Hong Liu, Rongrong Ji, Jie Li, Baochang Zhang, Yue Gao, Yongjian Wu, and Feiyue Huang. Universal adversarial perturbation via prior driven uncertainty approximation. In *Proceedings of the IEEE/CVF International Conference on Computer Vision*, pages 2941–2949, 2019.

[29] Pin-Yu Chen, Huan Zhang, Yash Sharma, Jinfeng Yi, and Cho-Jui Hsieh. Zoo: Zeroth order optimization based black-box attacks to deep neural networks without training substitute models. In *Proceedings of the 10th ACM workshop on artificial intelligence and security*, pages 15–26, 2017.

[30] Tao Bai, Jinqi Luo, Jun Zhao, Bihan Wen, and Qian Wang. Recent advances in adversarial training for adversarial robustness. *arXiv preprint arXiv:2102.01356*, 2021.

[31] Nicolas Papernot, Patrick McDaniel, Xi Wu, Somesh Jha, and Ananthram Swami. Distillation as a defense to adversarial perturbations against deep neural networks. In *2016 IEEE symposium on security and privacy (SP)*, pages 582–597. IEEE, 2016.

[32] Cihang Xie, Jianyu Wang, Zhishuai Zhang, Zhou Ren, and Alan Yuille. Mitigating adversarial effects through randomization. *arXiv preprint arXiv:1711.01991*, 2017.

[33] Hyungyu Lee, Ho Bae, and Sungroh Yoon. Gradient masking of label smoothing in adversarial robustness. *IEEE Access*, 9:6453–6464, 2021. doi: 10.1109/ACCESS.2020.3048120.

4 Transparency and Explainability

Let's talk about something called "Explainable AI", or XAI, using our smart traffic sign-reading computer as an example like in Figure 4.1.

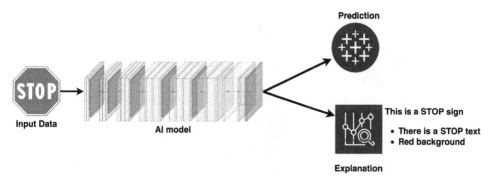

Figure 4.1: Explainable AI

Imagine your computer is like a super-smart friend who can tell you what traffic signs mean. Sometimes, it might give you an answer, but you're still wondering, "Why did it say that?" That's where XAI comes in.

XAI is like asking your computer friend not just to give you an answer, but to give you an answer and explain how it reached that conclusion. So, if it says, "Hey, that's a stop sign," you can ask, "Why do you think it's a stop sign?" And your computer friend will break it down for you, saying something like, "I saw the red color and the shape, just like the stop signs I learned from."

It's like making the computer's thinking process more transparent so you can understand why it made a particular decision. This is super important, especially when the computer does important stuff like helping with medical diagnoses or making decisions in self-driving cars. We want to know we can trust and understand the decisions it makes.

In other words, XAI is like talking with your computer, and it explains the outcomes of AI model to make it more understandable.

4.1 Introduction to Explainable Artificial Intelligence (XAI)

In recent years, AI has been applied in a variety of applications in healthcare, finance, and autonomous systems, which necessitates understanding the justification behind AI model decisions [1]. Therefore, the transparency and explainability of AI have become more important in improving the trust of AI, that is, trustworthy AI [2]. Advanced AI models, such as deep neural networks, can be highly accurate, but lack transparency and expandability, while other models, such as decision trees, are more interpretable but may be less accurate. XAI attempts to explore the gap between predictions and explainable reasoning to make AI models highly accurate and understandable [3]. To achieve this, XAI uses feature importance analysis, surrogate models, and attention mechanisms to make complex models more transparent and disclose their decision-making processes [4]. XAI also helps identify and correct any potential biases or errors in AI systems.

XAI is more essential in high-risk applications (healthcare [5], finance [6], autonomous systems [7] and energy [8]) and has the potential to make complex AI technologies more interpretable and understandable [9]. The authors in [10] have developed an XAI-based solution for healthcare applications, which provides global and local explanations based on the SHapley Additive exPlanations (SHAP) method. The results of the solution on real-life datasets, such as those related to COVID-19, demonstrate its effectiveness in creating trustworthy AI in healthcare. In finance, explainable financial market systems can provide justifications for creditworthiness decisions. The study [11] explores using a gradient boosting decision trees (GBDT) approach to predict significant drops in the S&P 500 stock index. The authors use 150 technical, fundamental, and macroeconomic features for their prediction. They find that GBDT outperforms other machine learning methods in accuracy when applied to S&P 500 futures prices. Shapley values from game theory help identify crucial variables for crisis prediction. They apply this to the March 2020 meltdown, showing tech equity's predictive role. Autonomous vehicles, a type of Intelligent Transportation System (ITS), can benefit from Explainable AI (XAI) to make clear why a self-driving car took a specific action, guaranteeing safety and responsibility. In [12], XAI is used for complex AI, i.e., deep learning models, to make them more understandable. The authors focus on Vehicular Adhoc Networks (VANET), which provide communication between AVs, and their performance is dependent on the exchanged data, such as detecting false or malicious information. The results show that the proposed decision tree-based random forest approach achieved a high accuracy and F1 score of 98.43% and 98.5%, respectively. The study [13] investigates a variety of cases for solar PV energy forecasting using XAI tools, i.e., LIME and SHAP. It also indicates that understanding a prediction model using AI/ML methods can significantly provide improvements to forecasting models as well as point out relevant parameters.

This chapter provides the fundamentals of XAI along with selected XAI tools, i.e., LIME and SHAP and CEM. It is for readers with a background in AI/ML but limited experience with XAI tools and methods. If you are already familiar with the transparency and explainability of AI, you can skip the initial sections and go to practical examples.

4.2 Types of Explainability Approaches

XAI is a field of AI that focuses on delivering transparent machine learning models and algorithms to be easily understood by humans. The aim of XAI is to provide explanations for the decisions made by AI systems, especially in critical applications where trust, accountability, and safety are essential. There are several approaches related to explainability techniques in XAI to facilitate interpretability, such as rule-based explanation, feature importance, model-specific and model-agnostic.

1. **Rule-based Explainability:** Rule-based models [14], such as decision trees, use a set of rules to make predictions. These models are inherently interpretable, as each rule represents a condition that influences the final prediction. Rule extraction techniques aim to extract human-readable rules from complex models, enhancing transparency and interpretability.

2. **Feature Importance:** Feature importance techniques aim to identify the most influential features in an AI model's decision-making process [15]. These techniques assign importance scores to each input feature, indicating their contribution to the model's output. Techniques like LIME (Local Interpretable Model-Agnostic Explanations) and SHAP (SHapley Additive exPlanations) estimate feature importance and provide explanations. Visualizations can further enhance the understanding of feature importance.

3. **Model-specific Approaches:** Different AI models have unique characteristics, and model-specific approaches aim to leverage those characteristics for interoperability. Model-specific approaches focus only specific ones,such as DNNs, support-vector machines (SVMs), or random forests [16], it also called transparent or whitebox. For instance, linear models' interpretability arises from the coefficients assigned to each feature. Decision trees can be visualized as a set of rules, making them easier to understand. SVMs provide interpretable explanations based on the support vectors' positions. It is crucial to be aware of the strengths and limitations of model-specific approaches when applying XAI techniques.

4. **Model-agnostic Approaches:** These approaches aim to explain the

decision of a model regardless of its architecture or type [17]. The main benefit of model-agnostic approaches is their adaptability. They can be used with many models, such as linear models, decision trees, support vector machines, deep neural networks, and more.

In addition, there are various methods for understanding an AI/ML model in terms of scope, i.e., locally (for a single prediction) or globally (for the entire model). It is essential to understand the local behavior to explain individual predictions and gain end-users trust. However, global explanations can provide a broader understanding of the model's behavior, which can be used to improve the model, select features, and guarantee fairness and transparency across the entire dataset. For example, it may be challenging to understand as a whole for a large decision tree, but it is still possible to trace the individual classifications it makes [16].

4.2.1 XAI Tools

XAI aims to provide end users with explanations about the outputs obtained from AI-based models. As mentioned earlier, it is essential for high-risk or critical applications, e.g., healthcare, finance, self-driving cars, and others, which can help users understand the rationale behind the decisions and actions taken by AI, as well as identify and rectify any mistakes made by the AI system. Over time, the field of XAI has become a significant area of research since the utilization of AI and ML technologies and their reliance grows. Researchers from different disciplines have created various XAI tools to help understand black-box models. LIME is a widely used XAI tool that creates an interpretable model to approximate any AI system, thereby giving an understanding of its decision-making process [18]. SHAP (SHapley Additive exPlanations) is a popular XAI tool that utilizes Shapley values to explain models and pinpoint significant features [19]. Contrastive Explanation Method (CEM) is a technique for producing instance-based, local black-box explanations for classification models. It is designed to be used locally and produces explanations in terms of Pertinent Positives (PP) and Pertinent Negatives (PN) [20].

It also exposes black-box models, which are machine learning models that are not designed for interpretability (e.g., random forests, neural networks). InterpretML is a Python package that provides machine learning interpretability algorithms. It provides two types of interpretability, i.e., glassbox models for machine learning models created for interpretability (e.g., linear models, rule lists, and generalized additive models), and black box models for machine learning models not designed for interpretability (e.g., random forests and neural networks) [21]. *Alibi Explain*, also known as Alibi, is an open-source Python library designed to inspect and interpret classification and regression models [22]. TreeInterpreter is a Python library to interpret and explain the decisions made by tree-based machine learning models, such as decision trees and random forests [23].

In this section, LIME, SHAP, and CEM are explored along with practical examples and provides a brief overview of these XAI tools.

4.2.2 Local Interpretable Model-agnostic Explanations (LIME)

LIME is one of the popular XAI techniques providing local interpretability for AI/ML models. The main idea behind LIME is to generate an interpretable model that explains the predictions of a black-box model for a specific instance of interest [24]. It achieves this by the steps as follows:

1. **Sampling:** Generate a set of samples from the instance to be explained. These samples are created by perturbing the features of the original instance while keeping the target label unchanged. Here, $S = \mathbf{x'}_{i\,i=1}^{n}$ can be defined as the set of samples, where $\mathbf{x'}_i$ represents a perturbed sample.
2. **Prediction:** Obtain a prediction for the samples in (S). $f(\mathbf{x'}_i)$ can be defined as the predicted labels, where f represents the black-box model.
3. **Weighting:** Assign weights to the samples in S based on their proximity to the explained instance. The weights reflect the importance of each sample in approximating the black-box model's behavior. These weights can be determined using various methods, such as distance-based or kernel-

based approaches. The weight is assigned to sample, i.e., $\mathbf{x}'_i$ as $w(\mathbf{x}'_i)$.

4. **Model Approximation:** Learn an interpretable model that approximates the black-box model's behavior within the local neighborhood of the instance. The goal is to find an interpretable model (g) from a set of possible interpretable models (G) that minimizes the loss function as follows:

$$g(z) = \arg\min_{g \in G} \sum_{\mathbf{x}'_i \in S} w(\mathbf{x}'_i) \cdot \text{dist}(z, \mathbf{x}'_i) \cdot \left(f(\mathbf{x}'_i) - g(z) \right)^2 \qquad (4.1)$$

where z represents the instance being explained, dist denotes a distance measure, and $f(\mathbf{x}'_i)$ is the predicted label for sample $\mathbf{x}'_i$.

5. **Explanation:** Once the interpretable model g is learned, it can be used to explain the predictions of the black box model. The explanation, denoted as $\text{Expl}(\mathbf{x})$, is simply the output of the interpretable model for the instance $\mathbf{x}$ being explained. It provides insights into the factors that contributed positively or negatively to the prediction for that instance.

LIME generates local explanations by perturbing the features of an instance, obtaining predictions from the black-box model, assigning weights to the perturbed samples, learning an interpretable model within the local neighborhood, and using this interpretable model to explain the predictions.

4.2.3 SHapley Additive exPlanation (SHAP)

SHAP is another popular XAI technique [25]. It is based on the concept of Shapley values from cooperative game theory. The main idea behind SHAP is to assign each feature a unique importance value by quantifying its contribution to the prediction. These importance values are calculated through Shapley values, representing a feature's average marginal contribution across all possible feature subsets.

Steps in calculating SHAP values are explained as follows:

1. **Define the Reference:** The first step is to define a reference or baseline point as a starting point for the explanation. It can be a default or average value of the training dataset. Let's denote the reference as $\mathbf{x}_{ref}$.

2. **Generate Coalitions:** The next step is to generate coalitions representing all possible combinations of features. Let's denote a coalition as C.

3. **Calculate Shapley Values:** For each feature i, SHAP calculates its Shapley value ϕ_i by considering all coalitions C that include feature i. The Shapley value represents the average marginal contribution of feature i across all possible coalitions. Mathematically, the Shapley value ϕ_i is calculated as:

$$\phi_i(x) = \sum_{C \subseteq N \setminus \{i\}} \frac{|C|!(|N| - |C| - 1)!}{|N|!} [f(C \cup \{i\}) - f(C)] \qquad (4.2)$$

where N is the set of all features, $f(C)$ represents the model's output prediction for the coalition C, and $|C|$ denotes the number of features in coalition C.

4. **Aggregate Shapley Values:** After calculating the Shapley values for each feature, they are aggregated to obtain the final feature importance scores. The aggregation method depends on the specific XAI implementation and can include methods such as taking the absolute value, averaging across multiple instances, or considering the sign of the Shapley values.

5. **Interpretation:** Once the SHAP values, i.e., positive and negative values, are obtained, they can be used to interpret the model's predictions. Here, positive SHAP values indicate a positive contribution of a feature to the results, while negative SHAP values indicate a negative contribution. The general magnitude of the SHAP value represents the importance of the selected feature in the prediction.

4.2.4 Contrastive Explanations Method (CEM)

The Contrastive Explanations Method (CEM) is a model-agnostic XAI tool, which was introduced by IBM Research, [26]. CEM approach provides an explanation based on missing values or features, i.e., pertinent negatives, by considering the present elements and the contrastive perturbations that should be absent. It is different from other methods, such as LIME and SHAP, as its focus is on justifying the classification of an input based on what should be minimally and sufficiently present and what should be necessarily absent. CEM is widely used in areas, such as healthcare and criminology. To generate this kind of explanation, CEM follows a three-step approach as follows [26]:

1. **Find the Pertinent Positives:** Find the characteristics of the input that are minimally sufficient to yield the same classification.
2. **Search the Pertinent Negatives:** Search for the minimal amount of features that should be absent from the input to prevent the classification result from changing.
3. **Interpretation:** Use a convolutional autoencoder to obtain explanations.

4.3 Practical Examples

This section provides the practical examples for the selected XAI tools, i.e., LIME, SHAP and CEM.

4.3.1 Practical Example for LIME

LIME produces local explanations by changing the characteristics of a single instance, getting predictions from the opaque model, assigning weights to the altered samples, training an understandable model within the local area, and using this understandable model to explain the predictions. By concentrating on the local behavior of the opaque model, LIME gives understanding into how the model comes to its predictions for individual cases.

The following Python code can serve as a foundation for training image classification models with interpretability. It lets users gain insights into the model's decision-making by generating LIME explanations for individual predictions. The code, Part 1 of the LIME example, can be explained as follows:

1. **Importing Libraries**: Import the necessary libraries, including *LIME, skimage, matplotlib, numpy, keras, and tensorflow.*

```
1  #============================================
2  ### Part 1
3  #Import libraries
4  import lime
5  from lime import lime_image
6  from skimage.segmentation import mark_boundaries
7  import matplotlib.pyplot as plt
8  import numpy as np
9  import keras
10 from keras.datasets import mnist
11 from tensorflow.keras.layers import Conv2D, MaxPooling2D,
      Flatten, Dense
```

2. **Data Loading and Preprocessing**: Load the the MNIST dataset, containing training and testing images and labels, then reshape the image data to (batch_size, 28, 28, 1).

```
1  # Load the MNIST digits dataset
2  (x_train, y_train), (x_test, y_test) = mnist.load_data()
3
4  # Preprocess the data
5  x_train = x_train.reshape((-1, 28, 28, 1)).astype('float32')
      / 255.0
6  x_test = x_test.reshape((-1, 28, 28, 1)).astype('float32') /
      255.0
```

3. **Defining the Function for Grayscale to RGB Conversion**: Define the function to convert grayscale images to RGB format, ensuring compatibility with the model.

```
1 #Define the Function for Grayscale to RGB Conversion
2 def to_rgb(x):
3     x_rgb = np.zeros((x.shape[0], 28, 28, 3))
4     for i in range(3):
5         x_rgb[..., i] = x[..., 0]
6     return x_rgb
```

4. **Converting Grayscale Images to RGB Format**: Convert the gray scale images to RGB format by using the defined function.

```
1 #Convert Grayscale Images to RGB Format
2 x_train = to_rgb(x_train)
3 x_test = to_rgb(x_test)
```

5. **Model Definition**: Define the CNN Model consisting of a 2D convolutional layer with 16 filters and ReLU activation, a max-pooling layer for dimensionality, and a dense layer with 10 units for digit classification.

```
1 #Define the Model
2 model = keras.Sequential(
3     [
4         Conv2D(16, 3, activation='relu', input_shape=(28, 28, 3)),
5         MaxPooling2D(),
6         Flatten(),
7         Dense(10)
8     ]
9 )
```

6. **Model Compilation**: Compile the model with settings including *sparse categorical cross-entropy loss, Adam optimizer, and accuracy* metric.

```
1 #Compile the Model
2 model.compile(
3     loss = keras.losses.SparseCategoricalCrossentropy(
           from_logits = True),
4     optimizer = keras.optimizers.Adam(),
5     metrics = ['accuracy']
6 )
```

7. **Model Training**: Train the model with 20 epochs and a batch size of 10,000 using the training data. Validation data is provided during training.

```
1 #Train the Model
2 model.fit(
```

```
3          x_train,
4          y_train,
5          epochs=20,
6          batch_size=10000,
7          validation_data=(x_test, y_test))
```

The following Python code, Part 2 of LIME example, serves as a foundation for training image classification models with interpretability. It provides a visual interpretation of how specific regions within images influence the predictions made by the machine learning model. Combining LIME explanations and image segmentation offers insights into the model's decision-making process for image classification tasks. It starts by setting up the LIME explainer object to help us generate explanations for model predictions and then configuring a segmentation algorithm for image segmentation. The 'quick-shift' algorithm is chosen with specific parameters, including kernel size, maximum distance, and ratio. A figure is created with subplots to visualize the results. The subplots will display the original images along with their corresponding explanations. Within a loop, we randomly select an image from the test dataset. For each selected image, the following steps will be conducted:

1. **Importing Libraies**: Import the necessary libraries, including *LIME, tqdm, keras, and label2rgb*.

```
1  #========================================
2  ### PART 2
3  from tensorflow import keras
4  from lime.wrappers.scikit_image import SegmentationAlgorithm
5  from tqdm.notebook import tqdm
6  from skimage.color import label2rgb
```

2. **Creating the Explainer Object:** Utilize the LIME explainer to generate an explanation for the selected image. This explanation highlights the image's most influential regions or features that contributed to the model's prediction. The *explanation* object is created using the *LIME explainer*, considering parameters such as the number of samples, segmentation function, and more.

```
1  # Create the explainer object
```

```
2 explainer = lime_image.LimeImageExplainer(random_state=42,
      verbose=False)
3 segmenter = SegmentationAlgorithm('quickshift',
      kernel_size=1, max_dist=200, ratio=0.2)
```

3. **Creating a Figure with Suplots:** Create a figure with 2 rows and 10 columns to display multiple subplots, i.e., *fig, axs = plt.subplots(2, 10, figsize=(12, 4))*. It utilizes the subplots function from the *matplotlib.pyplot* module to create a grid of subplots, and sets the dimensions of the entire figure. In this case, the figure will be 12 units wide and 4 units tall.

```
1 # Create a figure with subplots
2 fig, axes = plt.subplots(2, 10, figsize=(12, 4))
```

4. **Initializing an Empty List to Store Indices of Input Images:** Create an empty list *input_img_idx_list* to store indices of input images.

```
1 #Initialize an empty list to store indices of input images
2 input_img_idx_list = []
```

5. **Initializing a Loop to Iterate Each Subplot for Original Images:** Initiate a loop that iterates each element of *axes.flat* with *tqdm*. For image selection and prediction, randomly select an index *input_img_idx* from *x_test* and extract the corresponding image, retrieve the ground truth label *org_label* from *y_test* at the selected index, and make a prediction *pred_label* using the model on the selected image For generating explanation, use an *(explainer)* to generate an explanation for the model's prediction through *explain_instance* function that generates explanations for the model's prediction on a given input image. For visualizing explanation and original image, *explanation.get_image_and_mask()* function retrieves an image and mask from the explanation using specific parameters, and *ax.imshow()* and *label2rgb()* functions visualize the original image with the explanation overlay (mask). Set the subplot title to display the ground truth label and predicted label, turns off the axis for the subplot. For storing input image indices, append the index of the input image. *(input_img_idx)* to *input_img_idx_list* for reference or tracking purposes.

```
1 #Initialize a loop to iterate each element of axes.flat
2 for i, ax in tqdm(enumerate(axes.flat)):
3     # Randomly select an image
4     input_img_idx = np.random.randint(x_test.shape[0])
```

```
 5      input_img = x_test[input_img_idx:input_img_idx + 1]
 6
 7      # Get the ground truth and predicted labels
 8      org_label = y_test[input_img_idx]
 9      pred_label = model.predict(input_img,
        verbose=0)[0].argmax()
10
11      # Explain the instance
12      explanation =
        explainer.explain_instance(x_test[input_img_idx],
        model.predict,
13                                                  top_labels=10,
        hide_color=0, num_samples=100,
14
        segmentation_fn=segmenter)
15
16      # Retrieve an image and mask from the explanation
17      image, mask = explanation.get_image_and_mask(
18          model.predict(input_img).argmax(axis=1)[0],
19          positive_only=True, hide_rest=False,
20          num_features=10, min_weight=0.01
21      )
22
23      # Plot the original image with the LIME explanation
24      ax.imshow(label2rgb(mask, image, bg_label=0),
        interpolation='nearest')
25
26      #Set subplot
27      ax.set_title('GT:' + str(org_label) + ' Pred:' +
        str(pred_label))
28      ax.axis('off')
29
30      #Store Input Image Indices
31      input_img_idx_list.append(input_img_idx)
```

In summary, this code uses a *for* loop to iterate each subplot, selects a random image, predicts its label using a model, generates explanations for the predictions, and then visualizes the explanations overlaid on the original images in the subplots. Additionally, it stores the indices of the selected images for further analysis or reference.

6. **Displaying the Results:** Adjust the padding between the subplots for better visualization using *tight_layout* and display results.

```
 1  # Adjust the padding between the subplots
```

```
2 plt.tight_layout()
3 # Show the plot
4 plt.show()
```

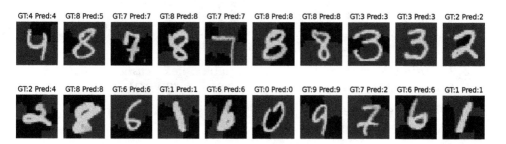

Figure 4.2: Interpretation of Model Predictions with LIME-Generated Explanations. This figure illustrates the interpretability of machine learning model predictions through LIME-generated explanations. Each subplot displays an original image with an overlaid explanation mask, highlighting significant regions influencing the model's predictions. Ground truth labels (GT) and predicted labels (Pred) are included in the subplot titles, providing insights into model decision-making.

The following code segment, Part 3 of the LIME example, combines adversarial attacks and interpretability techniques to gain insights into how the model's predictions change when input images are perturbed, shedding light on potential vulnerabilities and decision boundaries. After generating adversarial examples, the code interprets the model's predictions using LIME. For this purpose, a figure with subplots is created, where each subplot displays an original image with an overlaid explanation mask. These masks highlight regions that significantly influence the model's predictions. In each subplot, a random image is selected from the test dataset, and the selected image is subjected to the adversarial attack to modify its input and observe its impact on model predictions. Ground truth labels (GT) and predicted labels (Pred) are displayed in the subplot titles, providing insights into the model's decision-making process. The following Python code segment focusing on adversarial attacks and LIME will be explained in step-by-step below.

1. **Importing Libraries**: Import a specific library and function, i.e., *mo-*

mentum_iterative_method from the *CleverHans* library in *TensorFlow* 2.

```
1  #==============================================
2  ### PART 3
3  #Import Libraries
4  from cleverhans.tf2.attacks.momentum_iterative_method import
     momentum_iterative_method
```

2. **Defining Variable:** Define two variables, i.e., *"epsilon = 0.3"*, epsilon is a variable that is set to the value 0.3, and *"TARGET_CLASS = 5"*, a variable named *TARGET_CLASS* and assigning it the value 5.

```
1  # Define Variables
2  epsilon = 0.3
3  TARGET_CLASS = 5
```

3. **Creating a Figure with Suplots:** Create a figure with 2 rows and 10 columns to display multiple subplots, i.e., *fig, axs = plt.subplots(2, 10, figsize=(12, 4))*. It utilizes the subplots function from the *matplotlib.pyplot* module to create a grid of subplots, and sets the dimensions of the entire figure. In this case, the figure will be 12 units wide and 4 units tall.

```
1  # Create a figure with subplots
2  fig, axes = plt.subplots(2, 10, figsize=(12, 4))
```

4. **Initialing a Loop to Iterate Each Subplot for Adversarial Examples:** Initiate a loop that iterates each element of *axes.flat* with *tqdm*. For image selection and prediction, randomly select an index *input_img_idx* from *x_test* and extract the corresponding image. For adversarial examples, apply an adversarial attack *(momentum_iterative_method)* to the input image using parameters like *eps, eps_iter, nb_iter, etc.*, and modify the *input_img* with the result of the adversarial attack. For ground truth and predictions, retrieve the ground truth label *(org_label)* for the input image from *y_test*, and make a prediction *(pred_label)* using the modified input image and the model. For generating explanation, use an *(explainer)* to generate an explanation for the model's prediction through *explain_instance* function that generates explanations for the model's prediction on a given input image. For visualizing explanation and original image, *explanation.get_image_and_mask()* function retrieves an image and mask from the explanation using specific parameters, and *ax.imshow()* and *label2rgb()* functions visualize the original image with the explanation over-

lay (mask). Set the subplot title to display the ground truth label and predicted label, turns off the axis for the subplot. For storing input image indices, append the index of the input image. *(input_img_idx)* to *input_img_idx_list* for reference or tracking purposes.

```python
#Initialize a loop to iterate each element of axes.flat
for i, ax in tqdm(enumerate(axes.flat)):
    # Randomly select an image
    input_img_idx = input_img_idx_list[i]
    input_img = x_test[input_img_idx:input_img_idx + 1]

    # Apply Adversarial attack
    input_img = momentum_iterative_method(model, input_img,
    eps=epsilon, eps_iter=0.01, nb_iter=1000,
                                          decay_factor=1.0,
    clip_min=0.0, clip_max=1.0, y=[TARGET_CLASS],
                                          targeted=True,
    sanity_checks=False)

    # Get the ground truth and predicted labels
    org_label = y_test[input_img_idx]
    pred_label = model.predict(input_img,
    verbose=0)[0].argmax()

    # Explain the instance
    explanation =
    explainer.explain_instance(x_test[input_img_idx],
    model.predict,
                                          top_labels=10,
    hide_color=0, num_samples=100,

    segmentation_fn=segmenter)

    # Retrieve an image and mask from the explanation
    image, mask = explanation.get_image_and_mask(
        model.predict(input_img).argmax(axis=1)[0],
        positive_only=True, hide_rest=False,
        num_features=10, min_weight=0.01
    )

    # Plot the original image with the LIME explanation
    ax.imshow(label2rgb(mask,image, bg_label = 1),
    interpolation = 'nearest')
    ax.set_title('GT:' + str(org_label) + ' Pred:' +
```

```
      str(pred_label))
31    ax.axis('off')
```

5. **Displaying the Results:** Adjust the padding between the subplots for better visualization using *tight_ layout* and display results.

```
1 # Adjust the padding between the subplots
2 plt.tight_layout()
3 # Show the plot
4 plt.show()
```

As in the previous section, this code uses a *for* loop to iterate each subplot, applying an adversarial attack to the original image, generating explanations for the model's predictions on the modified images, and visualizing these explanations alongside the modified images for analysis or interpretation.

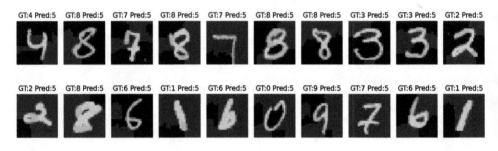

Figure 4.3: Adversarial Attack and Interpretation Results: The figure displays original images alongside their corresponding adversarial examples generated using the Momentum Iterative Method. Explanation masks, created using LIME, highlight the regions contributing to model predictions. Each subplot includes ground truth (GT) and predicted (Pred) labels for reference.

4.3.2 Practical Example for SHAP

In this practical example, the SHAP method is utilized to explain how a CNN model interprets and predicts digit images in MNIST dataset. The following source code, Part 1 of the SHAP example, is broken down into its parts and explained in detail.

1. **Importing Libraries:** Import libraries, including *NumPy Matplotlib, SHAP, and TensorFlow.*

```
1 #============================
2 ### Part 1
3 #Import libraries
4 import numpy as np
5 import matplotlib.pyplot as plt
6 import shap
7 from tensorflow import keras
```

2. **Data Loading and Preprocessing**: Load the MNIST dataset containing images of hand-written digits and their corresponding labels, and reprocess the data by reshaping the images and scaling pixel values to the range, i.e., 0, 1, to prepare the dataset for the model.

```
1 # Load the MNIST dataset
2 (X_train, y_train), (X_test, y_test) =
    keras.datasets.mnist.load_data()
3
4 # Preprocess the data
5 X_train = X_train.reshape((X_train.shape[0], 28, 28,
    1)).astype('float32') / 255.0
6 X_test = X_test.reshape((X_test.shape[0], 28, 28,
    1)).astype('float32') / 255.0
```

3. **Model Definition:** Define a convolutional neural network (CNN) model for image classification, consisting of convolutional layers, max-pooling layers, and dense layers designed to classify the input images, i.e, 0-9.

```
1 # Define the model architecture
2 model = keras.Sequential([
3     keras.layers.Conv2D(32, (3, 3), activation='relu',
       input_shape=(28, 28, 1)),
4     keras.layers.MaxPooling2D((2, 2)),
5     keras.layers.Flatten(),
6     keras.layers.Dense(64, activation='relu'),
7     keras.layers.Dense(10, activation='softmax')
8 ])
```

4. **Model Compilation:** Compile the model with appropriate loss and optimization functions.

```
1 # Compile the model
2 model.compile(optimizer='adam',
      loss='sparse_categorical_crossentropy',
      metrics=['accuracy'])
```

The following Python code, Part 2 of the SHAP example, will provide users with generated SHAP explanations for individual predictions. It provides a visual interpretation of how specific regions within images influence the predictions made by the machine learning model. It starts by setting up the SHAP explainer object to help us generate explanations for model predictions and then configuring a segmentation algorithm for image segmentation. A figure is created with subplots to visualize the results. The subplots will display the SHAP values overlaid on the images for interpretability or explanation of the model's predictions. Each step of Python code will be explained below.

1. **Creating SHAP Explainer:** Create a SHAP explainer called *"DeepExplainer"* for our trained model. This explainer will help us understand the model's predictions for individual images, and pass the first 1000 samples from the X_test dataset to the explainer for computing SHAP values.

```
1 #=========================
2 ### Part 2
3 # Create a SHAP explainer
4 explainer = shap.DeepExplainer(model, (X_test[:1000]))
```

2. **Initializing a Loop for 5 Iterations and Interpreting Model Predictions:** Initiate a loop for 5 iterations and interpret model predictions using SHAP values. For image selection and prediction, randomly select an index *(img_idx)* from the X_test dataset and retrieve a single image sample (sample) based on the selected index. For SHAP values computation, compute SHAP (SHapley Additive exPlanations) values for the selected sample using the explainer object. For prediction and true label retrieval, make a prediction *(pred_proba)* using the model for the selected image, and get the original true label *((org_y)* from the y_test dataset corresponding to the selected index. For formatting and printing

information, format information about prediction probabilities associated with different classes into strings *(index_ names)* for visualization or annotation purposes, and print the predicted label and the true label for diagnostic purposes. For plotting SHAP Values, plot the SHAP values for the sample image using *shap.image_ plot* with annotation information *(index_ names)* for the SHAP values. For displaying the plot, show the results through *plt.show()*.

```python
#Initialize a loop for 5 iterations
for i in range(5):
    # Randomly select the image
    img_idx = np.random.randint(X_test.shape[0])
    sample = X_test[[img_idx]]

    # Get SHAP values for the sample
    shap_values = explainer.shap_values(sample)

    # Predict the sample and get True Label
    pred_proba = model.predict(sample)
    org_y = y_test[img_idx]

    # Format and concatenate information about prediction
    probabilities associated with different classes
    index_names = np.array([str(x) + "\n" +
    '{:7.3%}'.format(pred_proba[0][x]) for x in
    range(10)]).reshape(1, 10)

    # Print the predicted label and the true label
    associated with an image
    print("Predicted label :{}\nTrue label
    :{}".format(pred_proba.argmax(), org_y))

    # Plot the SHAP values
    shap.image_plot(shap_values, -sample.reshape(1, 28, 28,
    1), index_names, show=False)

    # Show the plot
    plt.show()
```

The following Python code segment, Part 3 of the SHAP example, demonstrates the interpretation of adversarial images using SHAP. This code snippet showcases the interpretability of adversarial images, providing insights into how

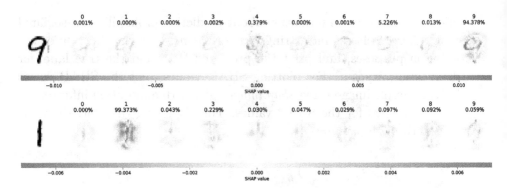

Figure 4.4: Visualization of SHAP Values for MNIST Image Explanations: Original Image and Corresponding SHAP Values Highlighting Pixel Importance.

AI/ML models make predictions even in the presence of adversarial attacks. SHAP values help visualize the contribution of each pixel in the adversarial image to the model's output. The code focuses on interpreting MNIST dataset images using SHAP values and explaining adversarial examples generated using the Momentum Iterative Method (MIM) attack, and each part of the Pyhton code will be explained below.

1. **Importing Libraries:** Import necessary libraries and modules, including *NumPy, Matplotlib, TensorFlow's Keras, SHAP, and CleverHans* (for adversarial attacks).

```
1  # ============================
2  ### Part 3
3  # Import libraries
4  import numpy as np
5  import matplotlib.pyplot as plt
6  import shap
7  from tensorflow import keras
8  from cleverhans.tf2.attacks.momentum_iterative_method import
       momentum_iterative_method
```

2. **Data Loading and Preprocessing:** Load the MNIST dataset, which contains images of hand-written digits and their corresponding labels, and preprocess the data by reshaping the images and scaling pixel values to

the range [0, 1] to prepare the dataset for use in the model.

```
1 # Load the MNIST dataset
2 (X_train, y_train), (X_test, y_test) =
    keras.datasets.mnist.load_data()
3
4 # Preprocess the data
5 X_train = X_train.reshape((X_train.shape[0], 28, 28,
    1)).astype('float32') / 255.0
6 X_test = X_test.reshape((X_test.shape[0], 28, 28,
    1)).astype('float32') / 255.0
```

3. **Model Definition:** Define a convolutional neural network (CNN) model for image classification. This model includes convolutional layers, max-pooling layers, and dense layers designed to classify the input images into one of ten classes.

```
1 # Define the model architecture
2 model = keras.Sequential([
3     keras.layers.Conv2D(32, (3, 3), activation='relu',
        input_shape=(28, 28, 1)),
4     keras.layers.MaxPooling2D((2, 2)),
5     keras.layers.Flatten(),
6     keras.layers.Dense(64, activation='relu'),
7     keras.layers.Dense(10, activation='softmax')
8 ])
```

4. **Model Compilation:** Compile the model with appropriate loss and optimization functions.

```
1 # Compile the model
2 model.compile(optimizer='adam',
    loss='sparse_categorical_crossentropy',
    metrics=['accuracy'])
```

5. **Model Training**: Train the model with 5 epochs and a batch size of 5000 using the training data. Validation data is provided during training.

```
1 # Train the model
2 model.fit(X_train, y_train, epochs=5, batch_size=5000,
    validation_split=0.1)
```

6. **Defining Adversarial Attack Parameters:** Define the parameters for an adversarial attack using the Momentum Iterative Method (MIM). Specify the perturbation strength *(epsilon)* and the target class *(TARGET_CLASS)* to generate adversarial examples.

```
1  # Define variables
2  epsilon = 0.1
3  TARGET_CLASS = 5
```

7. **Creating SHAP Explainer:** Create a SHAP explainer called *"DeepExplainer"* for our trained model. This explainer will help us understand the model's predictions for individual images, and pass the first 1000 samples from the *X_ test* dataset to the explainer for computing SHAP values.

```
1  # Create a SHAP explainer
2  explainer = shap.DeepExplainer(model, (X_test[:1000]))
```

8. **Interpreting Model Predictions of Adversarial Examples and Visualizing SHAP Values:** Initiate a loop for 5 iterations and interpret model predictions using SHAP values for adversarial examples. For each of five iterations, randomly select an image from the MNIST test dataset, apply the MIM attack to generate an adversarial example, calculate the SHAP values for the adversarial example to interpret the model's prediction, and display the predicted label, true label, and SHAP interpretation of the adversarial image using Matplotlib.

```
1  #Initialize a loop for 5 iterations
2  for i in range(5):
3      # Randomly select the image
4      img_idx = np.random.randint(X_test.shape[0])
5      sample = X_test[[img_idx]]
6
7      # Apply Adversarial attack
8      sample = momentum_iterative_method(model, sample,
       eps=epsilon, eps_iter=0.01, nb_iter=1000,
9                                    decay_factor=1.0,
       clip_min=0.0, clip_max=1.0, y=[TARGET_CLASS],
10                                        targeted=True,
       sanity_checks=False).numpy()
11
12     # Get SHAP values for the sample
13     shap_values = explainer.shap_values(sample)
14
15     # Predict the sample and get True Label
16     pred_proba = model.predict(sample)
17     org_y = y_test[img_idx]
18
19      # Format and concatenate information about prediction
       probabilities associated with different classes
```

```
20      index_names = np.array([str(x) + "\n" +
        '{:7.3%}'.format(pred_proba[0][x]) for x in
        range(10)]).reshape(1, 10)
21
22
23      # Print the predicted label and the true label
        associated with an image
24      print("Predicted label :{}\nTrue label
        :{}".format(pred_proba.argmax(), org_y))
25
26      # Plot the SHAP values
27      shap.image_plot(shap_values, -sample.reshape(1, 28, 28,
        1), index_names, show=False)
28
29      # Show the plot
30      plt.show()
```

4.3.3 Practical Example for CEM

Contrastive Explanation Method (CEM) produces local black-box explanations for classification models in terms of Pertinent Positives (PP) and Pertinent Negatives (PN) [20]. For a PP, the technique discovers the essential features that must be present to forecast the same class as the original example. For PN, it identifies the features that must be absent from the instance to keep the original prediction class.

In this practical example, the CEM library is used to explain the predictions made by a machine learning model trained on the MNIST dataset. In addition, the Alibi Python open source library is used to create a program that will illustrate CEM interpretations of images. The MNIST dataset will be implemented in an innovative way to find missing features to identify a number.

The code segment begins with importing the necessary libraries, loading and preprocessing the MNIST dataset, which consists of grayscale images of handwritten digits (0-9). These images are reshaped and normalized in preparation

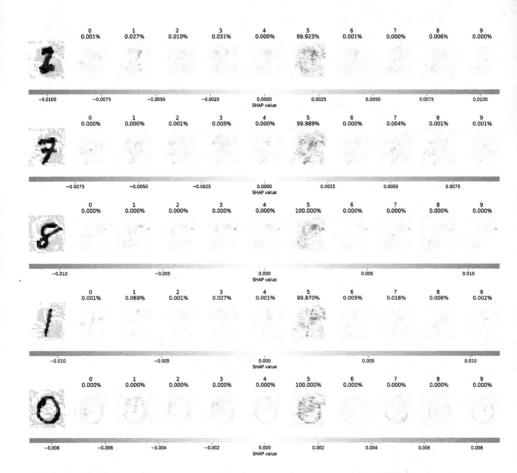

Figure 4.5: SHAP Interpretations of Adversarial MNIST Images: This series of images presents SHAP interpretations for adversarial images generated from the MNIST dataset. Each image displays the original digit (top) and the corresponding SHAP explanations, highlighting the pixels' contributions to the model's prediction after applying the Momentum Iterative Method attack.

for further processing. Subsequently, it is needed to convert the grayscale images into RGB format, a prerequisite for CEM. This conversion entails triplicating the single channel three times to ensure compatibility with the CEM explainer. A CEM explainer is instantiated for image data, configuring it with a random seed and deactivating verbose output to maintain code clarity. The core section of the code revolves around visualizing explanations for model predictions. A figure with subplots is generated to showcase these explanations. Within a loop, images are randomly selected from the test set, and CEM is employed to explain the model's predictions for these images. By visualizing these explanations, we gain insights into the regions of the image that influenced the model's decision-making process, thereby enhancing our understanding of the rationale behind the model's predictions. The following source code, Part 1 of the CEM example, will be explained below.

1. **Importing Libraries:** Import essential libraries and modules, such as *TensorFlow, NumPy, Matplotlib, Alibi, and CEM* for model loading, building, and machine learning model interpretation.

```
1  # ===================================
2  ### Part 1
3  #Import libraries
4  import tensorflow as tf
5  from tensorflow import keras
6  from tensorflow.keras.models import load_model
7  from tensorflow.keras.models import Model
8  import numpy as np
9  import matplotlib.pyplot as plt
10 import alibi
11 from alibi.explainers import CEM
```

2. **Disabling TensorFlow's eager execution and printing the version of TensorFlow:** Disable TensorFlow's eager execution. Eager execution allows for immediate evaluation of operations, making TensorFlow behave more like Python. Disabling eager execution means that TensorFlow operations will not be executed immediately; instead, they will be added to a computational graph and executed later when explicitly run within a tf.Session() context. Print the version of TensorFlow installed in your environment.

```
1  # ===================================
```

```
2 # Disable TensorFlow's eager execution and print the version
    of TensorFlow
3 tf.compat.v1.disable_eager_execution()
4 print(tf.__version__)
```

3. **Data Loading and Preprocessing:** Load the MNIST dataset, which contains images of hand-written digits and their corresponding labels, and preprocess image data contained in X_train and X_test for a convolutional neural network (CNN) by reshaping each image from a 3D array (height, width) to a 4D array (height, width, channels) where channels=1 (indicating grayscale images). Then, the pixel values of the images are normalized to a range between 0 and 1 by dividing each pixel value by 255, converting the data type to 'float32'

```
1 # Load the MNIST dataset
2 (X_train, y_train), (X_test, y_test) =
    keras.datasets.mnist.load_data()
3
4 # Preprocess the data, including scaling and shaping the data
5 X_train = X_train.reshape((X_train.shape[0], 28, 28,
    1)).astype('float32') / 255.0
6 X_test = X_test.reshape((X_test.shape[0], 28, 28,
    1)).astype('float32') / 255.0
```

4. **Model Definition:** Define a convolutional neural network (CNN) model for image classification. This model includes convolutional layers, max-pooling layers, and dense layers designed to classify the input images into one of ten classes. This architecture consists of convolutional layers for feature extraction and pooling layers for reducing spatial dimensions, followed by densely connected layers for classification, ending with a softmax layer to produce class probabilities.

```
1 # Define the cnn model architecture
2 model = keras.Sequential([
3     keras.layers.Conv2D(32, (3, 3), activation='relu',
        input_shape=(28, 28, 1)),
4     keras.layers.MaxPooling2D((2, 2)),
5     keras.layers.Conv2D(32, (3, 3), activation='relu',
        input_shape=(28, 28, 1)),
6     keras.layers.MaxPooling2D((2, 2)),
7     keras.layers.Flatten(),
8     keras.layers.Dense(64, activation='relu'),
9     keras.layers.Dense(10, activation='softmax')
```

```
10 ])
```

5. **Model Compilation:** Compile a convolutional neural network (CNN) model using the *Adam optimizer and sparse categorical cross-entropy loss.*

```
1 # Compile the model
2 model.compile(optimizer='adam',
    loss='sparse_categorical_crossentropy',
    metrics=['accuracy'])
```

6. **Model Training**: Train the model with 5 epochs and a batch size of 5000 using the training data. The training process aims to minimize the loss function and improve the model's accuracy. Validation data is provided during training.

```
1 # Train the model
2 model.fit(X_train, y_train, epochs=5, batch_size=5000,
    validation_split=0.1)
```

7. **Model Saving**: Save the trained model as *'mnist_ cnn.h5'.*

```
1 #Save the model
2 model.save('mnist_cnn.h5')
```

8. **Encoder and Decoder Model Definition:** Define an autoencoder architecture using *Keras.* An encoder model compresses the input image data into a lower-dimensional representation, and a decoder model attempts to reconstruct the original image from this compressed representation, both composed of convolutional layers for encoding and decoding operations.

```
1  # Define the encoder layers
2  encoder = keras.Sequential([
3      keras.layers.Conv2D(16, (3, 3), activation='relu',
          padding='same', input_shape=(28, 28, 1)),
4      keras.layers.Conv2D(16, (3, 3), activation='relu',
          padding='same'),
5      keras.layers.MaxPooling2D((2, 2), padding='same'),
6      keras.layers.Conv2D(1, (3, 3), activation=None,
          padding='same')
7  ])
8
9  # Define the decoder layers
10 decoder = keras.Sequential([
11     keras.layers.Conv2D(16, (3, 3), activation='relu',
          padding='same', input_shape=(14, 14, 1)),
```

```
12    keras.layers.UpSampling2D((2, 2)),
13    keras.layers.Conv2D(16, (3, 3), activation='relu',
      padding='same'),
14    keras.layers.Conv2D(1, (3, 3), activation=None,
      padding='same')
15 ])
16
17 # Combine encoder and decoder
18 autoencoder = keras.Sequential([encoder, decoder])
```

9. **Autoencoder Model Compilation** Compile the autoencoder by combining an encoder and a decoder. It aims to learn a compressed representation of the input data (through the encoding process) and reconstruct the original input data from this compressed representation (through the decoding process). The optimizer used is *'adam'*, which is a popular optimization algorithm for training neural networks. *'mse' (Mean Squared Error)* is used as the loss function, which measures the average squared difference between the reconstructed output and the original input.

```
1 # Combine encoder and decoder
2 autoencoder = keras.Sequential([encoder, decoder])
3
4 # Compile the autoencoder
5 autoencoder.compile(optimizer='adam', loss='mse')
```

10. **Model Training:** Train an autoencoder model using the MNIST dataset. The *autoencoder.fit()* function executes the training process for the specified number of epochs, updating the model's parameters to minimize the *mse* loss between the input *(X_ train)* and its reconstructed output. The autoencoder learns to compress and reconstruct the input data in a way that minimizes the reconstruction error. The validation data *(X_ test)* is used to monitor the model's performance.

```
1 # Train the autoencoder
2 autoencoder.fit(X_train, X_train, batch_size=128, epochs=4,
      validation_data=(X_test, X_test), verbose=0)
```

11. **Model Saving:** Save the trained autoencoder model as *'mnist_ autoencoder.h5'* in the current directory using the HDF5 format.

```
1 # Save the autoencoder
2 autoencoder.save('mnist_autoencoder.h5', save_format='h5')
```

12. **Comparing Original with Decoded Images:** Compare original images *(X_ test)* and their reconstructed counterparts *(decoded_ imgs)* produced by the loaded autoencoder model, i.e., *load_ model('mnist_ autoencoder.h5')*. It displays five pairs of images side by side-original images on the top row and their reconstructions on the bottom row-for visual inspection and comparison.

```
1  # Compare original with decoded images
2  ae = load_model('mnist_autoencoder.h5')
3  decoded_imgs = ae.predict(X_test)
4  n = 5
5  plt.figure(figsize=(20, 4))
6  for i in range(1, n+1):
7      # display original
8      ax = plt.subplot(2, n, i)
9      plt.imshow(X_test[i].reshape(28, 28))
10     ax.get_xaxis().set_visible(False)
11     ax.get_yaxis().set_visible(False)
12     # display reconstruction
13     ax = plt.subplot(2, n, i + n)
14     plt.imshow(decoded_imgs[i].reshape(28, 28))
15     ax.get_xaxis().set_visible(False)
16     ax.get_yaxis().set_visible(False)
17 plt.show()
```

The following Python code, Part 2 of the CEM example, focuses on utilizing the CEM to generate pertinent negative and pertinent positive examples that provide insights into a model's predictions. Each step of the Python code will be explained in the following.

1. **Selecting the Instance to Generate CEM Explanation:** Select and extract the data instance at index 5 from the *X_ test* dataset and reshape it to create a single-instance array *(X)*. The shape is adjusted to form a 1-sample array, which could be used for analysis or explanations.

```
1  #================================
2  ### Part 2
3  #Generate contrastive explanation
4  #Explained instance
5  idx = 5
```

```
6 X = X_test[idx].reshape((1,) + X_test[idx].shape)
```

2. **Setting up CEM Parameters:** Set CEM parameters, such as *mode, shape, kappa, beta, gamma, c_init, c_steps, max_iterations, feature_range, clip, lr, and no_info_val* to configure the CEM algorithm. These parameters control various aspects of the optimization process to generate pertinent negatives *(mode = 'PN')* or pertinent positives *(mode = 'PP')* for explaining model predictions.

```
1 # CEM parameters
2 #'PN' (Pertinent Negative) and 'PP' (Pertinent Positive). PN
     aims to find a counterfactual instance that leads to a
     different prediction, while PP aims to find a
     counterfactual that maintains the same prediction
3 mode = 'PN'
4 # Represent the shape of the instance for which the
     explanation is generated
5 shape = (1,) + X_train.shape[1:]
6 # Determine the minimum difference between the probability
     of the perturbed instance's predicted class and the
     maximum probability of other classes to be minimized
7 kappa = 0.
8 # Weight of the L1 loss term, encouraging sparsity in the
     perturbation
9 beta = .1
10 # Weight of an optional autoencoder loss term used to impose
     additional constraints on the perturbation
11 gamma = 100  # weight of the optional auto-encoder loss term
12 # Initial weight 'c' encouraging different predictions (PN)
     or the same predictions (PP) compared to the original
     instance
13 c_init = 1.
14 # Number of updates for 'c' during the optimization process
15 c_steps = 10
16 # Maximum number of iterations per value of 'c' in the
     optimization process
17 max_iterations = 1000
18 # Define the range of features for the perturbed instance
19 feature_range = (X_train.min(),X_train.max())
20 # Range for gradient clipping during optimization
21 clip = (-1000.,1000.)
22 # Initial learning rate used in optimization
23 lr = 1e-2
24 # A value or range considered as containing no information
```

```
      for prediction. Perturbations towards this value
      indicate feature removal or addition
25 no_info_val = -1.
```

3. **Initializing and Creating CEM explainer for PN:** Set the mode for generating a *Pertinent Negative (PN)* explanation, initialize the CEM explainer object and configure it with the specified parameters and models to generate CEM instances and explain model predictions based on the defined constraints and optimization criteria.

```
1 # Set the mode to pertinent negative
2 mode = 'PN'
3
4 #Initialize CEM explainer and explain instance
5 cem = CEM(cnn, mode, shape, kappa=kappa, beta=beta,
      feature_range=feature_range,
6           gamma=gamma, ae_model=ae,
      max_iterations=max_iterations,
7           c_init=c_init, c_steps=c_steps,
      learning_rate_init=lr, clip=clip,
      no_info_val=no_info_val)
8
9 # Explaination instance
10 explanation = cem.explain(X)
```

4. **Printing and Displaying Results for PN:** Print the predicted label associated with the generated Pertinent Negative instance *(explanation.PN_pred)*, and display the image representation of the Pertinent Negative instance *(explanation.PN)* reshaped to the original image dimensions (28x28 pixels).

```
1 # Print pertinent negative prediction
2 print('Pertinent negative prediction:
      {}'.format(explanation.PN_pred))
3
4 # Show the plot
5 pt.imshow(explanation.PN.reshape(28, 28));
6 plt.show()
```

5. **Initializing and Creating CEM explainer for PP:** Set the mode for generating a *Pertinent Positive (PP)* explanation, initialize the CEM explainer object and configure it with the specified parameters and models to generate CEM instances and explain model predictions based on the defined constraints and optimization criteria.

```
1  # Set the mode to pertinent positive
2  mode = 'PP'
3
4  # Initialize CEM explainer and explain instance
5  cem = CEM(cnn, mode, shape, kappa=kappa, beta=beta,
      feature_range=feature_range,
6            gamma=gamma, ae_model=ae,
      max_iterations=max_iterations,
7            c_init=c_init, c_steps=c_steps,
      learning_rate_init=lr, clip=clip,
      no_info_val=no_info_val)
8
9  # Explaination instance
10 explanation = cem.explain(X)
```

6. **Printing and Displaying Results for PP:** Print the predicted label associated with the generated Pertinent Negative instance *(explanation.PP_pred)*, and display the image representation of the Pertinent Negative instance *(explanation.PP)* reshaped to the original image dimensions (28x28 pixels).

```
1  # Print pertinent positive prediction
2  print('Pertinent positive prediction
      {}'.format(explanation.PP_pred))
3
4  # Show the plot
5  pt.imshow(explanation.PP.reshape(28, 28));
6  plt.show()
```

4.4 Summary

This chapter investigates the concepts of transparency and explainability in the context of AI, i.e., XAI. It introduces XAI and emphasizes the importance of understanding AI models' decision-making processes. Different types of explainability techniques are discussed, providing an extensive overview of approaches to improve the interpretability of AI models. Rule-based explainability methods are discussed, with a particular focus on LIME (Local Inter-

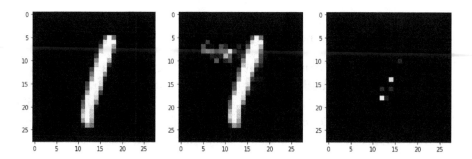

Figure 4.6: CEM Interpretations: This series of images presents CEM interpretations generated from the MNIST dataset. Each image displays the original digit "1" (top) and the pertinent negative prediction "7" from CEM explanations (middle), and pertinent positive prediction "1" from CEM explanations (bottom).

pretable Model-agnostic Explanations), a widely used technique for providing local-level explanations. The chapter also examines the practical application of LIME in explaining model predictions, followed by an introduction to SHAP (SHapley Additive exPlanations), a technique that offers both global and local interpretability. The application of LIME and SHAP in explaining adversarial image interpretations is also discussed, demonstrating how it helps to understand model predictions in the presence of adversarial attacks. Lastly, a practical example of Contrastive Explanation Method (CEM) is given along with its explanations.

Bibliography

[1] Wojciech Samek and Klaus-Robert Müller. Towards explainable artificial intelligence. *Explainable AI: interpreting, explaining and visualizing deep learning*, pages 5–22, 2019.

[2] Vinay Chamola, Vikas Hassija, A Razia Sulthana, Debshishu Ghosh, Di-

vyansh Dhingra, and Biplab Sikdar. A review of trustworthy and explainable artificial intelligence (xai). *IEEE Access*, 2023.

[3] Alejandro Barredo Arrieta, Natalia Díaz-Rodríguez, Javier Del Ser, Adrien Bennetot, Siham Tabik, Alberto Barbado, Salvador García, Sergio Gil-López, Daniel Molina, Richard Benjamins, et al. Explainable artificial intelligence (xai): Concepts, taxonomies, opportunities and challenges toward responsible ai. *Information fusion*, 58:82–115, 2020.

[4] Nida Aslam, Irfan Ullah Khan, Samiha Mirza, Alanoud AlOwayed, Fatima M Anis, Reef M Aljuaid, and Reham Baageel. Interpretable machine learning models for malicious domains detection using explainable artificial intelligence (xai). *Sustainability*, 14(12):7375, 2022.

[5] Salih Sarp, Murat Kuzlu, Emmanuel Wilson, Umit Cali, and Ozgur Guler. The enlightening role of explainable artificial intelligence in chronic wound classification. *Electronics*, 10(12):1406, 2021.

[6] Eric Benhamou, Jean-Jacques Ohana, David Saltiel, Beatrice Guez, and Steve Ohana. Explainable ai (xai) models applied to planning in financial markets. *Université Paris-Dauphine Research Paper*, (3862437), 2021.

[7] Jeff Druce, Michael Harradon, and James Tittle. Explainable artificial intelligence (xai) for increasing user trust in deep reinforcement learning driven autonomous systems. *arXiv preprint arXiv:2106.03775*, 2021.

[8] Eilert Henriksen, Ugur Halden, Murat Kuzlu, and Umit Cali. Electrical load forecasting utilizing an explainable artificial intelligence (xai) tool on norwegian residential buildings. In *2022 International Conference on Smart Energy Systems and Technologies (SEST)*, pages 1–6. IEEE, 2022.

[9] Julie Gerlings, Arisa Shollo, and Ioanna Constantiou. Reviewing the need for explainable artificial intelligence (xai). *arXiv preprint arXiv:2012.01007*, 2020.

[10] Carson K. Leung, Evan W.R. Madill, Joglas Souza, and Christine Y. Zhang. Towards trustworthy artificial intelligence in healthcare. In *2022 IEEE 10th International Conference on Healthcare Informatics (ICHI)*, pages 626–632, 2022. doi: 10.1109/ICHI54592.2022.00127.

[11] Jean Jacques Ohana, Steve Ohana, Eric Benhamou, David Saltiel, and Beatrice Guez. Explainable ai (xai) models applied to the multi-agent environment of financial markets. In *Explainable and Transparent AI and Multi-Agent Systems: Third International Workshop, EXTRAAMAS 2021, Virtual Event, May 3–7, 2021, Revised Selected Papers 3*, pages 189–207. Springer, 2021.

[12] Harsh Mankodiya, Mohammad S. Obaidat, Rajesh Gupta, and Sudeep Tanwar. Xai-av: Explainable artificial intelligence for trust management in autonomous vehicles. In *2021 International Conference on Communications, Computing, Cybersecurity, and Informatics (CCCI)*, pages 1–5, 2021. doi: 10.1109/CCCI52664.2021.9583190.

[13] Murat Kuzlu, Umit Cali, Vinayak Sharma, and Ozgur Guler. Gaining insight into solar photovoltaic power generation forecasting utilizing explainable artificial intelligence tools. *IEEE Access*, 8:187814–187823, 2020. doi: 10.1109/ACCESS.2020.3031477.

[14] Jasper van der Waa, Elisabeth Nieuwburg, Anita Cremers, and Mark Neerincx. Evaluating xai: A comparison of rule-based and example-based explanations. *Artificial Intelligence*, 291:103404, 2021.

[15] Xin Man and Ernest Chan. The best way to select features? comparing mda, lime, and shap. *The Journal of Financial Data Science Winter*, 3(1): 127–139, 2021.

[16] Timo Speith. A review of taxonomies of explainable artificial intelligence (xai) methods. In *Proceedings of the 2022 ACM Conference on Fairness, Accountability, and Transparency*, pages 2239–2250, 2022.

[17] Jesus M Darias, Belén Díaz-Agudo, and Juan A Recio-Garcia. A systematic review on model-agnostic xai libraries. In *ICCBR Workshops*, pages 28–39, 2021.

[18] Jürgen Dieber and Sabrina Kirrane. Why model why? assessing the strengths and limitations of lime. *arXiv preprint arXiv:2012.00093*, 2020.

[19] Michael Chromik. reshape: A framework for interactive explanations in xai based on shap. 2020.

[20] Jokin Labaien, Ekhi Zugasti, and Xabier De Carlos. Contrastive explanations for a deep learning model on time-series data. In *International Conference on Big Data Analytics and Knowledge Discovery*, pages 235–244. Springer, 2020.

[21] Harsha Nori, Samuel Jenkins, Paul Koch, and Rich Caruana. Interpretml: A unified framework for machine learning interpretability. *arXiv preprint arXiv:1909.09223*, 2019.

[22] Janis Klaise, Arnaud Van Looveren, Giovanni Vacanti, and Alexandru Coca. Alibi explain: Algorithms for explaining machine learning models. *The Journal of Machine Learning Research*, 22(1):8194–8200, 2021.

[23] Saikat Das, Namita Agarwal, Deepak Venugopal, Frederick T Sheldon, and Sajjan Shiva. Taxonomy and survey of interpretable machine learning method. In *2020 IEEE Symposium Series on Computational Intelligence (SSCI)*, pages 670–677. IEEE, 2020.

[24] Salih Sarp, Ferhat Ozgur Catak, Murat Kuzlu, Umit Cali, Huseyin Kusetogullari, Yanxiao Zhao, Gungor Ates, and Ozgur Guler. An xai approach for covid-19 detection using transfer learning with x-ray images. *Heliyon*, 9(4), 2023.

[25] Noratikah Nordin, Zurinahni Zainol, Mohd Halim Mohd Noor, and Lai Fong Chan. An explainable predictive model for suicide attempt risk using an ensemble learning and shapley additive explanations (shap) approach. *Asian journal of psychiatry*, 79:103316, 2023.

[26] Flavio Lorenzo. *Techniques for trustworthy artificial intelligence systems in the context of a loan approval process*. PhD thesis, Politecnico di Torino, 2019.

5 Privacy Preserving Artificial Intelligence: Federated Learning

Imagine your smart traffic sign-reading computer is like a helpful friend who wants to learn from different people to become even brighter. Now, let's talk about privacy-preserving AI and a cool concept called federated learning (FL).

So, your friend wants to learn about new types of traffic signs from people worldwide. But here's the thing, it cares about everyone's privacy. It doesn't want to know exactly where people live or all the details about them. It just wants to get more innovative in a way that keeps everyone's personal stuff private.

Here's where FL comes in like in Figure 5.1. Instead of bringing all the data to one central place, your friend sends a little helper to each person's device. This helper learns from the data on that device without actually taking it away. It's like your friend sending a mini-teacher to each person to learn about the traffic signs they've seen.

So, let's say someone in Japan has seen a unique traffic sign your friend's computer hasn't encountered before. The mini-teacher learns about that particular sign on the person's device without knowing anything else about them.

Then, all these mini-teachers share what they've learned with your friend's computer. It's like a big group chat where everyone contributes what they know without revealing personal details. Your friend's computer gets smarter

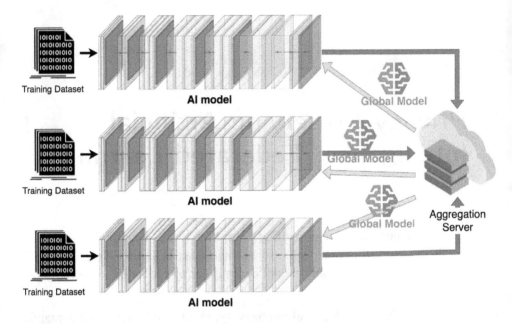

Figure 5.1: FL based Privacy Preserving

without ever seeing the individual data from each person.

This way, your friend learns from people's experiences worldwide, but everyone's personal information stays private. It's like a teamwork approach to getting brighter, where everyone helps without revealing their secrets. That's privacy-preserving AI and FL - making AI smarter while keeping your stuff safe.

5.1 Introduction to Privacy Preserving Artificial Intelligence

The use of Artificial Intelligence (AI) in many areas has already proven to be successful, and its integration continues to revolutionize a variety of industries

[1]. From healthcare [2] to finance [3], energy [4], transportation [5], and manufacturing [6], AI has become essential and one of the main tools. However, security and privacy concerns about the use of AI have increased in these high-risk domains. Fortunately, Privacy-preserving AI can deal with these concerns, which utilize AI algorithms, models, and systems while ensuring the protection and preservation of individuals' privacy rights and sensitive data [7]. In healthcare, it enables the development of AI models for diagnosis using patient records while safeguarding sensitive information. Financial institutions leverage privacy-preserving techniques for fraud detection and risk assessment, ensuring customer privacy. Within the Internet of Things (IoT), employing privacy-preserving AI allows devices to process data locally, mitigating the risk of data breaches. AI-powered personalized advertising thrives without disclosing individual user data, maintaining user privacy. Additionally, in smart cities, urban data analysis for city planning occurs without compromising citizens' privacy. Furthermore, in the realm of research, scientists collaborate on data-intensive projects while preserving dataset privacy, fostering knowledge dissemination and cooperation. Autonomous vehicles powered by AI are transforming transportation, offering safer and more efficient travel. In manufacturing, AI-enabled automation has optimized production lines, ensuring precision and reducing errors. AI's potential to revolutionize agriculture through predictive analytics, smart sensors, and automated machinery is also becoming increasingly evident, with the promise of higher crop yields and sustainability.

As AI algorithms continue to develop and learn from large datasets, their adaptability and problem-solving capabilities are increasing, opening up new possibilities across industries. AI algorithms require a great deal of data and computing power, which can lead to privacy issues due to the possibility of data breaches and changing regulations [8]. In addition, ethical issues such as data privacy, bias reduction, and responsible AI are still essential for its further development and approval. Privacy-preserving AI is a novel and developing area within AI that focuses on creating techniques and technologies to protect individual data and confidential information while still taking advantage of the power of AI and ML [9]. It meets the urgent need to reconcile the advantages of data-driven insights with ethical and legal concerns related to privacy.

Recently, several papers on privacy-preserving AI have been published in the literature. The study [10] provides a comprehensive survey of privacy-preserving techniques, focusing on Privacy-Preserving Deep Learning (PPDL) and Machine Learning as a Service (MLaaS) frameworks. Detailed comparisons between cutting-edge PPDL methods are presented, aiming to classify adversarial models in PPDL by identifying potential attacks and proposing corresponding solutions. The authors in [11] addressed threats (Reconstruction Attacks, Model Inversion Attacks, Membership Inference Attacks) and most widely used cryptographic-based solutions (Homomorphic encryption, garbled circuits, secret sharing, and secure processors) for privacy-enhancing AI/ML. Adversarial attacks on ML models also pose threats, necessitating privacy-preserving ML (PPML) solutions. The authors in [12] proposed a Phase, Guarantee, and Utility (PGU) triad-based model to evaluate and understand various privacy-preserving machine learning (PPML) solutions. This model aims to decompose and assess the privacy-preserving functionalities of different PPML approaches systematically. They also addressed the challenges and research directions in PPML while stressing the requirement of interdisciplinary effort from machine need for collaboration between the machine learning, distributed systems, and security-privacy communities. The study [13] presents CryptoDL, a framework designed to address privacy concerns associated with machine learning algorithms that access sensitive data, enabling the application of deep neural network algorithms to encrypted data. It demonstrates the feasibility and practicality of training neural networks using encrypted data, making predictions on encrypted data, and returning encrypted predictions. The framework's applicability is showcased through experiments with numerous datasets, demonstrating its ability to provide accurate privacy-preserving training and classification while maintaining data encryption.

This chapter provides an overview of AI to maintain privacy and meet trusting AI requirements. It introduces the concept of Privacy-Preserving AI, its significance, core techniques, and real-world applications performed in Python programming language. This chapter is designed for readers with a background in data privacy AI who have limited experience with privacy-preserving AI tools and methods. If you are already familiar with AI for data privacy, skip the initial sections and go straight to practical examples.

5.2 Significance of Privacy-Preserving AI and Core Techniques

Privacy-preserving AI methods have emerged to ensure the protection of the personal, and their impact has significantly increased in AI environments. This section briefly discusses the importance of privacy-preserving AI along with its core techniques.

5.2.1 Significance of Privacy-Preserving AI

Privacy-preserving AI is crucial for protecting sensitive data while leveraging AI technologies that ensure confidentiality, integrity and control over personal information in an era of increasing data-driven decision making and technological advancements [14]. The significance of AI that preserves privacy can be summarized in terms of data privacy, legal compliance, trust, and ethics.

■ **Data Privacy**: Privacy-preserving AI allows organizations and individuals to harness data without compromising privacy. It serves as a protection mechanism, ensuring that sensitive and personal information remains protected. By implementing techniques such as differential privacy, Federated Learning (FL), and homomorphic encryption (HE), AI systems can extract important information from data without compromising the confidentiality of personal information of individuals.

■ **Privacy Laws and Regulations**: Organizations must guarantee that the data utilized in AI systems are collected, stored, and processed in compliance with privacy laws and regulations to protect the privacy rights of individuals. Privacy-preserving AI helps organizations achieve that by integrating techniques that prioritize data privacy and confidentiality as well as avoid any law sanction due to data misuse or violations.

■ **Trustness**: In AI systems, multiple stakeholders may need to work together in a trusted environment. Privacy-preserving AI significantly contributes to establishing trust among these stakeholders by protecting the privacy rights of individuals from threats.

5.2.2 Core Techniques

The core techniques used in Privacy-Preserving AI include FL, differential privacy, HE, and secure multi-party computation (SMPC) [15]. Each core technique is briefly explained as follows:

■ **Federated Learning**: Federated learning (FL) is a type of machine learning that trains AI models on local devices and only exchanges model updates, instead of raw data, with the central server [16]. This approach significantly increases data security and privacy as well as allows the use of computing resources efficiently.

■ **Differential Privacy**: Differential Privacy is a mathematical framework that aims at ensuring the privacy of individuals in a dataset by adding noise to the data before processing AI algorithms [17]. This approach ensures that sensitive information will be removed from the data, while still allowing useful analysis to be performed properly.

■ **Homomorphic Encryption**: In the Homomorphic Encryption (HE) approach, the computations are performed directly on encrypted data without decryption. It means that sensitive information remains encrypted throughout processing, including model training, evaluation, and inference. Thus, privacy is maintained, and raw information is never exposed during these operations [18].

■ **Secure Multi-Party Computation**: Secure Multi-Party Computation (SMPC) technique facilitates the collaborative computation of AI models among multiple parties without revealing individual inputs [19]. Multiple parties are involved, and each holds its private dataset. SMPC enables computation of the collective data without sharing the raw information.

5.3 Federated Learning

FL is a distributed machine learning approach that enables multiple parties to collaborate on a machine learning model without sharing their raw data. In FL, each part keeps its data locally and independently trains a model using its respective dataset. After this local training phase, the models' updates and parameters are shared with the central server to be combined or aggregated to form a global model. This global model is then transmitted back to each party, allowing them to update their local model with the newly acquired global updates. The iterative process continues until the desired level of accuracy or performance is reached.

5.3.1 Process

The process can be divided into three fundamental stages, namely *Initialization, Local Training, and Aggregation*. This approach enables collaborative model training across decentralized environments while protecting data privacy, fostering collective learning from distributed datasets, and producing a refined global model representative of the aggregated knowledge from diverse sources. These stages are explained as follows:

■ **Initialization**: In this stage, the parties agree on the global model architecture and the hyperparameters, as well as exchanging information on the data distribution; however, it does not cover the actual data.

■ **Local Training**: In this stage, each party trains a local model on its own data. This phase is crucial as it enables learning from decentralized data sources while preserving data privacy and confidentiality.

■ **Aggregation**: In this stage, the local models are aggregated to create a global model using one of the FL strategies, e.g., Federated Averaging (FedAvg). Local models, independently trained on disparate datasets, are merged to create a global model. Through FL aggregation strategies, the updated model parameters or gradients from individual parties are integrated at a central server. The global model can also be refined through secure and privacy-preserving aggregation techniques, encapsulating collective knowledge from diverse local models without exposing raw data.

5.3.2 Types of Federated Learning

Federated Learning (FL) supports a variety of approaches for collaborative machine learning among multiple parties while preserving data privacy. There are two primary FL types: Horizontal FL and Vertical FL. They are briefly explained below.

5.3.2.1 Horizontal Federated Learning

In this FL type, the parties involved possess the same characteristics yet have different datasets. In this scenario, each party trains a local model on its data and then aggregates the models to create a global model. For example, in a healthcare application, each hospital may have data on the same medical conditions for different patients. This type of FL is beneficial when the parties involved wish to combine knowledge from various data sources without compromising individual data privacy.

A more detailed explanation is given with some math equations as follows:

Suppose we have N parties, and each party i has a dataset $\mathcal{D}_i = (\mathbf{x}_{i,j}, y_{i,j})_{j=1}^{m_i}$, where $\mathbf{x}_{i,j}$ is a feature vector and $y_{i,j}$ is the corresponding label. Let $f(\mathbf{x}; w)$ be a model parameterized by w, where w is the weight vector. The goal of FL is to find a global model w^* that minimizes the overall loss function:

$$w^* = \arg\min_{w} \sum_{i=1}^{N} \frac{1}{m_i} \sum_{j=1}^{m_i} \mathcal{L}(f(\mathbf{x}_{i,j}; \theta), y_{i,j}) \qquad (5.1)$$

where $\mathcal{L}(\cdot)$ is a loss function, such as mean squared error or cross-entropy loss.

In the horizontal FL setting, each party has the same feature space, so the model architecture is the same across all parties. Each party trains a local model w_i on its own data using the same model architecture and hyperparameters.

After local training, the parties aggregate their local models to create a global model. One popular algorithm for horizontal FL is Federated Averaging (FedAvg). In FedAvg, the global model is obtained by taking a weighted average of the local models:

$$\theta^+ = \sum_{i=1}^{N} \frac{n_i}{n} \theta_i, \qquad (5.2)$$

where n_i is the number of samples in party i, and $n = \sum_{i=1}^{N} n_i$ is the total number of samples. The parties then update their local models using the global model:

$$\theta_i' = \text{ClientUpdate}(\theta^+; \mathcal{D}_i), \qquad (5.3)$$

where ClientUpdate$(\cdot)$ is the local training function that updates the local model using the global model and the local data.

5.3.2.2 Vertical Federated Learning

Vertical FL (VFL) is a type of FL in which data from different sources is horizontally partitioned, but each partition has a different set of features.

In VFL, instead of horizontally partitioning the data (i.e., dividing data into non-overlapping subsets), the data is partitioned based on its features. In other words, each party has a unique set of features, but the data points themselves are shared across the parties.

Formally, let $\mathcal{D}$ be the dataset that needs to be learned and $P = \{P_1, P_2, ..., P_m\}$ be the set of m parties, where each party P_i holds a subset of features of the dataset $\mathcal{D}$. Then, the data can be represented as:

$$\mathcal{D} = \{(\mathbf{x}_1^1, \mathbf{x}_1^2, \ldots, \mathbf{x}_1^m, y_1), \ldots, (\mathbf{x}_n^1, \mathbf{x}_n^2, \ldots, \mathbf{x}_n^m, y_n)\} \tag{5.4}$$

where $\mathbf{x}_j^i$ is the ith feature of the jth data point at party P_i, y_j is the label of the jth data point, and n is the total number of data points in the dataset.

VFL can be used to learn a global model by utilizing the data from all parties. The goal is to train a model w that minimizes the following loss function:

$$\min_{w \in \mathbb{R}^d} \frac{1}{n} \sum_{j=1}^{n} \mathcal{L}(f(\mathbf{x}_j, w), y_j) \tag{5.5}$$

where $f(\mathbf{x}_j, w)$ is the output of the model w for the input $\mathbf{x}_j$, y_j is the label of the input, $\mathcal{L}$ is the loss function (e.g., cross-entropy loss), and d is the number of model parameters.

In VFL, each party P_i trains the local model with its feature subsets and iteratively updates the gradients with a coordinator or central server, who aggregates them to update a global model. w. The update rule is given as follows:

$$w_{t+1} = w_t - \eta \sum_{i=1}^{m} \frac{1}{|D_i|} \nabla_w \ell_i(w_t) \tag{5.6}$$

where t is the iteration number, η is the learning rate, $|\mathcal{D}_i|$ is the number of data points held by party P_i, and $\nabla_w l_i(w_t)$ is the gradient of the local loss function of party P_i at iteration t with respect to the model parameters w.

5.3.3 Federated Learning Algorithm Strategies

FL approach can be achieved through a variety of strategies, such as "FedAdagrad", "FedSGD" "FedAdam", "FedAvg", "FedProx", "FedYogi", and "Scaffold". Most of these strategies are briefly explained in [20]. This section focuses on two of them, FedAvg, and FedSGD, and investigates them.

5.3.3.1 Federated Averaging (FedAvg)

Federated averaging (FedAvg) is a ML approach that enables multiple parties to collaborate in training an ML model without sharing their local data. This technique is highly efficient in communication algorithms when dealing with a large number of clients. All communication is handled through the central client. The model parameters are then aggregated by taking the average across all parties.

Here is the FedAvg algorithm in detail:

1. **Initialization:** The central server initializes a global model with random weights, and sends it to all clients.
2. **Client Training:** Each client performs local training on its own data using the current model parameters. Specifically, each client i updates the model by computing the gradient of its local loss function $\mathcal{L}_i(w)$ with respect to the model parameters w, using a mini-batch of data $\mathcal{B}_i$:

$$g_i = \frac{1}{|\mathcal{B}_i|} \sum_{(\mathbf{x},y) \in \mathcal{B}_i} \nabla_w \mathcal{B}_i(w; \mathbf{x}, y) \qquad (5.7)$$

where $|\mathcal{B}_i|$ is the size of the mini-batch, and $\nabla_w \mathcal{B}_i(w; \mathbf{x}, y)$ is the gradient of the loss function with respect to w evaluated on the input-output pair $(\mathbf{x}, y)$.

3. **Model Aggregation:** Each client sends its updated model parameters w_i to the central server, which computes the new global model by averaging them:

$$w_{\text{new}} = \frac{1}{N} \sum_{i=1}^{N} w_i \qquad (5.8)$$

4. **Model Update:** The central server sends the new global model w_{new} back to all clients, which use it to initialize their models for the next round of training.
5. **Repeat:** Steps 2-4 are repeated for a number of iterations, until the global model converges to a good solution.

5.3.3.2 Federated Stochastic Gradient Descent (FedSGD)

In FedSGD, it is aimed to optimize a global model using local updates from multiple clients in a FL setting. Let's denote the set of clients as $\mathcal{C}$, and each client i has its own local dataset denoted as $\mathcal{D}_i$. The goal is to find the optimal global model weights w^* by aggregating the local updates from each client.

The FedSGD algorithm consists of the following steps:

1. Initialization: Initialize the global model weights w_0.
2. Client Update: For each client $i \in \mathcal{C}$, perform the following steps:
   - Sample a mini-batch $\mathcal{B}_i$ from the local dataset $\mathcal{D}_i$.
   - Compute the local gradient using the mini-batch:

$$g_i = \frac{1}{|\mathcal{D}_i|} \sum_{(\mathbf{x},y) \in \mathcal{B}_i} \nabla_w \mathcal{L}_i(w; \mathbf{x}, y), \qquad (5.9)$$

   where $\mathcal{L}_i(w; \mathbf{x}, y)$ is the loss function of client i for the model weights w and the input-label pair $(\mathbf{x}, y)$, and ∇w denotes the gradient with respect to the weights w.
3. Aggregation: Compute the average of the local gradients to obtain the aggregated gradient:

$$\bar{g} = \frac{1}{|C|} \sum_{i \in C} g_i \qquad (5.10)$$

4. Global Update: Update the global model weights using the aggregated gradient:

$$w_{\text{new}} = w - \eta \cdot \bar{g} \qquad (5.11)$$

where η is the learning rate.

5. Repeat Steps 2-4 for a certain number of iterations or until convergence.

5.4 Advantages and Challenges in Federated Learning

FL is considered one of the most promising techniques in the scope of trustworthy AI. Compared to traditional machine learning approaches, the FL approach has several advantages; however, it also presents challenges. This section summarizes them.

The main advantages in FL can be summarized as follows:

■ **Privacy**: FL approach ensures that sensitive information remains locally stored and is not exposed during the learning process. By exchanging only model updates rather than raw data, FL mitigates privacy risks and adheres to stringent data protection regulations.

■ **Scalability**: FL can be used to train models on a large amount of data that is distributed across multiple parties. This approach accommodates the training of machine learning models using data distributed across multiple devices, servers, or locations. FL enables collaborative learning from decentralized datasets without necessitating data aggregation into a central repository. This distributed nature of FL facilitates scalability, allowing models to be trained on a larger and more diverse dataset without centralizing sensitive information.

■ **Efficiency**: FL can reduce communication overhead compared to traditional distributed machine learning approaches since the parties only need to exchange the model parameters, not the data. Compared to conventional distributed machine learning frameworks, FL significantly reduces communication overhead. Instead of transmitting entire datasets across the network, FL leverages the transmission of lightweight model parameters or gradients among the participating parties. This streamlined communication protocol minimizes bandwidth usage and computational burden, resulting in more efficient model updates and faster convergence. As a result, FL offers a more resource-efficient approach, especially in bandwidth-constrained or latency-sensitive environments, by focusing communication solely on model updates rather than bulk data transfer.

During the AI/ML process, many challenges are present. These challenges underscore the delicate balance in ML between the need for extensive datasets to ensure model accuracy and the difficulties in data collection, managing, and utilizing large volumes of relevant and diverse data to prevent biases or inaccuracies in model predictions.

These challenges can be summarized as follows:

■ **Dependency on Data Volume**: Machine learning heavily relies on data, where larger datasets often lead to more accurate results. To achieve precision, substantial amounts of data are essential to train ML models effectively. They process extensive input data to derive accurate outcomes, aiming to replicate real-world scenarios.

■ **Advancements in Knowledge Extraction**: Recent advances in AI/ML have facilitated extensive learning from vast datasets. These developments have significantly improved storage efficiency, processing capabilities, and computational capabilities in substantial datasets, while raising challenges in collecting adequate data for specific projects due to data unavailability or scarcity.

■ **Dataset Collection**: Collecting a significant volume of datasets can be hard because of difficulties in finding all the different kinds of data required for comprehensive model training. Not having enough varied data can make the program less accurate and not work as well with new information.

■ **Impact of Limited Data**: A limited dataset may sometimes yield outputs that appear more accurate, but could lead to misleading or inaccurate outcomes. Insufficient data might result in overfitting, where the model performs exceptionally well on the limited data, but fails to generalize well to new, unseen data, thus providing misleading conclusions.

5.5 Practical Examples

This section will explore FL through practical implementations in Python using the Flower framework. Flower is a user-friendly and versatile framework that enables developers to construct FL systems with ease. It allows practitioners to create distributed ML setups where multiple devices or nodes can collaborate to train a global model while preserving data privacy. Examples of Flower's use will demonstrate how to organize FL workflows, coordinate communication between devices, and aggregate model updates securely. Flower is designed with several core principles in mind, such as flexibility, extensibility, framework-agnosticism, and codebase maintainability. The framework is intended to make FL accessible to a wide range of users. The Flower community actively creates tutorials and documentation to help users understand and implement FL. The tutorials cover fundamental concepts, strategies, and custom clients for FL. The framework also provides a collection of community-contributed experiments known as Flower Baselines. These experiments replicate the work of FL publications, allowing researchers to evaluate new ideas and build on existing baselines.

The following code segment is used to launch a Flower server, which is a component of the Flower (flwr) system for FL. The server is responsible for organizing and controlling FL activities. Let's go through the code line by line.

1. **Importing Libraries:** Import the flower framework library, i.e., *flwr*.

```
1 # Import libraries
2 import flwr as fl
```

2. **Starting Flower Server for FL:** Start Flower server.
   fl.server.ServerConfig class configures the server's behavior. In this code, a configuration object is created with a specified number of rounds *(num_-rounds)*. In FL, rounds typically represent iterations of model training and aggregation. The *server_address* parameter specifies the network address at which the server will listen for incoming connections. In this case, it is set to *0.0.0.0:8080* and *0.0.0.0* address means the server will listen on all available network interfaces. Port 8080 is the chosen port for commu-

nication. The *fl.server.start_server* function initiates the Flower server. This function takes the server's address and configuration as parameters.

```
1  # Import libraries
2  import flwr as fl
3
4  # Start Flower server
5  fl.server.start_server(
6    server_address="0.0.0.0:8080",
7    config=fl.server.ServerConfig(num_rounds=10),
8  )
```

Next, the script sets up a Flower client to participate in FL. This script creates a simple FL scenario with a server and a client. During each communication round, the client downloads the global model, performs local training on the MNIST data, and uploads the updated model to the server. This process is repeated for the configured number of rounds. First, it loads the MNIST dataset and creates a simple feedforward neural network model using TensorFlow. The Python source code will be explained line by line below.

1. **Importing Libraries:** Import required libraries, including *flwr, tensorflow and numpy*.

```
1  #Import libraries
2  import flwr as fl
3  import tensorflow as tf
4  import numpy as np
```

2. **Loading the Dataset:** Load the MNIST dataset, which contains images of hand-written digits and their corresponding labels.

```
1  # Load the MNIST dataset
2  (x_train, y_train), (x_test, y_test) =
       tf.keras.datasets.mnist.load_data()
```

3. **Defining the Model:** Define the model. The model consists of a flattening layer, a dense (fully connected) layer with *ReLU* activation, a dropout layer, and another dense layer without an activation function (for logits).

```
1  # Define the model architecture
2  model = tf.keras.Sequential([
3      tf.keras.layers.Flatten(input_shape=(28, 28)),
```

```
4        tf.keras.layers.Dense(128, activation="relu"),
5        tf.keras.layers.Dropout(0.2),
6        tf.keras.layers.Dense(10),
7 ])
```

4. **Model Compilation:** Compile the model using the *RMSprop optimizer and Sparse Categorical Crossentropy* loss function.

```
1 # Compile the model
2 model.compile(optimizer="rmsprop",
       loss=tf.keras.losses.SparseCategoricalCrossentropy(
       from_logits=True ), metrics=["accuracy"])
```

5. **Defining Flower Client Class:** Define a Flower Client class, which extends the *fl.client.NumPyClient* class. This client has the following methods for obtaining model parameters, fitting the model with local data, and evaluating the model:

   ■ *get_parameters(self, config)* : Returns the current model's weights.

   ■ *fit(self, parameters, config)* : Receives global model parameters, sets the local model's weights, and fits the local model with the MNIST training data.

   ■ *evaluate(self, parameters, config)* : Receives global model parameters, sets the local model's weights, evaluates the model on the MNIST test data, and saves the global model as *global-model.tf.*

```
1 # Define Flower client
2 class MnistClient(fl.client.NumPyClient):
3     def get_parameters(self, config):
4         return model.get_weights()
5
6     def fit(self, parameters, config):
7         model.set_weights(parameters)
8         model.fit(x_train, y_train, epochs=10,
    batch_size=2000, verbose=0)  # You can adjust batch_size
9         return model.get_weights(), len(x_train), {}
10
11     def evaluate(self, parameters, config):
12         model.set_weights(parameters)
13         loss, accuracy = model.evaluate(x_test, y_test)
14         model.save("global-model.tf")
15         return loss, len(x_test), {"accuracy": accuracy}
```

6. **Starting Flower Client:** Start a flower client. The Flower client is initiated and connected to the server at the specified server address. The 'server_address' argument specifies the address of the Flower server where the client will communicate.

```
# Start Flower client
fl.client.start_numpy_client(server_address="[::]:8080",
    client=MnistClient())
```

The following code snippet visualizes and prints the computed metrics, including *accuracy, precision, recall, and F1 score*. Additionally, the confusion matrix is printed for further analysis. To visualize the confusion matrix, a heatmap is plotted using Matplotlib. This analysis aids in understanding the global model's performance on the MNIST dataset, helping to identify areas for improvement and assessing its suitability for real-world applications.

The code is utilized to initiate a Flower server, which serves as a crucial element of the *Flower (flwr)* system for Federated Learning (FL). The server's primary role is to manage and oversee FL operations. The subsequent sections explain each part of the code segment.

1. **Importing Libraries:** Import libraries to perform numerical computations using *numpy*, machine learning or deep learning operations using *TensorFlow*, evaluate model performance using various metrics from *scikit-learn*, and create visualizations using *Matplotlib*.

```
# Import libraries
import numpy as np
import tensorflow as tf
from sklearn.metrics import accuracy_score, precision_score,
    recall_score, f1_score, confusion_matrix
import matplotlib.pyplot as plt
```

2. **Loading the Dataset:** Load the MNIST dataset, which contains images of hand-written digits and their corresponding labels.

```
# Load the MNIST dataset
(X_train, y_train), (X_test, y_test) =
    keras.datasets.mnist.load_data()
```

3. **Loading the Global Model:** Load the global model saved as *global-model.tf*. The global model has been previously trained in a FL setting and will be evaluated using the MNIST test data.

```
1  # Load the global model
2  loaded_model = tf.keras.models.load_model('global-model.tf')
```

4. **Predicting Labels:** Predict the label of each class for every sample in the test dataset, and *y_ pred_ classes* will hold the predicted class labels for each sample in *x_ test*. These predictions can be used for further analysis, evaluation, or visualization of the model's performance.

```
1  # Make predictions
2  y_pred = loaded_model.predict(x_test)
3  y_pred_classes = np.argmax(y_pred, axis=1)
```

5. **Evaluating the Model:** Evaluate model by calculating the metrics using *scikit-learn*, i.e., *accuracy_ score, precision_ score, recall_ score, f1_ score*, based on the true labels *(y_ test)* and predicted labels *(y_ pred_ classes)* obtained from the model predictions. These metrics provide insight into the model's overall performance and ability to classify digits in the MNIST dataset correctly.

```
1  # Calculate accuracy
2  accuracy = accuracy_score(y_test, y_pred_classes)
3  # Calculate precision, recall, and F1-score
4  precision = precision_score(y_test, y_pred_classes,
       average='weighted')
5  recall = recall_score(y_test, y_pred_classes,
       average='weighted')
6  f1 = f1_score(y_test, y_pred_classes, average='weighted')
```

6. **Computing the Confusion Matrix:** Compute the confusion matrix based on the true labels *(y_ test)* and the predicted labels *(y_ pred_-classes)*. It quantifies the number of true positive, true negative, false positive, and false negative predictions for each class (digit) in the dataset.

```
1  # Create a confusion matrix
2  conf_matrix = confusion_matrix(y_test, y_pred_classes)
```

7. **Displaying the Results:** Print out and display the results of some evaluation metrics, including *accuracy, precision, recall, F1-score, and the confusion matrix*.

```
1  # Display the results
2  print(f'Accuracy: {accuracy}')
3  print(f'Precision: {precision}')
4  print(f'Recall: {recall}')
5  print(f'F1-Score: {f1}')
6  print('Confusion Matrix:')
7  print(conf_matrix)
```

8. **Plotting Confusion Matrix:** Plot and display the results of the confusion matrix to visualize the overall performance of the model.

```
1  # Plot the confusion matrix
2  plt.figure(figsize=(8, 6))
3  plt.imshow(conf_matrix, interpolation='nearest',
       cmap=plt.cm.Blues)
4  plt.title('Confusion Matrix')
5  plt.colorbar()
6  tick_marks = np.arange(10)
7  plt.xticks(tick_marks, range(10), rotation=45)
8  plt.yticks(tick_marks, range(10))
9  plt.xlabel('Predicted')
10 plt.ylabel('True')
11
12 # Show the plot
13 plt.show()
```

5.6 Summary

This chapter overviews privacy-preserving AI and FL. It introduces the importance of privacy-preserving AI and its core techniques. Then, the chapter covers FL with its various types and strategies. Furthermore, it highlights the advantages associated with FL. Finally, the chapter provides practical examples to demonstrate Privacy-Preserving AI techniques using the Flower framework in Python.

Bibliography

[1] Yogesh K Dwivedi, Laurie Hughes, Elvira Ismagilova, Gert Aarts, Crispin Coombs, Tom Crick, Yanqing Duan, Rohita Dwivedi, John Edwards, Aled Eirug, et al. Artificial intelligence (ai): Multidisciplinary perspectives on emerging challenges, opportunities, and agenda for research, practice and policy. *International Journal of Information Management*, 57:101994, 2021.

[2] Salih Sarp, Murat Kuzlu, Manisa Pipattanasomporn, and Ozgur Guler. Simultaneous wound border segmentation and tissue classification using a conditional generative adversarial network. *The Journal of Engineering*, 2021(3):125–134, 2021.

[3] Longbing Cao. Ai in finance: challenges, techniques, and opportunities. *ACM Computing Surveys (CSUR)*, 55(3):1–38, 2022.

[4] Imran Rahman, Murat Kuzlu, and Saifur Rahman. Power disaggregation of combined hvac loads using supervised machine learning algorithms. *Energy and Buildings*, 172:57–66, 2018.

[5] Adel W Sadek. Artificial intelligence applications in transportation. *Transportation Research Circular*, pages 1–7, 2007.

[6] Bo-hu Li, Bao-cun Hou, Wen-tao Yu, Xiao-bing Lu, and Chun-wei Yang. Applications of artificial intelligence in intelligent manufacturing: a review. *Frontiers of Information Technology & Electronic Engineering*, 18:86–96, 2017.

[7] Saeed Iqbal, Adnan N Qureshi, Musaed Alhussein, Khursheed Aurangzeb, Khalid Javeed, and Rizwan Ali Naqvi. Privacy-preserving collaborative ai for distributed deep learning with cross-sectional data. *Multimedia Tools and Applications*, pages 1–23, 2023.

[8] Karl Manheim and Lyric Kaplan. Artificial intelligence: Risks to privacy and democracy. *Yale JL & Tech.*, 21:106, 2019.

[9] James Curzon, Tracy Ann Kosa, Rajen Akalu, and Khalil El-Khatib. Privacy and artificial intelligence. *IEEE Transactions on Artificial Intelligence*, 2(2):96–108, 2021.

[10] Harry Chandra Tanuwidjaja, Rakyong Choi, Seunggeun Baek, and Kwangjo Kim. Privacy-preserving deep learning on machine learning as a serviceâa comprehensive survey. *IEEE Access*, 8:167425–167447, 2020.

[11] Mohammad Al-Rubaie and J. Morris Chang. Privacy-preserving machine learning: Threats and solutions. *IEEE Security Privacy*, 17(2):49–58, 2019. doi: 10.1109/MSEC.2018.2888775.

[12] Runhua Xu, Nathalie Baracaldo, and James Joshi. Privacy-preserving machine learning: Methods, challenges and directions. *arXiv preprint arXiv:2108.04417*, 2021.

[13] Ehsan Hesamifard, Hassan Takabi, Mehdi Ghasemi, and Rebecca N Wright. Privacy-preserving machine learning as a service. *Proc. Priv. Enhancing Technol.*, 2018(3):123–142, 2018.

[14] Tjerk Timan and Zoltan Mann. Data protection in the era of artificial intelligence: trends, existing solutions and recommendations for privacy-preserving technologies. In *The Elements of Big Data Value: Foundations of the Research and Innovation Ecosystem*, pages 153–175. Springer International Publishing Cham, 2021.

[15] Elif Ustundag Soykan, Leyli Karaçay, Ferhat Karakoç, and Emrah Tomur. A survey and guideline on privacy enhancing technologies for collaborative machine learning. *IEEE Access*, 10:97495–97519, 2022.

[16] Priyanka Mary Mammen. Federated learning: Opportunities and challenges. *arXiv preprint arXiv:2101.05428*, 2021.

[17] Changchang Liu, Supriyo Chakraborty, and Prateek Mittal. Dependence makes you vulnberable: Differential privacy under dependent tuples. In *NDSS*, volume 16, pages 21–24, 2016.

[18] Febrianti Wibawa, Ferhat Ozgur Catak, Murat Kuzlu, Salih Sarp, and Umit Cali. Homomorphic encryption and federated learning based privacy-preserving cnn training: Covid-19 detection use-case. In *Proceedings of the 2022 European Interdisciplinary Cybersecurity Conference*, pages 85–90, 2022.

[19] Wajdi Alghamdi, Reda Salama, M Sirija, Ahmed Radie Abbas, and Kholmurodova Dilnoza. Secure multi-party computation for collaborative data analysis. In *E3S Web of Conferences*, volume 399, page 04034. EDP Sciences, 2023.

[20] Murat Kuzlu, Zhenxin Xiao, Maliha Tabassum, and Ferhat Ozgur Catak. A robust diabetes mellitus prediction system based on federated learning strategies. In *2023 International Conference on Intelligent Computing, Communication, Networking and Services (ICCNS)*, pages 246–253, 2023. doi: 10.1109/ICCNS58795.2023.10192981.

6 Privacy Preserving Artificial Intelligence: Homomorphic Encryption

Cryptography can keep secrets safe while sharing important information. Imagine you want to send a picture of a new traffic sign to your computer friend who can recognize traffic signs. You can put the picture inside a special envelope only your friend can open. It is like putting a secret code lock on the envelope. This way, even if someone tries to peek at the picture while it travels through the internet, they will not understand it because it is all coded up.

Now, let us talk about Homomorphic Encryption (HE) like in Figure 6.1. Your friend may want to learn something new from all the pictures it receives but still wants to keep everything secret. HE is like teaching the computer to do calculations on the coded-up pictures without actually decoding them.

When you send a coded-up picture of a new traffic sign, your friend's computer can still perform its recognition magic without knowing what the sign looks like. The computer can do math with a secret code and still get the correct answer without seeing the original picture.

This way, even if your friend's computer learns from pictures worldwide, it never sees real, uncoded pictures. It is like having a safe way to share and learn without revealing secrets.

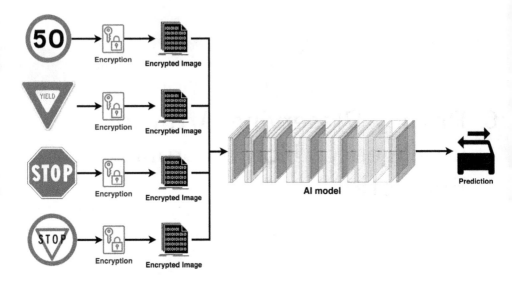

Figure 6.1: Homomorphic Encryption Based Privact Preserving AI

6.1 Introduction to Cryptography

Cryptography employs algorithms to protect the privacy of sensitive information in high-risk applications, providing confidentiality, integrity, and authenticity (CIA) [1]. Different security protocols like SSL/TLS use cryptography to create secure communications between parties by converting plaintext messages into ciphertext [2]. Several applications use cryptography, including symmetric/asymmetric encryption, digital signatures, and cryptographic hashing [3, 4]. Cryptography is also essential in numerous disciplines to protect data at rest, including online transactions, financial data, electronic health records, classified information, and digital documents and identities [5].

The recent developments in cryptographic techniques have particularly affected the development of secure data processing. HE enables secure AI applications in the training and prediction phases while preserving data privacy and integrity. The study [6] provides a comprehensive overview of HE, an encryption method that operates on ciphertext through public key algorithms. Unlike traditional encryption methods that secure data but do not maintain privacy during operations, HE enables performing simple arithmetic operations directly on encrypted data. The authors in [7, 8] address the criticality of sensitive medical data and propose a solution using HE and federated learning-based privacy-preserving training for AI models against privacy attacks. This privacy-preserving federated learning algorithm leverages a secure multi-party computation protocol to protect the DL model from adversaries to gain plain, sensitive information.

This chapter is a detailed exploration of HE. It highlights the importance of this approach, its fundamental principles, and how it guarantees data privacy during model training. The chapter also presents practical examples of HE's real-world applications using Python. It is designed for readers with basic cryptography knowledge interested in delving deeper into HE. For those already familiar with the algorithms, the chapter offers direct access to practical examples, allowing them to skip introductory sections and focus on implementing privacy-preserving DL training using HE.

6.2 Fundamentals of Encryption and Decryption

Encryption is the process of transforming plaintext messages into unbreakable ciphertext information. There are two main types of encryption methods: symmetric and asymmetric.

6.2.1 Symmetric Cryptography

A single secret key in symmetric cryptography encrypts ciphertext and decrypts plaintext messages. This key must be shared between all the parties to enable secure computation [9]. The encryption function can be represented by $ciphertext = Enc_{secret\_key}(plaintext)$. The encryption function Enc_{secret_key} is typically a permutation or substitution cipher, which operates on blocks of fixed-length data. On the other hand, the decryption function is expressed as $plaintext = Dec_{secret\_key}(ciphertext)$.

The security of symmetric encryption algorithms depends on the length of the key and the quality of the key generation process.

The encryption key length directly affects the number of possible keys for encryption and decryption. Generally, the longer the key, the more secure the encryption algorithm. However the quality of the key generation plays a significant role in overall security in cryptogprahy. If a weak (i.e. small length) key is generated, it can be easily guessed or brute-forced, which can compromise the ciphertext. Some widely used symmetric encryption algorithms are the Advanced Encryption Standard (AES), Data Encryption Standard (DES), and Blowfish.

6.2.2 Asymmetric Cryptography (Public-key cryptography)

Asymmetric encryption uses two different keys: the public key and the private key. The public key is used for encryption and is shared publicly, while the private key is kept secret and used for decryption [10]. The encryption process can be represented by the mathematical expression $c = E_{pk}(p)$, where pk is the public key, and p is the plaintext message to be encrypted. The decryption function is expressed as $p = D_{sk}(c)$, where sk is the private key used for decryption, and c is the ciphertext.

Asymmetric encryption uses complex mathematical problems for computers, making it difficult for attackers to decrypt ciphertext messages. RSA is one of the widely used algorithms. It generates a public and private encryption key. The encryption function uses modular exponentiation, while the decryption function uses modular inverse calculations.

6.3 Homomorphic Encryption

Collecting and analyzing sensitive information has become more common in most AI-based applications. While this data can be used to develop innovative and valuable AI-based applications, it also raises serious privacy concerns in the community. Using sensitive data without sufficient security protection can result in various damaging results, from identity theft to discriminatory algorithmic biases.

Researchers and industry practitioners have developed various privacy-preserving techniques to protect sensitive information in AI. These techniques aim to collect and analyse personal data without revealing sensitive information about individuals. HE allows data to be encrypted while still being processed meaningfully [11].

HE enables the processing of encrypted data using arithmetic operations. It allows for calculating a function $f()$ on a ciphertext x, which produces a ciphertext output y. When y is decrypted, it corresponds to the outcome of using the function to the plaintext of x. In other words:

$$f(\text{Decrypt}(x)) = \text{Decrypt}(y) \tag{6.1}$$

This is made possible through special encryption schemes like Paillier, CKKS and BFV. These algorithms allow for data encryption using arithmetic operations that preserve specific properties of the plaintext, such as its *additive* or *multiplicative* structure.

6.3.1 Additive and Multiplicative Homomorphic Encryption

Additive and multiplicative are two types of HE encryption types, which differ in the arithmetic operations performed on ciphertext. They are briefly explained in this subsection.

In the HE concept, additive HE uses addition-based arithmetic operations on the ciphertext as follows:

$$sum_{encrypted} = c_1 \oplus c_2 \tag{6.2}$$

The outcome of the addition operation can be decrypted to obtain the sum of the original plaintext messages as follows:

$$Dec(sum_{encrypted}) == m_1 + m_2 \tag{6.3}$$

In the HE concept, multiplicative HE uses addition and multiplication operations on their corresponding ciphertexts as follows:

$$mult_{encrypted} = c_1 \otimes c_2 \tag{6.4}$$

The product of the plaintext messages is obtained as follows:

$$Dec(mult_{encrypted}) == m_1 \times m_2 \tag{6.5}$$

Additive HE schemes are generally faster and require smaller key sizes than multiplicative HE schemes. However, they are more restricted in the types of computations that they can perform on encrypted data. On the other hand, multiplicative HE schemes can perform more complex computations, but are generally slower and require larger key sizes.

6.3.2 Types of Homomorphic Encryption

There are three main types of HE, i.e., fully (FHE), partially (PHE), and somewhat (SHE) [12, 13]. Each type has distinct capabilities and limitations.

6.3.2.1 Partially Homomorphic Encryption

Partially HE (PHE) supports only one operation on encrypted data, either addition or multiplication. Additive PHE supports only addition operations on ciphertexts. That is, given two ciphertexts c_1 and c_2 that correspond to plaintext messages m_1 and m_2, we can compute a new ciphertext $c_3 = c_1 \oplus c_2$ that corresponds to the sum $Enc(m_1 + m_2)$. In the multiplicative PHE case, the encryption scheme supports only multiplication operations on ciphertexts. That is, given two ciphertexts c_1 and c_2 that correspond to plaintext messages $m1$ and $m2$, we can compute a new ciphertext $c_3 = c_1 \otimes c_2$ that corresponds to the product $Enc(m_1 \times m_2)$.

6.3.2.2 Fully Homomorphic Encryption

Fully HE (FHE) schemes perform both additive and multiplicative arithmetic operations on ciphertext data. Addition and multiplication operations can be performed on encrypted data, and the result can be obtained as ciphertext without revealing the underlying plaintext values. FHE schemes can also support arbitrary polynomial computations, including exponentiation and modular operations [14]. However, FHE schemes come with certain limitations. First, there is a notable computational overhead. This arises from FHE schemes exhibiting a slower pace than alternative encryption methods due to their significant computational demands. Second, FHE schemes involve larger key sizes than other encryption schemes, and the keys employed in FHE schemes are typically much more extensive. Lastly, there is considerable memory usage associated with FHE schemes. The storage of encrypted data in these schemes requires substantial memory.

6.3.2.3 Somewhat Homomorphic Encryption

Somewhat HE (SHE) allows limited computations on ciphertext data and supports addition and multiplication operations [15]. Unlike FHE, which allows arbitrary computations on encrypted data, SHE only supports a limited number of computations. However, SHE is generally more efficient and practical than FHE.

SHE supports two types of operations: addition and multiplication. Addition can be performed without limitations, while multiplication can only be performed up to a certain number of times before the encrypted data becomes too large to compute.

6.4 Practical Examples

This section demonstrates the real-world applications of cryptographic techniques. It starts with partially HE, exemplified by methods such as the Paillier scheme, to execute simple arithmetic operations while preserving data confidentiality. This scrutiny of encryption's computational facilitation forms a foundational aspect of our discussion. Subsequently, it pivots towards cryptographic protocols that underpin secure communications, authentication mechanisms, and data integrity safeguards. Through these illustrative examples, we uncover the diverse and invaluable roles that cryptographic approaches play in ensuring the security and reliability of sensitive information within contemporary systems.

6.4.1 Simple Arithmetic Operations with Homomorphic Encryption

Simple arithmetic operations with HE refer to a cryptographic method that allows certain mathematical operations to be performed on encrypted data without decrypting it. HE schemes enable computations to be carried out directly on encrypted data, yielding an encrypted result that, when decrypted, matches the result of the operations performed on the plaintext data. However, not all encryption schemes are fully homomorphic, meaning that they can support unlimited operations of different types while preserving the encryption.

The following code segment demonstrates the use of the *Pyfhel* library for HE. Each part of the code segment will be explained below.

1. **Importing Libraries:** Import the necessary libraries, i.e., *Pyfhel* for encryption and *numpy* for numerical operations.

```
1 # Import Libraries
2 import numpy as np
3 from Pyfhel import Pyfhel
```

2. **Generating CKKS Key Pair:** Generate a CKKS public-private key pair. *HE.keyGen()* function generates a public-private key pair. The *public_key* is used for encryption, while the *private_key* is used for decryption.

```
1 # Generate CKKS Key Pair
2 HE = Pyfhel()              # Creating empty Pyfhel object
3 ckks_params = {
4     'scheme': 'CKKS',     # can also be 'ckks'
5     'n': 2**14,           # Polynomial modulus degree.
6     'scale': 2**30,       # All the encodings will use it for
      float->fixed point
7                           #  conversion: x_fix = round(x_float *
      scale)
8                           #  You can use this as default scale
      or use a different
9                           #  scale on each operation (set in
      HE.encryptFrac)
```

```
10    'qi_sizes': [60, 30, 30, 30, 60] # Number of bits of
      each prime in the chain.
11                        # Intermediate values should be
      close to log2(scale)
12                        # for each operation, to have small
      rounding errors.
13 }
14 HE.contextGen(**ckks_params)  # Generate context for ckks
      scheme
15 HE.keyGen()                   # Key Generation: generates a pair
      of public/secret keys
```

3. **Generating Random Values:** Generate random values. Two random float values *(val1 and val2)* are generated using *np.random.rand()* function to simulate plaintext data for encryption and operations.

```
1 # Generate Random Values
2 RANDOM_VAL_LENGTH = 5
3 ROUNDING_LENGTH = 5
4 val1 =
      np.random.rand(RANDOM_VAL_LENGTH).round(ROUNDING_LENGTH)
5 val2 =
      np.random.rand(RANDOM_VAL_LENGTH).round(ROUNDING_LENGTH)
```

4. **Displaying Plain Text Values:** Print the randomly generated *val1 and val2* values on the terminal, displaying the initial plain text data before any encryption or computation.

```
1 # Display Plain Text Values
2 print('*' * 50)
3 print('val1 \t:', val1, '\nval2 \t:', val2)
```

5. **Displaying Plain Domain Operations (Addition & Multiplication) and Results:** Display plain domain operations by performing basic arithmetic operations (addition and multiplication) on *val1 and val2* in the plaintext domain without encryption.

```
1 # Display Plain Domain Operations (Addition \&
      Multiplication) and Results
2 print('*' * 50)
3 print('Plain domain addition operation\nval1 + val2 :',
      (val1 + val2))
4 print('Plain domain multiplication operation\nval1 * val2
      :', (val1 * val2))
```

6. **Encrypting and Displaying Encrypted Values:** Ecrypt *val1 and val2* using the CKKS public key *(public_key)*. The *encrypt()* function from the *PyFHel* library is utilized to transform these plaintext values into encrypted ciphertexts *(val1_enc and val2_enc)* for secure computation. Displays the encrypted values of *val1 and val2*. It showcases the lengths of the ciphertexts *(len(str(val1_enc.ciphertext())))* and *len(str(val2_enc.ciphertext()))))* and provides a truncated representation of these ciphertexts for demonstration purposes.

```
1  # Encrypt and Display Encrypted Values
2  val1_enc = HE.encryptFrac(val1) # Encryption makes use of
   the public key
3  val2_enc = HE.encryptFrac(val2) # For integers, encryptInt
   function is used.
4
5  print('*' * 50)
6  print('Encrypted val1 \t: len(',
       len(str(val1_enc.to_bytes())), ')',
       str(val1_enc.to_bytes())[:40], '...',
       str(val1_enc.to_bytes())[-40:])
7  print('Encrypted val2 \t: len(',
       len(str(val2_enc.to_bytes())), ')',
       str(val2_enc.to_bytes())[:40], '...',
       str(val2_enc.to_bytes())[-40:])
```

7. **Performing Homomorphic Addition Operations and Displaying Encrypted Results:** Perform homomorphic addition operations and print encrypted results. Homomorphic addition operations are performed using encrypted values *(val1_enc, val2_enc)* and a mix of encrypted and plaintext values *(val1_enc, val2 or val1, val2_enc)*. It also prints the encrypted results of the homomorphic addition operations, providing the length of ciphertext and a glimpse of the encrypted data.

```
1  # Perform Homomorphic Addition Operations and Display
   Encrypted Results
2  sum1_enc = val1_enc + val2_enc
3  sum2_enc = val1_enc + val2
4
5  print('Encrypted sum1_enc \t: len(',
       len(str(sum1_enc.to_bytes())), ')',
       str(sum1_enc.to_bytes())[:40],
       '...',str(sum1_enc.to_bytes())[-40:])
```

```
6 print('Encrypted sum2_enc \t: len(',
      len(str(sum2_enc.to_bytes())), ')',
      str(sum2_enc.to_bytes())[:50],
      '...',str(sum2_enc.to_bytes())[-40:])
```

8. **Decrypting and Displaying Results:** Decrypt and display results. Decryption of the homomorphically computed results using the private key *(private_key)* to obtain the plaintext sums *(sum1, and sum2)*. Print the decrypted results of the homomorphic addition operations, showing the actual computed plaintext sums.

```
1 # Decrypt and Display Results
2 print('*' * 50)
3 sum1_dec = HE.decryptFrac(sum1_enc).round(ROUNDING_LENGTH)
4 sum2_dec = HE.decryptFrac(sum2_enc).round(ROUNDING_LENGTH)
5
6 print('Decrypted sum1 \t:', sum1_dec[:RANDOM_VAL_LENGTH])
7 print('Decrypted sum2 \t:', sum2_dec[:RANDOM_VAL_LENGTH])
```

9. **Performing Homomorphic Multiplication Operations:** Perform homomorphic multiplication operations using encrypted values *(val1_-enc, val2_enc)* and a mix of encrypted and plaintext values *(val1_enc, val2 or val1, val2_enc)*.

```
1 # Perform Homomorphic Multiplication Operations
2 print('*' * 50)
3 mult1_enc = val1_enc * val2_enc
4 mult2_enc = val1_enc * val2
```

10. **Performing Homomorphic Multiplication Operations and Displaying Results:** Perform homomorphic multiplication operations using encrypted values *(val1_enc, val2_enc)* and a mix of encrypted and plaintext values *(val1_enc, val2 or val1, val2_enc)*.

```
1 # Perform homomorphic multiplication operations
2 mult1_dec = HE.decryptFrac(mult1_enc).round(ROUNDING_LENGTH)
3 mult2_dec = HE.decryptFrac(mult2_enc).round(ROUNDING_LENGTH)
4
5 print('Decrypted sum1 \t:', mult1_dec[:RANDOM_VAL_LENGTH])
6 print('Decrypted sum2 \t:', mult2_dec[:RANDOM_VAL_LENGTH])
```

All results are given as follows:

```
**************************************************
val1  : [0.27403 0.00072 0.29825 0.18283 0.07851]
val2  : [0.73694 0.99903 0.94785 0.67683 0.1125 ]
**************************************************
Plain domain addition operation
val1 + val2 : [1.01097 0.99975 1.2461  0.85966 0.19101]
Plain domain multiplication operation
val1 * val2 : [0.20194367 0.0007193  0.28269626 0.12374483 0.00883237]
**************************************************
Encrypted val1   : len( 3434455 ) b'^\xa1\x10\x04\x00\x00\x00\x00q\x00\x10 ... 0\x00\x00\x00\x87ou\x05\x00\x00\x00\x00'
Encrypted val2   : len( 3436853 ) b'^\xa1\x10\x04\x00\x00\x00\x00q\x00\x10 ... 0\x00\x00\x00\x93)\xac9\x00\x00\x00\x00'
Encrypted sum1_enc  : len( 3435224 ) b'^\xa1\x10\x04\x00\x00\x00\x00q\x00 ... 0\x00\x00\x00\x1a\x99!?\x00\x00\x00\x00'
Encrypted sum2_enc  : len( 3436280 ) b'^\xa1\x10\x04\x00\x00\x00\x00q\x00 ... 0\x00\x00\x00\x87ou\x05\x00\x00\x00\x00'
**************************************************
Decrypted sum1   : [1.01097 0.99975 1.2461  0.85966 0.191 ]
Decrypted sum2   : [1.01097 0.99975 1.2461  0.85966 0.191 ]
**************************************************
Encrypted mult1_enc  : len( 5152500 ) b'^\xa1\x10\x04\x00\x00\x00\x00q\x00 ... x00\x00\x85E\x14\x00\x00\x00\x00\x00'
Encrypted mult2_enc  : len( 3435334 ) b'^\xa1\x10\x04\x00\x00\x00\x00q\x00 ... 0\x00\x00=\'\xf2\x1c\x00\x00\x00\x00'
**************************************************
Decrypted sum1   : [0.20194 0.00072 0.2827  0.12375 0.00883]
Decrypted sum2   : [0.20194 0.00072 0.2827  0.12375 0.00883]
```

6.4.2 Cryptographic Protocols

A cryptographic protocol is a set of rules and procedures that manage secure information exchange between several parties. The primary purpose of cryptographic protocols is to ensure that data transmitted between two or more parties remains confidential, authentic, and integral.

Cryptographic protocols secure communication channels between devices, authenticate users and verify data integrity [16]. Some examples of such protocols are Secure Socket Layer/Transport Layer Security (SSL/TLS), which is used for securing web communications, Secure Shell (SSH) for remote login sessions, and Internet Protocol Security (IPsec) for securing network communications.

6.4.2.1 Private set intersection (PSI)

Private set intersection (PSI) allows two or more parties to find the intersection of their respective sets without revealing the contents of their sets to each other [17].

In a PSI scenario, *Party A* has a set of elements $\{a_1, a_2, \cdots, a_n\}$, and *Party B* has another set of elements $\{b_1, b_2, \cdots, b_m\}$. These sets are represented as binary vectors of length N, where N is the maximum size of the sets. For each element in the set, the corresponding bit in the vector is set to 1 if the element is present in the set and 0 otherwise.

Here, the main goal is to compute the intersection of these two sets without revealing the contents of either set to the other party. To achieve this, HE can be used to perform the intersection operation on the encrypted sets. The first step in PSI using HE is to encrypt the binary vectors of the sets using an HE scheme. It is assumed that a fully HE (FHE) scheme is used to support addition and multiplication operations on encrypted data. Party A and Party B then exchange their encrypted sets with each other. Each party can perform the intersection operation on the encrypted sets using HE and multiplication operations. Specifically, the following steps are performed:

1. Party A encrypts its set $\{a_1, a_2, ..., a_n\}$ using HE:

$$\text{Enc}(A) = \{\text{Enc}(a_1), \text{Enc}(a_2), ..., \text{Enc}(a_n)\}$$

2. Party A sends the encrypted set $\text{Enc}(A)$ to Party B.
3. Party B encrypts its set $\{b_1, b_2, ..., b_m\}$ using HE:

$$\text{Enc}(B) = \{\text{Enc}(b_1), \text{Enc}(b_2), ..., \text{Enc}(b_m)\}$$

4. Party B sends the encrypted set $\text{Enc}(B)$ to Party A.
5. Party A and Party B then perform the following homomorphic operations:
   ■ They multiply the encrypted sets element-wise:

$$\text{Enc}(C) = \text{Enc}(A) * \text{Enc}(B)$$

   , where $*$ denotes element-wise multiplication.

   ■ They add up the elements of the resulting encrypted set:

$$\text{Enc}(D) = \sum \text{Enc}(C)$$

   , where $\sum$ denotes element-wise addition.

6. Party A decrypts the resulting encrypted set $\text{Enc}(D)$ using the decryption function $\text{Dec}(\cdot)$: $D = \text{Dec}(\text{Enc}(d_1)), \text{Dec}(\text{Enc}(d_2)), ..., \text{Dec}(\text{Enc}(d_N))$

The resulting set D is a binary vector of length N, where the i-th element is 1 if and only if the i-th element is present in both sets. In other words, D represents the intersection of the sets $a_1, a_2, ..., a_n$ and $b_1, b_2, ..., b_m$.

The privacy of the individual sets is preserved throughout the computation, as Party A and Party B never reveal their respective sets to each other. Furthermore, the HE ensures that the intermediate computations performed on the encrypted sets do not leak any information about the contents of the sets.

Note that this PSI protocol using HE assumes that the two parties are honest-but-curious, meaning that they follow the protocol but may try to learn additional information from the messages exchanged. If one or both parties are malicious, additional security measures such as secure multiparty computation may be necessary to ensure privacy.

The following code demonstrates a scenario where Alice and Bob use Paillier encryption to compute the intersection of their friend lists without directly sharing their lists, maintaining privacy while finding common elements. Each part of the code segment will be explained below.

1. **Importing Libraries:** Import necessary libraries,including *phe* for Paillier encryption, *random* for generating random numbers, and *numpy* as np for numerical operations.

```
1 # Import libraries
2 from phe import paillier
3 import random
4 import numpy as np
```

2. **Generating Paillier Key Pair for Alice:** Generate a Paillier key pair *(alice_pubkey* for public key and *alice_privkey* for private key) for Alice to perform encryption and decryption operations.

```
1 # Generate Paillier Key Pair for Alice
```

```
2 alice_pubkey , alice_privkey =
      paillier.generate_paillier_keypair()
```

3. **Defining Alice's and Bob's Friend Lists:** Define two sets representing the friend lists of Alice *(alice_friends) and Bob (bob_friends)*.

```
1 # Define Alice's and Bob's Friend Lists
2 alice_friends = [1, 2, 3, 4, 5]
3 bob_friends = [3, 4, 5, 6, 7, 8, 2]
```

4. **Encrypting Alice's Friend List:** Encrypt each friend ID in Alice's friend list using Alice's public key *(alice_pubkey)* and stores the encrypted values in *alice_enc_friends*.

```
1 # Encrypt Alice's Friend List
2 alice_enc_friends = [alice_pubkey.encrypt(friend) for friend
      in alice_friends]
```

5. **Computing Bob's Friends:** Compute the result of subtracting *bob_friend* from *alice_enc_friend*. Each element in Bob's friend list *(bob_friends)* multiplied by the random integer r.

```
1 # Compute the result of subtracting Bob's friends from
      Alice's friends
2 r = random.randint(1, alice_pubkey.n - 1)
3 bob_results = [(alice_enc_friend - bob_friend) for
      alice_enc_friend in alice_enc_friends for bob_friend in
      bob_friends]
```

6. **Checking Intersection:** Check the intersection by iterating through the *bob_results* and decrypting each result using *alice_privkey*. Alice decrypts each result obtained from Bob's computations using her private key *(alice_privkey)*. If the decrypted result is equal to 0, it implies an intersection between Alice's and Bob's friend lists. Alice then identifies the index of the intersecting friend and prints the message *Intersection found*.

```
1 # Check Intersection
2 idx = 0
3 for result in bob_results:
4     dec_result = alice_privkey.decrypt(result)
5     if dec_result == 0:
6         found_friend_idx = np.floor(idx /
      len(bob_friends)).astype(int)
```

```
7        print("Intersection found:",
     alice_friends[found_friend_idx])
8        idx = idx + 1
```

All results are given as follows:

```
Intersection found:  2
Intersection found:  3
Intersection found:  4
Intersection found:  5
```

6.4.2.2 Private Preserving Logistic Regression

The provided code demonstrates a secure machine-learning scenario, specifically a privacy-preserving logistic regression using HE. In this scenario, Alice possesses a trained logistic regression classifier, and Bob has personal data that he wishes to classify without revealing it to Alice. The classifier is designed to predict binary outcomes, such as classifying data points into two categories. In our demonstration, the binary classification could represent, for instance, identifying emails as spam or not spam. Alice, who has the classifier, wants to apply this model to Bob's emails. However, both parties aim to maintain privacy: Bob does not wish to reveal the content of his emails to Alice, and Alice does not want to expose the details of her trained model to Bob.

The code proceeds with the following steps:

1. **Paillier Encryption Setup**: It is initialized the Paillier encryption scheme, generating public and private keys. Alice will use this to encrypt the model's computations, while Bob will use the public key to encrypt his data.

2. **Alice's Model**: Alice has a logistic regression model with predefined

weights and an intercept. These represent the trained parameters of her spam classifier.

3. **Bob's Data**: Bob's emails are numerical data in an array. Bob encrypts his email data using Alice's public key, thus maintaining the confidentiality of his emails.

4. **Encrypted Classification**: Alice receives Bob's encrypted data and performs the classification using her model. The computation is done on the encrypted data, ensuring that Alice cannot access the actual content of Bob's emails.

5. **Result Decryption:** The encrypted classification result is returned to Bob, who then decrypts it using his private key. This decryption step reveals the classification result (spam or not spam) of his emails without Alice ever having access to the content of the emails.

6. **Preserving Privacy:** Throughout this process, the privacy of both parties is preserved. Bob's emails remain confidential, and the details of Alice's model are not exposed to Bob.

This code simplifies how privacy-preserving techniques can be applied in ML, mainly when data confidentiality is crucial. It highlights the potential of HE in enabling secure and private data analysis, a key consideration in the growing field of privacy-preserving AI.

1. **Importing Libraries:** Import various Python modules essential for different functionalities. The code imports *phe*, a library supporting HE using the Paillier cryptosystem, and *numpy* for numerical computations.

```
1 # Import libraries
2 from phe import paillier
3 import numpy as np
```

2. **Initializing Paillier Encryption System:** Initialize the Paillier cryptosystem. This step involves generating a pair of keys - a public key and a private key. The public key will be used by Bob to encrypt his data, and the private key will be used by Bob to decrypt the results.

```
1 # Initialize the Paillier cryptosystem
2 public_key, private_key =
      paillier.generate_paillier_keypair()
```

3. **Creating Alice's Part (Model Owner):** Create Alice's part with a trained logistic regression model. For this demonstration, we're using predefined weights and an intercept. In a real-world scenario, these would be the learned parameters from Alice's model training process.

```
# Create Alice's part
weights = np.array([0.5, -0.3])   # Example weights
intercept = 0.1  # Example intercept
```

4. **Defining Logistic Function:** Define the logistic function used in logistic regression for binary classification. It maps any input value to a value between 0 and 1, which is interpreted as the probability of belonging to a particular class.

```
# Define the logistic function
def logistic_function(z):
    return 1 / (1 + np.exp(-z))
```

5. **Defining Encrypted Prediction Function:** Define an encrypted prediction function taking the model's weights, intercept, and Bob's encrypted data to compute the encrypted prediction. The prediction is done using a linear combination (dot product) of the weights and the data, to which the intercept is then added. The entire computation is performed on encrypted data, thus preserving privacy.

```
def encrypted_prediction(weights, intercept, encrypted_data):
    # Encrypted dot product of weights and data
    encrypted_dot_product = sum([w * x for w, x in
    zip(weights, encrypted_data)])
    # Adding the intercept to the dot product
    encrypted_linear_combination = encrypted_dot_product +
    intercept
    return encrypted_linear_combination
```

6. **Creating Bob's Part (Data Owner):** Create Bob's part having some personal data that he wants to classify using Alice's model. However, he does not want to reveal his data to Alice. For this demonstration, we're using a small array to represent Bob's data. Bob encrypts his data using Alice's public key. This ensures that his data stays confidential, and only encrypted data is shared with Alice.

```
# Create Bob's part
bob_data = np.array([1.2, 0.4])   # Example data
encrypted_data = [public_key.encrypt(x) for x in bob_data]
```

7. **Computing the Encrypted Prediction:** Compute the encrypted prediction. In this process, Alice receives the encrypted data from Bob. She then computes the encrypted prediction using her model's weights and intercept. This computation is entirely performed on encrypted data, ensuring that Alice does not gain access to Bob's actual data.

```
1 # Compute the encrypted prediction
2 encrypted_result = encrypted_prediction(weights, intercept,
    encrypted_data)
```

8. **Performing Decryption:** Perform the decryption. In this process, after receiving the encrypted result from Alice, Bob decrypts it using his private key. This step reveals the classification result (in an encrypted form) of his data, without Alice ever having access to the actual data..

```
1 # Perform the decryption
2 decrypted_result = private_key.decrypt(encrypted_result)
```

9. **Finalizing Prediction and Printing the Result:** Finalize the prediction. In this process, Bob applies the logistic function locally to convert the decrypted result into a probability. He then classifies the data based on this probability. For instance, if the probability is 0.5 or higher, the data is classified into one class (e.g., *spam*), otherwise, it's classified into the other (e.g., *not spam*). Print the result based on the prediction.

```
1 # Finalize the prediction
2 prediction = logistic_function(decrypted_result)
3 predicted_class = 1 if prediction >= 0.5 else 0
4
5 # Print the classification result
6 print("Predicted Class:", predicted_class)
```

6.5 Summary

This chapter offers an insightful exploration into HE, a pivotal advancement in cryptographic techniques enhancing data security. The chapter begins with an introductory overview of cryptography, explaining fundamental concepts such as encryption and decryption. Subsequently, it delves into the core of HE, laying the foundations and detailing its Additive and Multiplicative forms, clarifying their significance in preserving data privacy during AI computations and predictions. Furthermore, the chapter covers various HE methods, underscoring their diverse applications in secure data processing. The chapter highlights example applications, including simple arithmetic operations leveraging Partially HE, exemplified by Paillier encryption and cryptographic protocols.

Bibliography

[1] Bhushan Kapoor, Pramod Pandya, and Joseph S Sherif. Cryptography: A security pillar of privacy, integrity and authenticity of data communication. *Kybernetes*, 40(9/10):1422–1439, 2011.

[2] Ashraf Elgohary, Tarek S Sobh, and Mohammed Zaki. Design of an enhancement for ssl/tls protocols. *computers & security*, 25(4):297–306, 2006.

[3] Vidushi Agarwal, Ashish K Kaushal, and Lokesh Chouhan. A survey on cloud computing security issues and cryptographic techniques. In *Social Networking and Computational Intelligence: Proceedings of SCI-2018*, pages 119–134. Springer, 2020.

[4] Shivani Sharma and Yash Gupta. Study on cryptography and techniques. *International Journal of Scientific Research in Computer Science, Engineering and Information Technology*, 2(1):249–252, 2017.

[5] Anindita Sarkar, Swagata Roy Chatterjee, and Mohuya Chakraborty. Role of cryptography in network security. *The" Essence" of Network Security: An End-to-End Panorama*, pages 103–143, 2021.

[6] Namrata Patel, Parita Oza, and Smita Agrawal. Homomorphic cryptography and its applications in various domains. In *International Conference on Innovative Computing and Communications: Proceedings of ICICC 2018, Volume 1*, pages 269–278. Springer, 2019.

[7] Febrianti Wibawa, Ferhat Ozgur Catak, Salih Sarp, and Murat Kuzlu. Bfv-based homomorphic encryption for privacy-preserving cnn models. *Cryptography*, 6(3):34, 2022.

[8] Febrianti Wibawa, Ferhat Ozgur Catak, Murat Kuzlu, Salih Sarp, and Umit Cali. Homomorphic encryption and federated learning based privacy-preserving cnn training: Covid-19 detection use-case. In *Proceedings of the 2022 European Interdisciplinary Cybersecurity Conference*, pages 85–90, 2022.

[9] Hans Delfs, Helmut Knebl, Hans Delfs, and Helmut Knebl. Symmetric-key encryption. *Introduction to cryptography: principles and applications*, pages 11–31, 2007.

[10] S Suguna, V Dhanakoti, and R Manjupriya. A study on symmetric and asymmetric key encryption algorithms. *Int Res J Eng Technol (IRJET)*, 3 (4):27–31, 2016.

[11] Lifang Zhang, Yan Zheng, and Raimo Kantoa. A review of homomorphic encryption and its applications. In *Proceedings of the 9th EAI International Conference on Mobile Multimedia Communications*, pages 97–106, 2016.

[12] Abbas Acar, Hidayet Aksu, A Selcuk Uluagac, and Mauro Conti. A survey on homomorphic encryption schemes: Theory and implementation. *ACM Computing Surveys (Csur)*, 51(4):1–35, 2018.

[13] Ayman Alharbi, Haneen Zamzami, and Eman Samkri. Survey on homomorphic encryption and address of new trend. *International Journal of Advanced Computer Science and Applications*, 11(7), 2020.

[14] Paulo Martins, Leonel Sousa, and Artur Mariano. A survey on fully homomorphic encryption: An engineering perspective. *ACM Computing Surveys (CSUR)*, 50(6):1–33, 2017.

[15] Jung Hee Cheon and Jinsu Kim. A hybrid scheme of public-key encryption and somewhat homomorphic encryption. *IEEE transactions on information forensics and security*, 10(5):1052–1063, 2015.

[16] Md Abu Faisal. *Design and Implementation of a Secure Communication Architecture*. PhD thesis, Queen's University (Canada), 2022.

[17] Emiliano De Cristofaro, Paolo Gasti, and Gene Tsudik. Fast and private computation of cardinality of set intersection and union. In *International Conference on Cryptology and Network Security*, pages 218–231. Springer, 2012.

7 Opportunities, Challenges, and Future Directions in Trustworthy AI

The use of AI-based models has been widespread in many high-risk applications [1], such as healthcare diagnostics and treatment planning, autonomous vehicles, criminal justice and law enforcement, financial and investment decisions, critical infrastructure and utilities, national security and defense, education and employment decisions, and many more. These models have been highly successful in their respective fields, yet they also raise questions about trustworthiness, that is, trustworthy AI (TAI). In addition to the properties of the traditional computing system of reliability, security, privacy, and usability, AI-based models must also be probabilistically accurate in uncertain conditions, fair, robust, accountable, and explainable to be considered trustworthy. Unfortunately, AI-based models can be fragile and unfair, as evidenced by corporate recruitment tools that are biased against a specific gender [2]. This chapter will explore opportunities, challenges, and future directions in trustworthy AI.

7.1 Opportunities

The use of AI has been beneficial both to academia and industry in many ways. However, there is always the question of how much we can trust it. To be able to depend on AI, we must understand the rationale behind its decisions. This is known as "Trusted AI" or "Trustworthy AI". Having this kind of AI can be advantageous, especially for the reputation of a company and a university, and increase the trust and support of stakeholders in the organization, including academia. The selected main opportunities in trustworthy AI are discussed below.

Improved Decision-Making

AI systems have become increasingly common in everyday life and business settings, often to support human decision making. These systems have become more sophisticated and effective, offering the potential to uncover valuable information in a variety of applications [3]. However, AI systems must be trusted with their output to be widely adopted. When people understand how technology works and can evaluate its safety and dependability, they are more likely to trust it. Many AI systems have been "black boxes" up to this point, where data is input and results are produced. To trust a decision made by an algorithm, we need to be sure that it is fair, reliable, accountable, and will not cause any harm [4], that is, AI should not be manipulated, and the system itself is secure. AI-based model/system developers should be able to look inside systems to understand the model outcome. Trustworthy AI has the potential to lead to more reliable and accurate outcomes, particularly in critical areas such as healthcare, finance, and autonomous systems. Integration of XAI-based tools will play a crucial role in building trust and improving decision-making [5]. Users can gain insight into the process by providing explanations for AI-based decisions. Furthermore, the ability to create a collaborative environment between AI systems and human experts can further enhance the reliability and accuracy of the results, particularly in complex domains such as autonomous systems.

Responsible AI Deployment

Responsible AI deployment is one of the main opportunities in trustworthy AI, which allows AI development and deployment in a safe, trustworthy, and ethical way. Responsible AI can proactively guide AI model decisions toward more beneficial and equitable outcomes. There are several frameworks and tools to enable responsible AI deployments. Microsoft has developed a framework for the building of AI systems, which addresses six principles of trustworthy AI, i.e., fairness, reliability and safety, privacy and security, inclusion, transparency and accountability[1]. In addition, collaboration among stakeholders from different areas, such as ethics, law, psychology, sociology, and technology, is essential to provide ethical decisions and predictions for responsible AI deployments. This multipartner collaboration may help reduce risks and build trust among stakeholders by enabling ethical practices.

Improved Transparency and Accountability

Together, transparency and accountability can contribute to achieving trustworthy AI goals by facilitating a fairness assessment to identify and mitigate any biases in the data and model, and providing interfaces for understanding the functions of the AI system. They increase usability and encourage wider adoption, presenting an opportunity to expand the positive impact of AI. The study [6] provides a comprehensive framework for the governance of digital data along with future trends and directions in the trustworthy AI concept. It defines the roles and responsibilities to monitor, evaluate, and address ethical or privacy concerns within organizations. Continuous monitoring and auditing processes with transparency and accountability can help track AI system performance in terms of accuracy and vulnerability. This ongoing evaluation also offers the opportunity to adapt the systems.

Reduced Bias
Reduced bias or reducing bias is essential for trustworthy AI to create more equitable and responsible AI-based systems [7]. AI systems can be biased for several reasons, such as biased data, poor algorithms, or improper implementation. It directly affects the trustworthiness of AI. Reducing bias in AI models increases trust in AI systems in terms of accuracy. AI systems can also extend their full potential in various fields by reducing bias, including healthcare, education, and recruitment. For example, medical diagnoses can lead to more accurate and effective healthcare outcomes by reducing bias. Another exam-

---

[1]https://learn.microsoft.com/en-us/azure/machine-learning/concept-responsible-ai?view=azureml-api-2

ple can be given from education, i.e., AI-based tools can be designed to offer personalized learning experiences to the diverse needs of students. Additionally, AI systems can make unbiased hiring decisions, offering candidates fair opportunities regardless of their demographic background. Various stakeholders, including companies, academia, government, multilateral institutions, and non-governmental organizations (NGOs), are taking action to reduce bias in AI[2].

7.2 Challenges

In recent years, AI-based applications have been widely accepted as reliable due to the advancement of trustworthy AI. Although significant progress has been made in developing trustworthy AI, several challenges still exist. In order to ensure trustworthy AI, it is necessary to address a number of challenges from data quality and bias, interpretability and explainability, robustness and adversarial attacks, adaptability, standardization and regulation, and security and privacy. This subsection briefly discusses these challenges for trustworthy AI.

Data Quality and Bias
Data quality and bias together are combined concerns for AI systems to properly train the model and provide accurate output, that is, low-quality and biased data can provide unfair results and damage the trustworthiness of AI systems [8]. Data quality and bias are essential for creating and deploying trustworthy AI systems. There are various approaches and tools for trustworthy AI, with a focus on data quality, bias detection, and mitigation. It is essential to use best practices for continuous detection and mitigation of bias during algorithm training, deployment, and operation. Bias can be introduced at the training stage through data manipulation, fine-tuning steps, the definition of objective functions, or using specific algorithmic techniques. Even during deployment, AI-based systems can be affected by bias through potential feedback

---

[2]https://haas.berkeley.edu/wp-content/uploads/UCB_Playbook_R10_V2_spreads2.pdf

loops, improper evaluation techniques and benchmarks, or adversarial attacks. Standardized methods and tools, particularly to detect and mitigate bias, are also essential to ensure trust in AI. This is especially valid for high-risk sectors, such as healthcare, law enforcement, finance, education, and employment, and industrial automation and robotics [9]. Each sector has its own unique data quality and bias issues, e.g., trustworthiness, transparency, and privacy are very important in healthcare. It is necessary to adopt specific best practices, such as those related to fairness, transparency, explainability, robustness, and sustainable monitoring and evaluation techniques.

Interpretability and Explainability
Together, interpretability and explainability are the main challenges in the trustworthy AI concept. Interpretability refers to how an AI-based model makes a decision or prediction, while explainability refers to further one by providing a clear and understandable explanation for the model's output. Both parts are necessary for trustworthy AI [10], which is especially important in high-risk applications, such as healthcare, autonomous vehicles, or finance. In both cases, interpretability and explainability increase the transparency and accountability of AI systems and enable the understanding and validation of AI decisions for building trustworthy AI. Although there are several interpretability and explainability methods in AI, such as intrinsically interpretable models and post hoc explanations, a comprehensive guideline is still required for developers designing AI systems with a focus on interpretability and explainability for trustworthy AI applications. The study [11] provides a framework to balance explainability and predictive performance to ensure the reliability and trustworthiness of AI systems. It offers a step-by-step framework, particularly in healthcare or similar domains where explainability is essential. The framework addresses trade-offs between explainability and predictive performance, advises on awareness of post hoc explanations' limitations, and considers the balance between complexity and interpretability, interpretability, and local vs. global explanations. This structured approach helps developers make the right decisions about trustworthy AI.

Robustness and Adversarial Attacks
Robustness in AI is one of the main issues. The ongoing improvement between

adversarial attacks and defenses reflects our changing understanding. Newly developed attacks can easily bypass traditional adversarial training. This requires a flexible approach to defensive strategies. The rapid growth of AI technology has made systems vulnerable to imperceptible attacks and biases. Adversarial attacks are designed to manipulate the output of the model and present a significant challenge. From an algorithmic point of view, the effect of different trustworthiness objectives on model performance has still been explored [12]. Adversarial robustness increases generalizability but may reduce overall accuracy. AI models must be reliable for critical decision making and resource protection. Robustness against adversarial attacks is a crucial requirement. However, there is a lack of standardized evaluation metrics. The study [13] proposed the Sophisticated Adversarial Robustness Score (SARS), which provides a comprehensive assessment and helps identify vulnerabilities. Adversarial attacks and defenses have received considerable attention. They cover different types of attack, timing, and spaces. Attacks range from perturbations at decision time to injections at training time. Evaluating robustness requires considering practical attack scenarios. Adversarial training is a recognized approach to defense. Enhancing the training data with adversarial samples can reduce certain attacks. However, it may leave models exposed to other attack types.

Standardization and Regulation
Many parallel activities characterize the global landscape of AI standards, regulations, and organizational policies. Since 2017, there has been an exponential growth in AI initiatives worldwide. As of February 2021, the Council of Europe has identified over 450 such initiatives globally, primarily driven by national authorities, international organizations, and the private sector[3]. These initiatives predominantly address critical subjects like privacy, human rights, transparency, responsibility, trust, accountability, freedom, fairness, and diversity. Prominent works such as the IEEE EAD, the EU's High-Level Expert Group on AI, and the OECD often frame these issues within the context of ethical or trustworthy AI. The Trustworthiness Working Group (WG 3) within SC 42 is actively engaged in pre-standardization and standardization activities. Their roadmap is guided by comprehensive analyses of existing work and cur-

---

[3]https://www.coe.int/en/web/artificial-intelligence/national-initiatives

rent policy documents, including those from IEEE EAD, HLEG, and OECD. Establishing industry-wide standards and regulations for Trustworthy AI is a continuous challenge, requiring explicit guidelines to guarantee compliance [14]. The existing regulatory framework, including acts like the Data Act, Data Governance Act, and AI Act, offers possibilities to establish standards in line with legal requirements. This alignment could lead to widespread adoption in the AI community. Some standards are urgently needed and can be implemented in the short term, while others, such as constructing standardized software tools for data analysis and defining a unified taxonomy for AI data, are more difficult due to a lack of consensus [9]. Standardized approaches must guarantee that AI models are inclusive, non-biased, and trustworthy, along with data quality. Regulation of AI systems is actively pursued, and the regulation of other safety-critical applications suggests that it can successfully build trust in the long run. Different potential forms of regulation for AI have been suggested [15], such as mandating that the AI system meets certain pre-defined criteria, controlling the development process with standard development guidelines, and introducing a licensing system for developers. Each of these approaches has its own benefits and challenges, and it is essential to tailor regulation to the adaptive nature of AI systems.

Security and Privacy Concerns
In trustworthy AI, ensuring privacy and security is essential [16]. Privacy revolves around protecting sensitive data and model parameters to prevent leaks, which includes personal information such as names, ages, and images. This is essential not only for preserving data, but also for compliance with regulatory and legal requirements. Security, in contrast, focuses on measures to prevent unauthorized access to data. Threats are prevalent in AI, making it susceptible to information leakage and adversarial attacks. Security strengths are classified based on attributes like abort, fair, and guaranteed output delivery. They can be categorized into data security, model security, and system security, with Partially/Fully Secure Federated Training (P/FSFT) offering varying levels of protection. Federated learning is a machine learning approach that allows a model to be trained across multiple decentralized devices or servers holding local data samples, without exchanging them. Trustworthy Federated Learning (TFL) is a cornerstone of AI to address security and privacy concerns in trust-

worthy AI [17]. Although significant progress has been made in TFL, there are still challenges, such as identifying threats and developing mechanisms toward trustworthy AI.

7.3 Future Directions

The pursuit of trustworthy AI has continued along with the development of new AI technologies and a better understanding of their effects on society. To achieve this, a long-term research vision is necessary. The possible main directions for the future advancement of trustworthy AI are discussed below.

Advancements in Explainable AI
One of the main future directions is to create more sophisticated Explainable AI (XAI) techniques, which can explain the output of the AI model in a way being easily understandable and actionable by humans [18]. XAI-based solutions can also be supported by interactive frameworks or tools along with advanced user interfaces, data visualization for users, operators, and developers. In addition, future research in XAI can focus on methods to be applied for a variety of domains and applications. It is clear that advancement in XAI can significantly contribute to trustworthy AI systems and lead to responsible and ethical AI deployments.

Ethical AI Frameworks
The development of ethical AI frameworks is essential to build trustworthy AI [19], which addresses ethical issues in the use of AI methods. These frameworks typically encompass the main components and principles of trustworthy AI, such as transparency, explainability, fairness, bias mitigation, accountability, security, and privacy. They are also compatible with AI standards, regulations, and governance [20]. A comprehensive ethics guide was released for US intelligence community personnel, covering goals and risks in AI systems, legal obligations, mitigating bias, testing, and evaluations of AI systems, transparency, account-

ability[4].

Mitigation Bias

Mitigating bias in trustworthy AI is crucial in achieving fair and equitable outcomes [21]. In the literature, several approaches have been recommended to achieve this [12], i.e., advanced algorithms, tools and frameworks, feedback mechanisms, and continuous monitoring and adaptation. Advanced algorithms and models, e.g., adversarial training, are the key approaches to accurately identify and reduce biases in AI systems. Tools and frameworks, i.e., XAI methods, can be utilized to investigate AI models, and assess AI models in terms of potential biases. Feedback mechanisms are also crucial to allow users to report biases in AI outputs. Continuous monitoring and adaptation is the other key process to monitor AI output and adapt to new data and contexts. All these approaches will be a significant step towards trustworthy AI.

Enhanced Secure System

Integrating secure computing techniques into AI systems is an important research area to protect AI systems against adversarial attacks and unauthorized access [22]. Enhancing security is necessary to ensure the reliability and safety of AI systems. There are some key future directions in security for trustworthy AI [17]. Secure federated learning enables models to be trained on multiple decentralized devices or servers with local data samples. Differential privacy adds noise or randomness to data before AI models process it. Secure model updates ensure that updates to AI models are performed securely. Multi-Party Computation allows multiple parties to jointly compute a function over their inputs, while keeping those inputs private. Secure hardware provides secure enclaves where sensitive operations can be performed, i.e., such as Trusted Execution Environments and Hardware Security Modules. Adversarial Defense Strategies develop more robust defenses against adversarial attacks. Of course, Regulatory and Compliance Standards is to establish industry-specific standards and regulations to guarantee that AI systems meet minimum security requirements. These future directions in trustworthy AI can make AI systems powerful, accurate, highly secure, and resilient to threats, thus helping to build trust and

---

[4]https://www.intelligence.gov/artificial-intelligence-ethics-framework-for-the-intelligence-community

confidence in the widespread adoption of AI technologies.

Interdisciplinary, International Collaboration and Standardization
The future of trustworthy AI will require interdisciplinary, global collaboration, and standardization. This includes harmonizing ethical and technical standards, interdisciplinary collaboration between experts from various fields, and developing international agreements and frameworks [9]. Cross-border data governance protocols and standardized evaluation metrics will be established to assess the trustworthiness of AI systems. Mutual recognition of compliance with ethical and technical standards will be the cornerstone of global collaboration. This includes working with domain experts from different countries and fields need to work together. The development of reliable AI is not a problem exclusive to any single country, and its potential positive or negative effects do not respect geopolitical boundaries [12]. Therefore, international collaboration is necessary to combine diverse ideas from different backgrounds. It is also essential for the development of reliable AI technology, which will benefit humanity as a whole.

7.4 Summary

This chapter emphasizes the importance of trustworthy AI, discussing the opportunities, challenges, and future directions. In order to ensure confidence in AI decision-making, it is essential to understand its functioning and use transparent, interpretable models, particularly in critical areas such as healthcare and finance. Additionally, ethical and responsible deployment of AI is necessary, which requires transparency, accountability, and proactive measures to prevent bias and discrimination. To ensure AI is seamlessly integrated into our lives, it is essential to build user confidence, which involves addressing data quality and bias, interpretability and explainability, resilience against adversarial attacks, the need for global standards and regulations, and the assurance of privacy and security. To make AI a trusted and essential part of decision-making, there must be progress in Explainable AI (XAI) techniques, robust ethical frameworks, ongoing bias detection and mitigation, heightened security measures, and global collaboration and standardization efforts. Moreover, it is important to raise end-user awareness and education on AI trustworthiness and promote interdisciplinary and international collaboration.

Bibliography

[1] Samar Fatima, Kevin C Desouza, and Gregory S Dawson. National strategic artificial intelligence plans: A multi-dimensional analysis. *Economic Analysis and Policy*, 67:178–194, 2020.

[2] Raja Chatila, Virginia Dignum, Michael Fisher, Fosca Giannotti, Katharina Morik, Stuart Russell, and Karen Yeung. Trustworthy ai. *Reflections on Artificial Intelligence for Humanity*, pages 13–39, 2021.

[3] Petri Helo and Yuqiuge Hao. Artificial intelligence in operations management and supply chain management: An exploratory case study. *Production Planning & Control*, 33(16):1573–1590, 2022.

[4] Bruno Lepri, Nuria Oliver, Emmanuel Letouzé, Alex Pentland, and Patrick Vinck. Fair, transparent, and accountable algorithmic decision-making processes: The premise, the proposed solutions, and the open challenges. *Philosophy & Technology*, 31:611–627, 2018.

[5] Mark Sendak, Madeleine Clare Elish, Michael Gao, Joseph Futoma, William Ratliff, Marshall Nichols, Armando Bedoya, Suresh Balu, and Cara O'Brien. " the human body is a black box" supporting clinical decision-making with deep learning. In *Proceedings of the 2020 conference on fairness, accountability, and transparency*, pages 99–109, 2020.

[6] Hossein Hassani and Steve MacFeely. Driving excellence in official statistics: Unleashing the potential of comprehensive digital data governance. *Big Data and Cognitive Computing*, 7(3):134, 2023.

[7] Ying-Tung Lin, Tzu-Wei Hung, and Linus Ta-Lun Huang. Engineering equity: How ai can help reduce the harm of implicit bias. *Philosophy & Technology*, 34(Suppl 1):65–90, 2021.

[8] Donatella Firmani, Letizia Tanca, and Riccardo Torlone. Ethical dimensions for data quality. *Journal of Data and Information Quality (JDIQ)*, 12(1):1–5, 2019.

[9] Martin Ebers. Standardizing ai-the case of the european commission's proposal for an artificial intelligence act. *The Cambridge handbook of artificial intelligence: global perspectives on law and ethics*, 2021.

[10] Erico Tjoa and Cuntai Guan. A survey on explainable artificial intelligence (xai): Toward medical xai. *IEEE transactions on neural networks and learning systems*, 32(11):4793–4813, 2020.

[11] Aniek F Markus, Jan A Kors, and Peter R Rijnbeek. The role of explainability in creating trustworthy artificial intelligence for health care: a comprehensive survey of the terminology, design choices, and evaluation strategies. *Journal of biomedical informatics*, 113:103655, 2021.

[12] Bo Li, Peng Qi, Bo Liu, Shuai Di, Jingen Liu, Jiquan Pei, Jinfeng Yi, and Bowen Zhou. Trustworthy ai: From principles to practices. *ACM Computing Surveys*, 55(9):1–46, 2023.

[13] Eungyu Lee, Yongsoo Lee, and Taejin Lee. Adversarial attack-based robustness evaluation for trustworthy ai. *Computer Systems Science & Engineering*, 47(2), 2023.

[14] David Filip, L Dave, and P Harshvardhan. An ontology for standardising trustworthy ai. *cited on*, page 102, 2021.

[15] Mariano-Florentino Cuéllar and Aziz Z Huq. Toward the democratic regulation of ai systems: A prolegomenon. *U of Chicago, Public Law Working Paper*, (753), 2020.

[16] Davinder Kaur, Suleyman Uslu, and Arjan Durresi. Requirements for trustworthy artificial intelligence–a review. In *Advances in Networked-Based Information Systems: The 23rd International Conference on Network-Based Information Systems (NBiS-2020) 23*, pages 105–115. Springer, 2021.

[17] Yifei Zhang, Dun Zeng, Jinglong Luo, Zenglin Xu, and Irwin King. A survey of trustworthy federated learning with perspectives on security, robustness, and privacy. *arXiv preprint arXiv:2302.10637*, 2023.

[18] Hans de Bruijn, Martijn Warnier, and Marijn Janssen. The perils and pitfalls of explainable ai: Strategies for explaining algorithmic decision-making. *Government information quarterly*, 39(2):101666, 2022.

[19] Manoj Kumar Kamila and Sahil Singh Jasrotia. Ethical issues in the development of artificial intelligence: recognizing the risks. *International Journal of Ethics and Systems*, 2023.

[20] Saud Hakem Al Harbi, Lionel Nganyewou Tidjon, and Foutse Khomh. Responsible design patterns for machine learning pipelines. *arXiv preprint arXiv:2306.01788*, 2023.

[21] Runshan Fu, Yan Huang, and Param Vir Singh. Artificial intelligence and algorithmic bias: Source, detection, mitigation, and implications. In *Pushing the Boundaries: Frontiers in Impactful OR/OM Research*, pages 39–63. INFORMS, 2020.

[22] Iqbal H Sarker, Md Hasan Furhad, and Raza Nowrozy. Ai-driven cybersecurity: an overview, security intelligence modeling and research directions. *SN Computer Science*, 2:1–18, 2021.

Appendix-A

Table 7.1: Summary of mathematical notations used in the book.

Symbol	Description
x, y, z	Scalar variables
$\mathbf{x}, \mathbf{y}, \mathbf{z}$	Vectors
$\mathbf{X}, \mathbf{Y}, \mathbf{Z}$	Matrices
$f(\cdot), g(\cdot), h(\cdot)$	Functions
$\nabla_{\mathbf{x}} f$	Gradient of function f with respect to vector $\mathbf{x}$
$\mathcal{L}(\theta)$	Loss function with parameters θ
$\mathcal{D}$	Dataset
$\mathcal{N}(\mu, \sigma^2)$	Normal distribution with mean μ and variance σ^2
ϵ	Perturbation magnitude in adversarial attacks
η	Learning rate
$P(\cdot)$	Probability of an event
$\mathbb{E}[\cdot]$	Expectation of a random variable
∂	Partial derivative symbol
$\sum$	Summation symbol
$\prod$	Product symbol
$\int$	Integral symbol
$\Rightarrow$	Implies or leads to
$\Leftrightarrow$	If and only if (equivalence)
∞	Infinity symbol
$\lim$	Limit symbol

www.ingramcontent.com/pod-product-compliance
Lightning Source LLC
Chambersburg PA
CBHW071238050326

40690CB00011B/2166